The Taylorized Beauty of the Mechanical

The Taylorized Beauty of the Mechanical

Mauro F. Guillén

Scientific Management
and the Rise of
Modernist Architecture

Princeton University Press
Princeton and Oxford

Published by Princeton University Press, 41 William Street, Princeton, New Jersey 08540
In the United Kingdom: Princeton University Press, 3 Market Place, Woodstock, Oxfordshire OX20 1SY

Library of Congress Cataloging-in-Publication Data

Guillén, Mauro F.　　　　　•
 The Taylorized beauty of the mechanical : scientific management and the rise of modernist architecture / Mauro F. Guillén.
　　p. cm.
 Includes bibliographical references.
 ISBN-13: 978-0-691-11520-7 (cloth : alk. paper)
 ISBN-10: 0-691-11520-6 (cloth : alk. paper)
1. Modern movement (Architecture)　2. Architectural practice—History—20th century.　3. Architecture—Social aspects.　4. Architecture—Economic aspects.　5. Industrial management. 6. Engineering—Management.　I. Title.
 NA682.M63G85 2006
 720.1'0509041—dc22　　　　2005029498

British Library Cataloging-in-Publication Data is available

Printed on acid-free paper. ∞

pup.princeton.edu

Printed in the United States of America

10　9　8　7　6　5　4　3　2　1

Contents

List of Plates

(See insert following text page 80)

List of Tables and Figures

Preface

ARCHITECTURE OCCUPIES a unique position in society. It is both an art and an important economic activity, and must attend to both aesthetic and practical considerations. As if that were not enough, architecture also is an extremely politicized realm because it has major implications for the distribution of power in society. In this book I contend that architecture became more economically and socially important with its embrace of the principles of method, standardization, and planning that it borrowed from engineering and scientific management some one hundred years ago. Modernism in architecture is the movement and period that changed theory and practice in ways that were consistent with an industrial age. In this book I document and explain exactly how modernism in architecture emerged as an aesthetic implementation of ideas first developed by engineers and scientific managers.

I started to work on this research project back in 1992, after finishing my dissertation at Yale, which focused on the cross-national spread of various theories of organization, including scientific management, and appeared in 1994 as *Models of Management: Work, Authority, and Organization in a Comparative Perspective*. After moving to MIT to start my teaching career, I was lucky to receive funding from the Marion and Jasper Whiting Foundation, which enabled me to travel to France, Germany, Italy, and Spain to conduct research on modernism. My Latin American exposure to architecture was facilitated by another project, on organizational change over the course of economic development, which resulted in the 2001 book *The Limits of Convergence: Globalization and Organizational Change in Argentina, South Korea, and Spain*. My research on models of management and on economic development made me aware of the importance of placing architecture in the managerial and economic context of its time, the key theme of this book.

I would like to thank a relatively small number of people for their unwavering support during the long years that led to the completion of this manuscript. As the editor of the *Administrative Science Quarterly*, where I published an article-length analysis of the relationship between scientific management and architecture, Steve Barley of Stanford University helped me refine the main argument. Without his superb editorial advice and intellectual support, I do not think I would have persisted long enough to bring this project to fruition.

Equally supportive during the early years was John van Maanen of MIT. Anonymous reviewers for the *Latin American Research Review*, in which I published a condensed version of chapter 6, also provided useful insights and information. I am also indebted to Paul DiMaggio of Princeton, who encouraged me to pursue a book-length manuscript on the topic. Paul has been a wonderful source of theoretical inspiration and career advice. Charles Perrow and Juan Linz of Yale, and Jesús de Miguel of the University of Barcelona reminded me several times that this was an important topic worthy of my time and attention. In his characteristic style, Chick helped me ground my arguments in terms of key sociological debates. Victoria Alexander of the University of Sussex, Steve Brint of the University of California at Riverside, Randy Collins of Penn, and Mayer Zald of Michigan also helped me clarify some of the arguments. Magali Sarfatti Larson of Temple and Dick Scott of Stanford read the manuscript as referees, and supplied me with excellent suggestions for improvement. Sandy Lee, Linda Cohen, and Teddy Slowik provided me with excellent research assistance. At Princeton University Press, Ian Malcolm displayed his boundless enthusiasm as an editor, and improved the prose, especially of chapter 1. Kathleen Cioffi copyedited the manuscript, saving me from making rather embarrassing mistakes. Librarians at Yale, Harvard, MIT, and Penn provided me with the lifeblood of a scholar: a never-ending supply of books, articles, photographs, pamphlets and other materials. I must also express my gratitude to the Wharton School of the University of Pennsylvania, my employer during much of the time I have spent working on this project. Undeniably, it is a good sign of things to come when one of the world's leading business schools not only allows but also supports a faculty member to do research on aesthetics.

I would like to dedicate this book to the three women that give my life aesthetic meaning: my wife Sandra and my daughters Daniela and Andrea. I fully realize that working on this project has meant spending less precious time with them. I am deeply grateful for their generosity.

Philadelphia, Pennsylvania, April 2005

The Taylorized Beauty of the Mechanical

Organization, Modernism, and Architecture

> Form follows function.
> —Louis H. Sullivan

> Less is more.
> —Ludwig Mies van der Rohe

MODERNIST ARCHITECTURE is the child of industry and engineering. Its rise during the early twentieth century dovetailed with the spread of scientific management, historically the most controversial and influential approach to the organization of work. The modernist architects read about scientific management, thought of buildings as machines, embraced the ideas of waste reduction and order, used such notorious efficiency techniques as time-and-motion study, collaborated with industrialists and firms, and strived to turn architecture into a science driven by method, standardization, and planning. They yearned to create houses, public buildings, factories, artifacts, and durable consumer goods combining beauty with technical, economic, and social efficiency. They became technicians, organizers, and social reformers as well as artists, adding the stopwatch, the motion picture camera, the slide rule, and the psycho-physiological test to their toolkit. Architecture and our experience of the built environment changed in ways still discernible today. Technology merged with style, science with history, efficiency with creativity, and functionality with aesthetics.

In this book I examine the parallels between scientific management and architecture in a variety of countries in Europe and the Americas between 1890 and 1940. I provide the first systematic assessment of the economic, social, and political conditions that prompted architects to pursue a modernist approach to design. It was the crucial influence exerted by engineering and scientific management that helps explain the emergence of modernist architecture. The link developed in the historical context of the appearance of new sponsors—industrial firms and the state—and of the professionalization of architecture following an engineering model rather than the traditional Beaux-Arts one. In some countries the modernists succeeded at reconfiguring architecture, especially by changing the way in which architects were trained.

Among the various arts, architecture proved most receptive to the new methods and ideas emerging from industry in the early twentieth century. Architecture and its associated activities—design of interiors, furniture, and household objects—produced an aesthetic companion to the influential technical and ideological messages of scientific management. Like organizational methods, architecture carries consequences for people's lives at home and at work (Smith 1993, 399). As Siegfried Giedion ([1941] 1982, 705) has pointed out, "architecture is a complex activity; it works in the boundary area halfway between the regions of aesthetic feeling and practical doing." Similarly, Magali Sarfatti Larson (1993, 16) noted that architecture is a peculiar "social art" because it contributes to the culture not only "discourse and codified practices . . . but also, and crucially . . . *artifacts* that are useful and can be beautiful." Architecture is "a public and useful art . . . that must convince a client, mobilize the complex enterprise of building, inspire the public (and not offend it), and work with the culture, visual skills, and symbolic vocabulary not of the client but of its time." In addition, the architect has become a professional expert who must strike a delicate balance between enjoying a "latitude for judgment and artistic freedom of expression" and complying with the "limits imposed by the client, the character of the site, the cost of construction, and materials" (Blau 1984, 28).

This book's journey through the times and places at which scientific management and modernist architecture blended into a single endeavor begins with a general characterization of the modernist movement in architecture. I focus attention on the ideas of method, standardization, and planning, initially developed in the United States, that the modernist architects borrowed from the world of industry and scientific management (chapter 2). I then characterize the various explanations offered by architectural historians and social scientists for the emergence of modernist architecture. What invited some architects to look into engineering and scientific management for ideas about method, standardization, and planning? Did modernist architecture emerge simply as a natural consequence of industrialization, or was it the result of an unusual degree of sociopolitical upheaval that encouraged new experiments in art, architecture, and urban planning? Was modernism made possible by specific class dynamics during the formation of the mass consumption market for artistic artifacts? How important were the state and industrialists as new sponsors of architecture interested in affordable housing for the masses and better, more efficient workplaces? Or was it the joint training of engineers and architects that helped the latter produce a new approach to design?

These questions and themes are outlined in chapter 3, and then assessed in chapters 4–6 using evidence drawn from the six largest European countries (Britain, France, Germany, Italy, Russia, and Spain), and the three largest Latin American ones (Mexico, Brazil, and Argentina). The case of the United States is covered in this first chapter because American managerial and architectural achievements represented an antecedent to modernist architecture rather than a culmination: it was European architects who developed the key insights pioneered in the United States and arrived at the new aesthetic that one associates with modernism in architecture. Specifically, modernist architecture was first formulated by German, Italian, Russian, and some early French architects educated as such in an engineering tradition, whereas most architects in Britain and Spain were not exposed to such an influence. In the Americas, a similar argument holds in that the reception of European modernism was more enthusiastic among architects exposed to industry and engineering during their education or early on in their careers (chapter 7). Thus, modernist architecture emerged when architects influenced by engineering and scientific management obtained commissions for "useful" buildings like factories, schools, or apartment buildings from patrons such as industrial companies or the state. In tracing the connections between scientific management and modernist architecture around the world, this book seeks to explain the shift in architectural leadership from France and Britain to Germany, Russia, and Italy during the early twentieth century, a process that produced a modernist approach that was reexported back to the United States in the years just before World War II.

It is precisely because aesthetics should be studied not in splendid isolation but in its historical and institutional context that I compare architectural movements in ten countries in Europe and the Americas between the turn of the century and World War II. I will follow the typical analytical approach in the sociology of cultural production, namely, to examine a new artistic movement as "both a social and an ideational phenomenon" because "it involves a new world view, new techniques, a community of interacting artists and a support structure," which in the case of architecture consists of theorists, practitioners, critics, sponsors, and educators (Crane 1989, 270). Finally, chapter 8 delves into the long-term consequences of the emergence and consolidation of modernist architecture as a public, moral, and social art, exploring such an important issue in the sociology of culture as the consumption of modernist architecture. The book ends with a reconsideration of the aesthetic dimension of scientific management and other organizational theories. In examining one specific link between organization and aesthetics, I suggest that we have misunderstood the theoretical meaning and social impact of such a key organizational theory as scientific management.

The chapters that follow do not amount to a comprehensive treatise on the history of modernist architecture. Rather, the analysis is mainly concerned with the critical junctures and processes in the development of a new vision of architecture as an activity and a profession based on ideas about method, standardization, and planning. While I pay some attention to the cross-national diffusion of modernist architecture as an institutionalized pattern, I focus on the emergence of the pattern itself, that is, on the process of institutionalization. And although the link between scientific management and modernist architecture has been observed by many art historians, critics, and sociologists—as well as by the modernist architects themselves—I offer the first comprehensive conceptual treatment and the first systematic cross-national comparison of the causes that produced it.

A key development initially unrelated to architecture was reaching a climax in the United States just before World War I: the formulation of a new model of industrial management known as scientific management, which highlighted method, standardization, and planning, elements that would later appeal to the modernist architects. The scientific managers believed that analytical methods such as the division of labor (or specialization), time-and-motion study, and flowchart analysis would help optimize the production process and the utilization of labor, making them more efficient. They also focused their attention on the standardization of products, tools, and equipment so as to achieve the highest possible degree of mechanization. Product standardization essentially meant simplification and interchangeability of parts and components. The scientific managers insisted on separating task conception from execution, thus elevating the role of planning above that of implementation. They initially applied these ideas to the organization of simple tasks. Later, it occurred to them that entire production processes, companies, cities, and even countries were amenable to the same principles and methodologies.

Like the scientific managers, the modernist architects initially sought to improve building practices but soon realized that method, standardization, and planning enabled them to formulate a new approach to architecture. The overarching idea in scientific management was that of order, one that subsequently captivated the modernist architects because it enabled them to move away from the prevailing eclecticism and to present themselves as organizers, as technocrats who could ameliorate social conflict and improve standards of living.[1] The modernist architects were frustrated at the inability of existing architectural approaches and practices to take advantage of the aesthetic possibilities offered by industrialization, and to tackle the social problems engendered by the growth of cities. Scientific management offered a set of ideas and methods that promised to reduce chaos and waste. Armed with them, the modernist architects thought they could arrive at an "orderly" theory and practice of architecture firmly rooted in the industrial era (see chapter 2).

The origins of scientific management date back to the second half of the nineteenth century. After the Civil War, American industry grew in size and bureaucratization, and managers and engineers began to complain about how difficult it had become to run complex enterprises and to keep the workforce disciplined and motivated. In fact, the period between 1890 and 1910 was one of acute labor turmoil. Unlike most business owners, whose instincts led them

---

[1] Technocracy is an important concept in sociology, one that includes two components: the use of technical knowledge, especially in a bureaucratized setting; and the appeal to an ideology of objectivity or neutrality to justify the power structure that results from the rise of the technocrats (Larson 1972–73).

to confront worker insubordination with force, American engineers and managers attempted to meet the challenge through innovation (Bendix 2001; Guillén 1994). The "American System" of interchangeable parts was an early attempt to solve the problem through labor savings (Hounshell 1984). In a related development, the so-called movement of systematic management of the late nineteenth century focused on increasing efficiency and reducing waste (Bendix 2001; Shenhav 1999).

It was Frederick Winslow Taylor, a self-made engineer, who came up with a coherent synthesis of these diverse efficiency ideas, which he felicitously labeled "scientific management" (plate 1.1; see insert). I will use the term "Taylorism" to refer to the "Taylor System," although Taylor himself preferred to present his own ideas as "scientific management" (Taylor [1912] 1972, 6). For the purposes of this book, scientific management is a much broader set of ideas and techniques that came to be identified with Taylorism as well as with the achievements of other efficiency experts and practitioners, including Frank and Lillian Gilbreth, Henry Gantt, Hugo Münsterberg, and Henry Ford, all of them deeply admired by the modernist architects (see chapter 2).

After having discovered high-speed steel in the 1890s, Taylor envisaged the gains that could be derived from the speed-up of the work process if tools and machinery were standardized, machine times estimated, and the human factor adapted to an ever faster work pace (Nelson 1980, 80–103). As novelist John Dos Passos wryly observed, he was called "Speedy Taylor" in the shop, and "couldn't stand to see an idle lathe or an idle man"; "production was an itch under his skin" (Dos Passos [1933] 1979, 44, 45). In 1903 Taylor published his first book, *Shop Management*. He recommended that all manual tasks be studied, divided, and, when necessary and economical, performed by different workers. Taylor's model of organization combined four elements, as enunciated in his famous *Principles of Scientific Management*: time-and-motion studies to standardize work tools and working conditions, and to divide the process into its simplest constituent tasks; selection of the cheapest yet adequate worker to perform each of the divided tasks; the "bringing together" of the scientifically determined task and the scientifically selected worker by means of functional foremanship and an incentive system based on differential rates; and the separation of the execution of work by the workers from its conception, which belonged to a "planning department" (Taylor [1911] 1967, 85; [1903] 1972, 4–45).

Although Taylor's ideas were met by managerial skepticism and worker fury, he succeeded at placing efficiency and planning at the top of the agenda for social and business reform in the United States and around the world (Guillén 1994; Merkle 1980). Meanwhile, Taylor's many followers refined several theoretical and methodological aspects of scientific management. The Gilbreths improved the methodology of time-and-motion study, introducing the cyclograph and the chronocyclograph (Gilbreth 1909, 1911, 1912; Gilbreth and Gilbreth 1917; see also Giedion [1948] 1969, 17–30, 101–13; plates 1.2 and 1.3). Motion study using motion picture cameras became much easier and cheaper to implement with the introduction of 16-millimeter film in 1921, and the Gilbreths used them assiduously (plate 1.4). "Scientific management, . . . early cinematography, Cubism, and Futurism reflect aspects of each other across the cultural spectrum like images of a house of mirrors. As the Cubists broke up and recreated bottles and guitars, Gilbreth broke down and reconstructed work processes" (Kern 1983, 117). Tellingly, Frank Gilbreth's first book (1909) was a treatise on efficient bricklaying for the construction industry, in which he proposed a new, adjustable scaffold to improve productivity. Gantt developed work flowcharts to optimize the use of resources over time (Gantt 1911, 1919), a technique that has become widely used in the construction industry.

Another prominent contributor to scientific management was Hugo Münsterberg whose 1913 book, *Psychology and Industrial Efficiency*, developed and systematized Taylor's observations about worker selection in *The Principles of Scientific Management*. These two books read more like manifestos than scientific treatises, perhaps one of the reasons why the avant-garde modernist architects were so fond of them. The modernists in Europe would find theoretical and practical inspiration in both books' insights, techniques, and overall ideology of order. Beyond its technical promises, scientific management proved influential because of its ideological claim to a superior scientific approach to work and organization, one that the modernist architects extended to the world of design and building.

Scientific management was fundamental to the development of what came to be known as Fordism, that is, mass production based on the assembly line, another system of management that was to capture the imagination of modernist architects. Like Taylor, Henry Ford was a self-made mechanic (Sward 1972; plate 1.5). "The American Plan; automotive prosperity seeping down from above, . . . But that five dollars a day paid to good, clean American workmen who didn't drink or smoke cigarettes or read or think . . . made Henry Ford the automobileer, the admirer of Edison, the birdlover, the great American of his time" (Dos Passos [1933] 1979, 73). He made extensive use of Taylorite techniques at his new factory at Highland Park in Detroit, hiring the best mechanics and scientific-management experts in the area. Ford's plant managers improved the production process on a trial-and-error basis, making use of standardization, time study, and systematic planning techniques. Gravity-slides, automatic conveyors, overhead conveyors, and the endless-chain conveyor for final assembly (1914) were the major technological innovations that resulted from their attempts to optimize the production of Model T cars (plate 1.6). Ford envisaged that "the big money was in economical quantity production, quick turnover, cheap interchangeable easilyreplaced standardized parts" (Dos Passos [1933] 1979, 72). For him, mass production was "power, accuracy, economy, system, continuity and speed" (Ford 1926), themes that would appeal to the modernist architects because of their inherent promise to reduce chaos and improve life.[2] The only Taylorite principles that Ford did not implement were functional foremanship and the differential wage rate, mainly because the speed of the assembly line and the feeder routes dictated the pace of work. Thus, the need for incentives and continuous supervising was greatly reduced or even eliminated. Like Taylorism, Fordism was also an ideology promising great gains for workers, managers, owners, and consumers alike, and it was perhaps this aspect that ultimately influenced the modernist architects most.

Scientific management made an enormous impact on American industry, government, and nonprofit organizations. While a group of notorious engineers active at the turn of the century provided a set of methods and metaphors to make organizational practices more "systematic" and "scientific," an equally prominent group of social and political reformers known as the Progressives extended the same set of principles to education, the government, and culture (Callahan 1962; Haber 1964; Fairfield 1994; DiMaggio 1991). The writings and practical accomplishments of Taylor, the Gilbreths, Münsterberg, and Ford provided the modernist architects with an endless supply of inspiration. The ideas of method, standardization, and planning came in handy when looking for ways to develop an approach to architecture consistent with the age of machines.

CONSTRUCTION AND ARCHITECTURE: AMERICA VERSUS EUROPE

In the midst of such an outburst of organizational innovation in the factory, much of the world of architecture remained anchored in the past. Historians agree that before the arrival of modernism, the theory and practice of architectural design prevalent on both sides of the Atlantic were conspicuously inconsistent with the increasingly pervasive reality of machines and industrial production. They also suggest that an inordinate enthusiasm for revivalism and historical styles had thrown architecture into such a creative deadlock and chaos that reform and renewal were unlikely to emerge easily from within. The historiography shows that the first designers to take advantage of the principles of machine production and of such new construction materials as steel, glass, cement, and plastics were not architects but engineers (Jencks 1973; Benevolo [1960] 1977, 219–50; Banham [1960] 1980; Curtis [1982] 1996).

Although the first major innovation in industrial-age building that captured the world's attention was the impressive Crystal Palace at the London Universal

[2] This article by Ford, prepared for the 1926 edition of the *Encyclopaedia Britannica* and later published in the *New York Times*, was in fact written by a collaborator of his, William J. Cameron. See Hounshell 1984, 304.

Exhibition of 1851, American constructors and engineers had taken the lead by the 1880s. They built massive factories, silos, grain elevators, bridges, and other types of industrial structures emphasizing efficiency, rationality, and functionality.[3] The Chicago architects—especially Louis H. Sullivan—used the new engineering techniques and construction materials outside the realm of industry, erecting the first skyscrapers and modernist office buildings (plate 1.7). Sullivan formulated the famous modernist principle of "form follows function." Most of his contemporaries, however, clung to the old-fashioned taste for superfluous ornamentation and fell short of producing an overarching theory of aesthetic design, a new vocabulary to guide the architect's work (Banham [1960] 1980; Benevolo [1960] 1977). Thorstein Veblen complained that the new industrial bourgeoisie regarded as beautiful artifacts that were rarely useful, and frequently wasteful of labor and materials (Veblen [1899] 1934). And when it came to designing useful artifacts, American designers and architects were forced to cater to the needs of a large mass consumption market that put ornament and kitsch ahead of rationality and functionality (Gartman 2000). Most importantly, the leaders of the Chicago Movement, Adler and Sullivan, and their most distinguished disciple, Frank Lloyd Wright, failed to nurture a college of followers or to influence architectural education (Benevolo [1960] 1977, 191–250, 629–83; Hitchcock and Johnson [1932] 1995, 38–54; Pevsner [1936] 1960, 32). Sullivan and Wright "had to live almost as exiles in their own country" (Giedion [1941] 1982, 391, 425, 500; Wright [1928] 1992, 257).

Wright occupies a prominent place in American architecture. Some historians argue that there were two Wrights, the forward-looking architect who developed an "architectural system" of his own by departing from the prevailing eclecticism, and the traditionalist who wished to preserve regional styles and craftsmanship (Curtis [1982] 1996, 113). Wright, heir to a long American tradition of rationalism, "became the prophet and genius of the so-called organic trend." He extolled "the horizontal, the ground line, unfinished materials sometimes crude and telluric, and the house anchored in the soil as a factor of a reintegrated landscape" (Zevi [1973] 1994, 210; plate 1.8). While the European modernists would receive and further develop some of these themes, they would reject others, including his organic expressionism. It should also be remembered that Wright ([1929] 1944, 129) did not fully come to terms with mechanization, which he "dreaded" and found "malevolent."

The World's Columbian Exposition of 1893 in Chicago illustrates why the incipient American architectural modernism of Sullivan and Wright failed to inspire his compatriots at the critical juncture of the turn of the century. The fair

[3] Pevsner ([1936] 1960, 126) has dutifully noted that the Chinese had successfully undertaken metallic construction of suspended bridges prior to the eighteenth century, and this was known in Europe and the United States.

offered architects a unique opportunity to influence tastes and trends in design. And yet, instead of finding inspiration in the works of the engineers, most of the architects commissioned to design the buildings looked towards France and the Beaux-Arts tradition. Sullivan criticized the exposition for being like an academic "plague," although his own contribution, the Transportation Building, was eclectic in that it combined Roman, Romanesque, Gothic and Islamic influences (Tselos 1967, 263–67). Wright lamented in his autobiography that "[t]he Fair is going to have a great influence in our country. The American people have seen the 'Classics' on a grand scale for the first time. . . . I can see all America constructed . . . in noble 'dignified' classic style" (quoted in Giedion [1941] 1982, 396). The Fair represented the "triumph of Beaux-Arts Classicism" (Pevsner, as quoted in Pfammatter 2000, 289).

History books profusely document that the first architects to fully grasp the significance of the industrial era, of the new methods and materials it offered, were European. They avidly learned from American industrial construction and from scientific management, applying engineering methods to all sorts of buildings and designs, and carrying the new principles to their ultimate aesthetic consequences. In the United States construction and building practices evolved to meet the requirements of mass production, while in Continental Europe—where large-scale industrialization was slower to develop than in the land of Taylor and Ford—modernist architecture emerged much more unconstrained, and played an independent role in shaping life at the factory, the home, and the public building (Smith 1993, 92, 398; Gartman 2000).

Modernist architecture in the relatively backward and politically troubled Continental European countries was in a position to lead rather than follow, allowing the architect to exert a tremendous influence over social and industrial organization as the designer and planner of dwellings, cities, and workplaces. While the American architect of the turn of the century caught up with developments in industry as an individualist and marginal player, and the British architect reacted against the machine age altogether, the architect in the relatively backward Continental European countries actively advocated and planned for a transformation of society. The emerging modernist architecture in Europe thus stood in sharp contrast to American architecture in that it was avant-garde, though not in the simplistic sense that it espoused art for art's sake but rather in that it was revolutionary, that is, moving at the forefront of social and economic change rather than following it.

The links between modernist architecture and engineering are hard to miss. "The engineer is the hero of our age," stated the German architect and product designer Peter Behrens in the early 1900s. He was one of the key pioneers of modernism in architecture and design. Upon being appointed chief architect and designer at the large electrical appliances company AEG—a firm fully committed to the implementation of Taylorism and Fordism—he promised to work toward the "most intimate union possible between art and industry"

(Buddensieg 1984, 207–19). Together with other leading German architects of the time, he took part in the Werkbund—the German version of the English Arts and Crafts movement—founded in 1907 to "introduce the idea of standardization as a virtue, and of abstract form as the basis of the aesthetics of product design" (Banham [1960] 1980, 72; Campbell 1978; Buddensieg 1984, 46).

European modernism did not arrive at an entirely novel approach to architecture and design until the 1920s, with the Bauhaus in Germany, constructivism in the Soviet Union, rationalism in Italy, and purism in France (see chapters 4–5). It was at this point that European architects made their revolutionary reinterpretation of scientific management in aesthetic terms. Walter Gropius, the founder of the Bauhaus school of art and architecture in Germany, was a firm believer in scientific management and became one of the most influential architects of the twentieth century. He wished to formulate a new theory of architecture and to develop "practical designs for present-day goods" that could be mass-produced (Buddensieg 1984, 18). He and his colleagues designed all manner of buildings, decorated interiors, and collaborated with many German manufacturing firms on product design. Most importantly, they proposed a new way to train the architect that departed from classicism and eclecticism, and emphasized method and utility.

As a result of German influence, the Russian arts and crafts movement had been toying with the artistic possibilities of mass production since the turn of the century (Lodder 1983, 74). While the Bolshevik revolution spurred myriad competing avant-garde movements, constructivism quickly gained sway over its alternatives (Bowlt 1988, 204–61). The constructivists proposed the ideals of the "artist-constructor" and the "artist-engineer," arguing for a functional and engineering-oriented approach to design, with extensive use of prefabricated housing, standardization, modular coordination, efficient building methods, new materials, and industrial production. As in Germany, the Soviet modernists created a state-sponsored school of art to realize their dreams, the Higher State Artistic-Technical Workshops, founded in 1920 to train "highly qualified master artists for industry" (Kahn 1982; Lodder 1983, 109–44).

In 1909 Italian futurism was launched as a literary movement by F. T. Marinetti, who entertained a political agenda of nationalism, violence, war, and destruction (Bowler 1991). Futurist ideas were developed and put into practice by the "rationalist" architects of the 1920s and '30s, who were interested in low-cost housing and furniture design, urban planning, prefabricated construction, factory architecture, and standardization (Banham [1960] 1980, 98–137; Etlin 1991, 53–100). Meanwhile, French architecture was revolutionized by Le Corbusier, a tireless advocate of scientific management. He was influenced by German, Russian, and Italian modernism. In the early 1920s he published what many regarded as the most revolutionary and influential modernist manifestos on architecture and city planning (Le Corbusier [1923] 1986,

[1924] 1987). Drawing on his experiences with manufacturers and his reading of Taylor and Ford, Le Corbusier developed and popularized the concepts of the "machine for living," the standardized "dwelling unit," and the "mass-produced house" (Benevolo [1960] 1977, 435–49; Brooks 1987, 107–25, 203–40).

The European architects and designers turned the mechanical into a metaphor for beauty and form as well as order and function. As a volume created by simple lines and plain surfaces, with seamless and unadorned shapes, the machine was raised to the status of symbol and muse. The Italian architect Antonio Sant'Elia put it concisely in 1914: "Just as the ancients drew inspiration for their art from the elements of nature, we . . . must find that inspiration in the elements of the utterly new mechanical world we have created, and of which architecture must be the most beautiful expression, the most complete synthesis, the most efficacious integration" (Sant'Elia [1914] 1973, 171–72).

A DEFINITION OF MODERNIST ARCHITECTURE

It should be carefully noted that the emergence of a discernible and unified "modernist architecture" in Europe during the early twentieth century is a matter of debate among art historians and critics. The chronicler-historians of the modern movement believed that a new, well-defined architectural style started to emerge in the late nineteenth century, and crystallized by the early 1920s if not prior to World War I, as reflected in the very titles of their books: Hitchcock and Johnson's *The International Style* ([1932] 1995), Pevsner's *Pioneers of Modern Design* ([1936] 1960), and Giedion's *Space, Time, and Architecture: The Growth of a New Tradition* ([1941] 1982). For instance, Pevsner ([1936] 1960, 38) asserted that "the new style, the genuine and legitimate style of our century, was achieved by 1914."

In contrast to contemporary accounts of the modern movement, more recent historical analyses have argued that "modern architecture" never was the "true style of our century." Rather, modernism includes several "discontinuous movements" not always fully compatible with each other (Jencks 1973, 11–13; see also Banham [1960] 1980; Benevolo [1960] 1977; Frampton [1980] 1992; Curtis [1982] 1996). This fragmentation was largely due to the ways in which architects combined the ideas coming from the world of industry with other trends they were exposed to. For instance, the English Arts and Crafts movement contributed to modernism the ideas of the well-crafted object, art for the people (as opposed to for the elite), coherence and simplicity in design, and architecture's moral role in setting the tone of the entire modern town (see chapter 4). Art nouveau, in spite of its conspicuous (though disciplined) use of naturalistic decoration, incorporated iron columns and frames allowing for the "free disposition of the rooms at the different levels, and the independence of the partitions one from another" (Giedion [1941] 1982, 305), as in Victor Horta's Tassel House of 1893 (plate 1.9).[4] Cubism offered architects new conceptions of light and space, turning the picture and the building into autonomous artifacts that depicted the psychic or the social rather than the physical, representing three dimensions on the flat canvas "without recourse to perspective illusions," (Weston 1996, 62; Banham [1960] 1980; Benevolo [1960] 1977; Kern 1983, 143–48).[5] Abstract art also exerted an influence on modernist architecture, with its conception of "art as 'research,' art as an end in itself, art as an expression of 'modernity,' art as 'avant-gardisme,' art as a means of creating 'surprise,' art as 'not-art,' and art as 'pure art' " (Collins [1965] 1998, 274).[6]

In spite of its manifold roots and resulting fragmentation, it is possible to highlight some of the aesthetic qualities of modernism in architecture. The institutionalized concept of modernist architecture included first and foremost the trinity of "unity, order, purity" as the guiding principles of any design, from the building itself to the furniture and paintings inside it. Clean shapes and clarity of form became paramount; "less is more," declared one leading architect of the period (Mies van der Rohe), invoking a sort of economy of taste. The aesthetic order that emerged from European modernism in architecture has been defined by its three main principles: "Emphasis upon volume—space enclosed by thin planes or surfaces as opposed to the suggestion of mass and solidity; regularity as opposed to symmetry or other kinds of obvious balance; and, lastly, dependence on the intrinsic elegance of materials, technical perfection, and fine proportions, as opposed to applied ornament" (Barr 1995, 29).

Modernism was a reaction against the imitation of the classical canons and

[4] A key precursor of art nouveau was Eugène Viollet-le-Duc, who abhorred eclecticism, promoting instead the idea that architecture should be honest, truthful, and authentic in that it should reflect the conditions and materials of its time, without decorating them in artificial ways. He was "disturbed by the inability of the nineteenth century to find its own style" (Curtis [1982] 1996, 24, 27). Besides Horta, the other great art nouveau architect was his Belgian compatriot Henry Van de Velde ([1907] 1971, 18): "Thou shalt comprehend the form and construction of all objects only in the sense of their strictest, elementary logic and justification for their existence."

[5] Several modernist architects and designers started their careers as painters (e.g., Behrens, Chernikhov, Lissitzky, Tatlin, Le Corbusier, Chiattone, Terragni, O'Gorman, van de Velde), and many painters (Léger, Boccioni, Severini, Malevich, Kandinsky, Klee, the Mexican muralists) collaborated assiduously with the architects. The links between painting and architecture perhaps reached their zenith with the De Stijl movement in Holland, founded in 1917 on the basis of the abstractions of Theo van Doesburg and Piet Mondrian (Padovan 2002).

[6] Galison (1990) has observed the parallels between modernist architecture and logical positivism in philosophy, with both emphasizing the simple and the functional. The logical positivist philosophers visited with the Bauhaus frequently.

approaches rescued from oblivion during the Renaissance.[7] Many historians see in architectural modernism an attack on classicism's arbitrariness, emphasis on perspective and proportion, insistence on symmetry, and pervasive use of ornament. They single out symmetry as the key problem, for it "sacrifices the particular and individual on the altar of overall design, which is uniform, hierarchical, and unalterable" (Zevi [1973] 1994, 83; see also Giedion [1941] 1982, lvi). Thus, abandoning symmetry was one way to reintroduce the idea of order. The endless repetition of architectural elements became the modernists' technique for achieving an effect similar to symmetry. The departure from the principle of perspective owes much to cubism, which introduced time as a third dimension in painting, setting objects in motion, displaying their interior and exterior simultaneously and from several angles (Giedion [1941] 1982, 446–47, 521). With the elimination of the vantage point, one needs to walk around the building in order to grasp it, resulting in "space in time," a clear departure from the "compositional unity" of classicism, so entrenched in architectural practice since the Renaissance (Zevi [1973] 1994, 33; Giedion [1941] 1982, 529; Moore 1977). Like cubism, architectural modernism uses thin walls and large windows to blur the distinction between the inside and the outside, the inner and the outer reality (see plate 1.10).

In 1925 the Italian critic Roberto Papini described "modern European architecture" as having "these essential characteristics: a tendency toward the rational, the expression of structure, a free movement of masses, the emancipation from academic canons, an adherence to purely geometric forms, and independence from conventional proportions, and the maximum parsimony in ornamentation" (quoted in Etlin 1991, 238). Perhaps Giedion ([1941] 1982, 484–85) captured it best when he argued that modernism presented a "new conception of space," that instead of emphasizing the "supports of projecting parts such as . . . staircases," allowed for "freely hovering parts and surfaces." The modernist aesthetic sensation is triggered when "the relation between load and support is no longer traditionally obvious."

Modernism in architecture, however, was more than an aesthetic proposal. It included ideological and technical elements as well. European modernism sought to achieve order through the systematic application of method, standardization, and planning, embracing the "idea of technology as a social arbiter" (Maier 1970). Ideologically, modernism was antitraditional, antiromantic, futurist (i.e., forward-looking), and somewhat utopian. It was rational in the sense that "architectural forms not only required rational justification, but could only be so justified if they derived their laws from science" (Collins

---

[7] In philosophy and literature the reaction against the imitation of the classics took place during the eighteenth century, much earlier than in architecture. In each of these fields the modern movement was associated with an attack on imitation (Gomá Lanzón 2003, 22, 156, 167–68).

[1965] 1998, 198). It was functional in the dual sense of making "full use of modern technology and its honest expression in design . . . and [embracing] a scientific approach to human needs and uses in programming, planning and design" (Wurster 1965, 48; Poggioli 1968; Tafuri 1976).[8] Moreover, modernism aspired to revolutionize the process of artistic creation itself by applying method and science to both the design and construction of buildings and other artifacts. Traditional building practices—performed by a small number of craftsmen—were to be replaced by modern construction methods involving dozens of specialized subcontractors working independently, as in automobile manufacturing.

European machine-age modernism embraced scientific management in part because cost and efficiency were socially and politically constructed as important concerns. However, the romance of modernism with scientific organizational ideas went well beyond immediate economic considerations, leading to the formulation of an aesthetic based on the idea of order, on the promise of efficiency, and on technical virtuosity. The modernists "sought to merge aesthetic innovation with economic rationality" (Larson 1993, 50). By applying a mechanical metaphor to the design of houses, public buildings, schools, factories, and everyday objects, European modernism magnified the impact of scientific management, extending it into new realms. If scientific management argued that organizations and people in organizations worked, or were supposed to work, like machines (Morgan 1986; Perrow 1986; Schein 1988; Scott 1995b), European modernism insisted on the aesthetic potential of efficiency, precision, simplicity, regularity, and functionality; on producing useful and beautiful objects; on designing buildings and artifacts that would look like machines and be used like machines; on infusing design and social life with order.

Modernism, consistent with its emphasis on the technical rather than the humanistic or the social-psychological, aimed at democratizing good artistic taste (DiMaggio 1987, 448), making it available to the population at large, especially through housing projects, urban planning, and everyday objects for use in the home, the office, and the factory. The architect was to shift from being an aesthete to a reformer (Wurster 1965), to have in mind the user of the building rather than the client or sponsor; architecture was to be used, not admired or contemplated (Scully [1961] 1974, 42). In the end, modernism proposed an aesthetic companion to scientific management's rationalized machine world, a Taylorized sense of the beautiful. It contained a set of ideological, technical and aesthetic proposals that altered the way in which buildings were designed, constructed and used, as the next chapter documents.

[8] By "rationality" I mean the systematic application of method and planning, and by "functionality" the description and organization of elements of a system by reference to their needs and their mutual interaction.

CHAPTER TWO
The Taylorized Beauty of the Mechanical

> Building norms and construction times
> must be worked out, so that building
> can be transferred to mass-production
> factories and houses ordered from a
> catalogue.
> —El Lissitzky (quoted in
>   Lissitzky-Küppers 1967, 374).

> . . . In order to BUILD: STANDARDIZE to be
> able to INDUSTRIALIZE AND TAYLORIZE.
> —Le Corbusier (quoted in McLeod
>   1983, 143).

MODERNISM IN ARCHITECTURE emerged in a context of increasingly rational-ized industrial activity, one that offered new materials, techniques, and moti-vations for a method-driven, standardized, and planned approach to design, building, and the organization of space. While most architectural historians have noted the influence of scientific management on modernist architecture, they do not analyze in detail the specific ideological, technical, and aesthetic connections between the two movements.

The evidence of the relationship between scientific management and mod-ernism is based on the writings and works of the one hundred most influential architects during the 1890–1940 period, ten in each of the six largest countries in Europe (France, Germany, Great Britain, Italy, Russia/Soviet Union, and Spain), and the four largest countries in the Americas (Argentina, Brazil, Mexico, and the United States). I relied on the most important histories and encyclopedias of architecture, and on specialized country sources, to identify the most influential architects (see the appendix). Drawing on these documen-tary sources and on primary research at several archives,[1] I assigned each ar-chitect a code on a four-point scale depending on whether he welcomed or op-posed mechanization and standardization in art and architecture and whether he explicitly accepted or rejected scientific management. My coding reflects the architects' statements and writings about architecture and organization,

---

[1] The archives were the Bauhaus-Archiv, Museum für Gestaltung, Berlin; Busch-Reisinger Museum, Harvard University, Cambridge, MA; Biblioteca Nacional, Madrid; and Fundació Joan Miró, Barcelona.

their patterns of collaboration with industrialists and firms that were pioneers in the introduction of scientific management, their explicit endorsement and/or implementation of key scientific management techniques, and their actual projects and completed buildings, if applicable.

The appendix includes architects who proved influential in a variety of roles, including theorists and critics, propagators, designers of projects, urban planners, actual builders, and teachers. Some of the architects (e.g., Gropius, Le Corbusier) played most or all of these different roles, while others were also influential but in a more circumspect way. For instance, Ruskin and Sant'Elia were primarily theorists and designers (see chapters 4 and 5). My approach parallels that of historians of modernist architecture, who also discuss the influence of each of these types and roles of the architect (Banham [1960] 1980; Benevolo [1960] 1977; Curtis [1982] 1996; Hitchcock [1958] 1971; Pevsner [1936] 1960).

Histories and encyclopedias of modernist architecture provide coverage of the countries considered in this book to quite different degrees. Table 2.1 shows how many of the hundred leading architects listed in the appendix are actually cited in five key histories of modernist or twentieth-century architecture (Banham [1960] 1980; Benevolo [1960] 1977; Curtis [1982] 1996; Hitchcock [1958] 1971; Weston 1996), or included as a main entry in five encyclopedias of architecture (Lampugnani [1964] 1986; Midant 1996; Muriel [1980] 1994; Placzek 1982; Sharp [1967] 1981). The architects not cited or referenced in any of these ten histories or encyclopedias were identified using country-specific sources (see the appendix). While the achievements of French, German, British, and American architects are well represented in the ten histories or encyclopedias, those of Italian, Russian, Spanish, or Latin American architects tend not to be. This is quite surprising in the cases of Italy and Russia because avant-garde artists and architects in both countries played a key role in the international modernist movement. Still, Banham ([1960] 1980) and Hitchcock ([1958] 1971) cite only a few of the leading Italian and Russian architects, although the latter is, together with Benevolo ([1960] 1977), the only historian to cite as many as five of the ten leading Brazilian architects. Among historians, only Curtis ([1982] 1996) cites at least one of the ten leading architects for each country. The sources used are highly correlated with each other in terms of the architects cited, except for two of the encyclopedias (Midant 1996; Muriel [1980] 1994), as indicated in table 2.2.

Histories of architecture, and to a lesser extent, encyclopedias tend to be focused on a few highly influential architects. Of the one hundred architects listed in the appendix, only nine are cited in the ten histories or encyclopedias, including five Germans, two French, one Italian, and one American (see table 2.3). An analysis of the writings, statements, designs, and buildings of the most influential architects will serve in subsequent chapters to provide

TABLE 2.1
Number of Leading Architects Cited in Ten Histories or Encyclopedias of Architecture

Country	Total	Histories of Architecture						Encyclopedias of Architecture			
		Banham [1960]	Benevolo [1960]	Curtis [1982]	Hitchcock [1958]	Weston 1996	Lampugnani [1964]	Midant 1996	Muriel [1980]	Placzek 1982	Sharp [1967]
France	10	8	7	8	6	9	7	7	3	10	4
Germany	10	9	9	9	7	9	9	10	7	10	9
Great Britain	10	7	9	6	6	9	7	5	1	8	4
Italy	10	3	6	7	2	5	5	9	3	9	5
Russia/USSR	10	1	4	5	0	9	2	8	0	7	3
Spain/Catalonia	10	0	1	2	1	2	2	4	3	5	2
Argentina	10	0	0	1	0	0	1	10	1	9	0
Brazil	10	0	5	3	5	2	3	10	9	10	1
Mexico	10	0	0	2	1	0	3	9	4	5	1
United States	10	1	6	10	10	6	10	10	7	10	7
Total	100	29	47	53	38	51	49	82	38	83	36

Sources: Banham [1960] 1980; Benevolo [1960] 1977; Curtis [1982] 1996; Hitchcock [1958] 1971; Weston 1996; Lampugnani [1964] 1986; Midant 1996; Muriel [1980] 1994; Placzek 1982; Sharp [1967] 1981.

TABLE 2.2

Correlations of Citations between Pairs of Histories or Encyclopedias of Architecture (N = 100)

	1	2	3	4	5	6	7	8	9
1. Banham									
2. Benevolo	.43*								
3. Curtis	.40*	.53*							
4. Hitchcock	.33*	.56*	.47*						
5. Weston	.39*	.49*	.36*	.24*					
6. Lampugnani	.38*	.42*	.54*	.50*	.27*				
7. Midant	.07	.19	.15	.21*	.15	.35*			
8. Muriel	.07	.25*	.16	.47*	.01	.44*	.35*		
9. Placzek	.27*	.44*	.50*	.45*	.13	.54*	.23*	.44*	
10. Sharp	.37*	.50*	.41*	.47*	.44*	.61*	.28*	.44*	.32*

Note: *Significant at the 5 percent level or better based on a chi-squared test for the *phi* or Cohen's w correlation coefficient between two dichotomous variables.

Sources: See table 2.1.

TABLE 2.3

Architects Cited by All Ten Histories or Encyclopedias of Architecture

Architect	Country
Peter Behrens	Germany
Walter Gropius	Germany
Le Corbusier	France
Erich Mendelsohn	Germany
Hannes Meyer	Germany
Ludwig Mies van der Rohe	Germany
Auguste Perret	France
Giuseppe Terragni	Italy
Frank Lloyd Wright	United States

Sources: See table 2.1.

answers to the question of what motivated them to apply method, standardization, and planning to architecture.

SCIENTIFIC MANAGEMENT AND MODERNIST ARCHITECTURE

Some may find it surprising, even disquieting, that many of the most influential architects in Europe and some of those in Latin America—who were artists, after all—took sides with the proponents of such an individualistic, mechanistic, and engineering-based model of organization as scientific management. Their enthusiasm for Taylorism and Fordism surfaced at three levels.

First, they exhibited a technocratic ideological approach to problem solving inspired by the principles of neutrality, efficiency, and planning. Second, they worked for firms that were deeply committed to scientific management, endorsed and used the most important scientific management techniques in their architectural projects, and took part in organizations promoting the diffusion of scientific management. And third, they reinterpreted scientific management in aesthetic terms. I have organized the evidence of the relationship between scientific management and modernism analytically rather than chronologically so that the aesthetic inspiration that the modernist architects drew from the scientific managers becomes readily apparent from a comparison of their ideological and technical inclinations. Table 2.4 summarizes the key characteristics of scientific management (Guillén 1994, 8–11) and describes why they appealed to the modernist architects.

The affinities between modernism and scientific management begin with the assessment of the problem of chaos as one requiring method and organization. Le Corbusier read Taylor's *Principles of Scientific Management* in 1917. At first, Taylorism struck him as a "horrifying and inevitable path towards the future," but it did not take him long to see in engineering a possible "return to order," by applying the "scientific principles of analysis, organization, and classification" (CGP 1987, 191, 398; see also Forty 1986). Scientific management promised to reduce waste and cut costs, and glorified regularity and standardization, aspects that were in line with the aesthetic concerns of the modernists (Larson 1993, 3–33). According to scientific management, chaos, disorder, waste, and soldiering by workers, coupled with management's arbitrariness, greed, and lack of control, seriously constrained production and social welfare (item A1 in table 2.4). A "mental revolution" was proposed to tackle such evils. The modernists believed that traditional modes of thought (i.e., "orthodox intellectual activity" and "academic design") limited rationalization and social liberation (Tafuri 1976, 50–77). Le Corbusier argued that architects were "enslaved to the past" and mounted a blistering attack on "the narrowness of commonplace conceptions" in architecture (Le Corbusier [1923] 1986, 103). One manifesto of the Russian modernists started by reaffirming the goal of the "factual rationalization of artistic labor" (Bowlt 1988, 241), and of a utilitarian conception of art and scientific research into art (Kopp 1985, 10). In general, modernism reasserted the principle of form as an organizing device to avoid disorder (Tafuri 1976, 93).

The scientific managers focused on the analysis of tasks and individual performance, and so did the modernists, who were eager to redefine the different artistic and technical aspects of the job of the architect (A2 in table 2.4). In addition, both groups believed in hierarchy (A3), in a vertically stratified organization of work and decision making based on the principle of specialization. Finally, the scientific managers and the architects shared an admiration for method and calculation as essential to solving the problems of the day (A4). These parallels will become more readily apparent with a

TABLE 2.4
Key Features of Scientific Management, and Why They Appealed to the European Modernist Architects

Scientific Management	Basis of Appeal to the Modernists
A. General features	
1. Perceived problem: Workers' soldiering, waste, disorder; management's arbitrariness and greed, lack of control.	Traditional modes of thought (orthodoxy) are limiting economic rationalization and social liberation.
2. Basic units of analysis: Individuals and tasks.	Need to find alternatives to the "old individual work."
3. Predominant social relationships: Authority, hierarchy, subordination.	Belief in artistic and social hierarchy.
4. Formal knowledge bases: Engineering, psychology, ergonomics, physiology.	Architecture as a technical as well as artistic endeavor.
B. Ideological features	
1. Rationality assumptions: All actors can behave rationally.	Belief in rationality and planning.
2. Predominant conditions: Technical.	Belief in technocracy.
3. View of industrial conflict: Avoidable; increased surplus benefits workers, managers, and society at large.	Technocratic elites (including artists) can help solve social and industrial problems.
4. View of workers: Blindly driven by self-interest.	Need to change traditional modes of thought.
5. How to manage workers: Tell them what to do, and supervise them.	Need to inculcate a new ideology of work.
6. Social and intellectual agenda: Futurism, human mastering of nature; material advance; the engineer as visionary.	Desacralization of intellectual activity, permanent social change, elevation of public taste; the artist as visionary.
C. Technical features	
1. General form of solution: Normative, one best way of organizing.	Normative: one best way of designing and of performing production tasks.
2. Methodology: Experimentation, time-and-motion studies, job analysis.	Experimentation with forms, materials, and techniques; job analysis.
3. Selection of workers: On-site, scientific psycho-physiological testing.	Talent-based selection to arrive at artistic and productive excellence.
4. Distribution of tasks: Task conception and execution separated; division of labor among individual workers, specialization.	The artist designs the product, the components, and the production process; the worker performs prescribed tasks.

TABLE 2.4 (*Continued*)

Scientific Management	Basis of Appeal to the Modernists
5. Authority structures: Simple managerial hierarchy.	Need to plan, administer, and control efficiently.
6. Concentration of authority: Unity of command, control of supervisory authority.	Need to centralize design activities and to control the production process.
7. Organization of the process of work: Work simplification, mechanization, assembly-line work.	Belief in planning, simplification, and standardization; prefabrication; "artistic assemblage."
8. Preferred rewards: Piecework wages, bonuses.	Need to motivate and economize on labor.
D. *Evoked imagery* 1. Order, system, objectivity, machinery, mass production.	Regularity, continuity, speed, technology, mass production, machine aesthetic.

Source: Adapted and expanded from Guillén 1994, 1997.

comparison of the ideological and technical coincidences between the two groups.

IDEOLOGICAL AFFINITIES BETWEEN SCIENTIFIC MANAGEMENT AND MODERNISM

The scientific managers and the modernists agreed in their technocratic approach to industrial and social problems (see panel B of table 2.4): everybody can behave rationally (item B1); technical improvements and "social engineering" will solve social problems, including class conflict (B2 and B3); and a new "ideology of work" needs to be inculcated into workers (B4 and B5; Tafuri 1976, 57). The famous dictum by Le Corbusier ([1923] 1986, 289) on social problems illustrates this ideological agenda: "Architecture or revolution. Revolution can be avoided." In his writings Le Corbusier ([1924] 1987) championed the belief in the capacity of rational planning to improve efficiency, welfare, and standards of living in the city (Brooks 1987, 206). Like the scientific managers, the modernist architects claimed the right to organize life at the factory as well as the home. The Russian architect El Lissitzky explained: "As a result of the precise allotment of time and work rhythms and by giving each individual an important role of responsibility, the factory has become the true home of education. . . . The factory has become the melting pot of the socialization of the urban population; its architecture is not merely the wrapping for a group of machines but something completely new and different" (quoted in Kopp 1985, 103).

The modernist architects saw themselves as much more than mere designers of good-looking buildings. According to Hannes Meyer, the architect "was an artist and is becoming a specialist in organization. . . . [B]uilding is only organization: social, technical, economic, mental organization" (quoted in Whitford 1984, 180). Aleksei Gan went even further: "Art is finished! It has no place in the human labor apparatus. Labor, technology, organization!" (quoted in Bowlt 1988, 223). Moisei Ginzburg argued that the "architect will no longer think of himself as the decorator of life but as its organizer" and ought to find "types of housing that will help develop a way of life for the workers that is of a socially superior type." "From a garden one can teach many lessons, and encourage people to live better," argued Brazilian modernist landscape designer and longtime Socialist Party member, Roberto Burle Marx (Fraser 2000, 179). "Maximum efficiency and minimum effort," cried the Mexican architect Juan O'Gorman; "maximum comfort for minimum cost," demanded Gregori Warchavchik (quoted in Luna Arroyo 1973, 271; Fraser 2000, 47, 165). In O'Gorman's view, composition was to follow a simple plan: "the spaces for circulation which served to unite and separate, the useful places for work and those for rest, separated by walls so that [each] should be efficient" (quoted in Fraser 2000, 52).

In a powerful, if scary, metaphor, houses and buildings became "social condensers," which would instill in their dwellers new social habits (Kopp 1985, 22, 64). The architects of Brasília, Brazil's new capital city, situated buildings in the midst of communal spaces to emphasize collective interaction as opposed to private life and property. They actively sought to reduce the impact of social stratification, to equalize, to harmonize (Holston 1989, 74–91), but with the (technocratic) architect planning for everything and everyone. Lúcio Costa, who designed the pilot plan for Brasília, intended the city to be "an exemplar, or enclave, or beachhead, or blueprint of radiating change which creates a new society on the basis of the values that motivate its design," that is, equality, standardization, and progress (quoted in Holston 1989, 77). The modernist architects wished to break with their old role of catering to the tastes of the monarch, the Church, or the upper class, and this desire paralleled the scientific manager's goal to make mass consumption widely available and to fix social problems by increasing the size of the pie. As Hannes Meyer stated in 1926, *The new artwork is a collective work and intended for all*; it is neither a prize for the collector nor an individual's private privilege." He suggested that in the new architectural era, "the artist's atelier becomes a scientific laboratory" (quoted in Kaes, Jay, and Dimendberg 1994, 445–49). Peter Behrens, the chief architect and designer at AEG, stated that "through the mass-production of objects of use corresponding to an aesthetically refined order, it is possible to carry taste into the broadest sections of the population" (quoted in Weston 1996, 50). These views of the role of the architect in shaping life at home and at the factory developed in the midst of rapid economic and social change, as noted by Hungarian-born László Moholy-Nagy, a teacher at the Bauhaus school of modernist design in Germany: "This is our century: technology—machine—socialism. Come to terms with it, and shoulder the tasks of the century" (quoted in Wingler 1983, 28).

Le Corbusier's "free plan" has often been referred to as an arrangement highlighting the central theme of rationalized space in which work, or life in general, takes place (see chapter 4). The free plan makes it possible to accommodate high turnover rates of workers or residents, and hence sends the message that people are interchangeable and replaceable. Le Corbusier himself argued that in modernist buildings "labor will shift about as needed, and must be ready to move, bag and baggage" ([1924] 1987, 231). In addition, the modernist architects were quick to point out that open, free spaces inside buildings, achieved through pillar-based construction and the relegation of walls to the role of separation rather than support, "eliminated workers' privacy and facilitated their constant surveillance by the gaze of technocratic reason" (Gartman 2000, 89). As Mies van der Rohe ([1923] 1971, 74) once argued, "the office building is a house of work, of organization, of clarity, of economy. Bright, wide workrooms, easy to oversee, undivided except as the organism of the undertaking is divided. The maximum effect with the minimum expenditure of means." In a more worker-friendly vein, Walter Gropius realized as early as 1911 the potential contribution of a modernist architecture to the rationalization of industry: "A worker will find that a room well thought out by an artist, which responds to the innate sense of beauty we all possess, will relieve the monotony of the daily task and he will be more willing to join in the common enterprise. If the worker is happy, he will take more pleasure in his duties, and the productivity of the firm will increase" (quoted in Banham 1986, 201).

As true technocrats, the modernists followed the scientific managers in assuming that workers shared their ideas: "These millions of workers must unquestionably be considered supporters of modern architecture" (Ginzburg, quoted in Starr 1976, 206). Following the classic Fordist logic, however, they thought of workers not only as producers but also as consumers. For the Russian architect Yakov Chernikhov, the new modernism "can, and must, take into consideration all the concrete needs of contemporary life and must answer in full the needs of the mass consumer, the collective 'customer'—the people" (quoted in Bowlt 1988, 260–61). The modernists promised great improvements in the quality of life (e.g., Soria y Mata 1894, 11; Behrens, as quoted in Buddensieg 1984, 208; Cooke 1995), just as Taylor did.

The modernists and the scientific managers clearly viewed themselves as visionaries equipped with a "futurist," forward-looking agenda focused on material progress and on achieving change (B6 in table 2.4). Thus, O'Gorman pointed to architecture's end "to be useful to man in a direct and precise way. The difference between a technical architect and an academic or artistic architect will be perfectly clear. The technician is useful to the majority and the academic useful to the minority. . . . An architecture which serves humanity, or an architecture which serves money" (quoted in Fraser 2000, 52).

THE TECHNICAL PARALLELS

One could argue that it was not really that surprising to find these radical modernists using colorful rhetoric in order to liberate themselves from the chains of tradition, bolster their creativity, and attract attention to their cause. However, there was much more than creative thirst or rhetorical fluff in modernism. The modernists not only glorified planning and the beauty of the machine in their writings and architectural works but also endorsed and used the new scientific methods of labor management and organization originally developed in the United States at the turn of the century. The similarities between the techniques used by the scientific managers and by the modernists are stunning— and perhaps troubling.

Normative solutions (item C1 in table 2.4) were favored by both groups, and the "one best way" of producing, building, or designing was believed to be both feasible and attainable (Nerdinger 1985, 11). Many modernists endorsed and personally used the scientific management methodology of experimentation, time-and-motion studies, and even work flowcharts à la Gantt (C2). Thus, in 1927 Gropius recommended the "determination of the expenditure of time and energy for each individual part of the production process during manufacture and assembly of the buildings," and the "preparation of flow charts of work on the site according to scientific business principles" (quoted in Wingler 1983, 127; Nerdinger 1985, 18, 20). Following the archetypal Taylorite logic, he further observed: "Precise numerical records by the famous American scientific managers Taylor and Gilbreth, show that the average American bricklayer is not more productive than the German bricklayer. Rather, the reason for the astonishing double efficiency in the United States lies in the adoption of appropriate building methods" (Gropius 1927, no page).

Gropius and his collaborators introduced time-and-motion study at the Dessau and Praunheim housing projects using photo cameras and stopwatches.[2] Other German architects had long been in favor of applying scientific management. Max Mayer lectured in 1914 on "Taylor's Suggestions for the Construction Business," while Martin Wagner edited a journal during the 1920s that published many reports on Taylorism and Gilbreth's motion studies

[2] See Bauhaus-Archiv Berlin, Schrank 34, Inv.-Nr. 9153/1-12; RFG 1929; RFGWBW 1929, 92–130.

(Nerdinger 1985, 11–12).[3] In the early Soviet Union the modernists used time-and-motion study to plan the allocation of space in public and residential buildings, and were in touch with the main Taylorite organization, the Scientific Organization of Work or NOT. "On the basis of the new processes of domestic work and way of life, we then devised new sizes and forms of accommodation, analyzing the forms we had built up on the basis of movement diagrams and of the schemes of equipment that will serve the accommodation" (quoted in Cooke 1995, 112, 115). In Spain, the urban planner and industrialist Arturo Soria advocated and actually implemented methods of scientific management in the tramway shops at Madrid's Ciudad Lineal (Linear City), his chief contribution to urban planning (Soria y Mata 1894, 1907; Collins and Flores 1968; Benevolo [1960] 1977, 358–61; García Hernández and Calvo Barrios 1981; Maure Rubio 1991, 302–4).

The modernist architects sometimes got carried away by the promises of scientific management. At the International Congress for Modern Architecture of 1928, Gropius, May, and Le Corbusier each presented papers discussing how to use time-and-motion study to arrive at the so-called "minimum existence housing unit," that is, the smallest possible apartment that an average family could comfortably inhabit (CIAM [1928a] 1979; Mumford 2000, 30). Similar proposals were put forward by Ginzburg in the Soviet Union, and by Bottoni and Griffini in Italy (Kopp 1985, 64; Etlin 1991, 227–28). The Mexican government in 1932 organized a competition for the "minimum worker's house" (Fraser 2000, 53).[4] German and Russian architects even delved into the "question of getting some order into the kitchen" with the aid of time-and-motion study (Kaes, Jay, and Dimendberg 1994, 461–62, 465; Cooke 1995, 115–16; see also Bauer 1934). May, for instance, taylorized the kitchen by standardizing doors, windows, work surfaces, and hardware (Mumford 2000, 29). These utopian ideas found their way into the design of apartment units, bathrooms and kitchens, and remain influential to this day (Giedion [1948] 1969; Nolan 1994, 206–26).

Heavily influenced by the modernist architects, other artists also found in Taylorism a source of inspiration and creative techniques. The Russian art theoretician Nikolai Chuzhak used time-and-motion study to improve performance skills in drama through the elimination of redundant or inefficient motions, gestures, and expressions (Lodder 1983, 170–80). His compatriot Vsevelod Meyerhold arrived at a science of "biomechanics" or application of

---

[3] See Reichsforschunggesellschaft für Wirtschaftlichkeit im Bau- und Wohnungswesen, *Mitteilungen*, no. 5 (February 1928): 2; no. 31 (April 1929): 7; no. 40 (April 1929): 1–6; no. 42 (April 1929): 1–6.

[4] See also *Revista Mexicana de Ingeniería y Arquitectura* 13 (1935): 168–86. Evidence of Spanish efforts in this respect can be found in *AC*, no. 6 (1932): 21 and no. 8 (1932): 21 (reprinted as *AC/GATEPAC 1931–1937* [Barcelona: Gustavo Gili, 1975]).

Taylorism to the theater. In his view, research could help "discover those movements in work which facilitate the maximum use of work time," so as to improve acting skills and reduce play duration from four hours to one "without lessening aesthetic content or form" (quoted in Stites 1989, 161; see also Reeves, Duncan, and Ginter 2001).

Scientific management stressed the careful selection of the most adequate worker for each task, and so did the modernist architects (C3 in table 2.4). They believed in a talent-based selection of apprentices to bring forth artistic excellence and channel good design to industry (Bayer, Gropius, and Gropius 1975, 22). Le Corbusier extended the principle to the workers who were to perform the tasks of production:

> Industry has brought us to the mass-produced article; machinery is at work in close collaboration with man; the right man for the right job is coldly selected; laborers, workmen, foremen, engineers, managers, administrators— each in his proper place. . . . Specialization ties man to his machine; an absolute precision is demanded of every worker, for the article passed on to the next man cannot be snatched back in order to be corrected and fitted; it must be exact in order . . . to fit automatically into the assembling of the whole; . . . a strange foreman directs severely and precisely the restrained and circumscribed tasks. ([1923] 1986, 274–75)

These Taylorite ideas about work simplification and specialization were embraced by the International Congress of Modernist Architecture (CIAM) in its La Sarraz Declaration of 1928, which advocated the "simplification of working methods on the site and in the factory," and "the employment of less specialized labor working under the direction of highly skilled technicians" (CIAM 1928b, 110). The Declaration was signed by Le Corbusier, May, García Mercadal, and Meyer, among other leading architects.

Some modernist architects were drawn to the scientific methods of modern psychology. In 1926 the architect Nikolai Ladovsky created a psychotechnical laboratory at the Higher State Artistic-Technical Workshops (VKhUTEMAS), the Soviet equivalent of the Bauhaus, borrowing from the theories of the father of industrial psychology, Hugo Münsterberg. The laboratory was initially used to select the best students, do research on the amount of energy required to perceive different architectural forms, and experiment with devices to measure various dimensions of human visual capacity. The key recommendation to architects was to handle complexity with discipline and restraint, because more regular and simple forms were found to be easier to perceive and therefore to produce more satisfaction. As Ladovsky observed, "Psychotechnics cannot create artists . . . but it can give them all a solid starting point from which they can achieve the aims to which they aspire by the most scientifically correct means" (quoted in Ginzburg 1982, 97; Kopp 1985, 136; Senkevitch 1983; Cooke 1995, 98, 184–85).

The modernist architects also subscribed to scientific management's proposal to totally separate task conception from task execution (C4 in table 2.4). Le Corbusier's quotation above is explicit in this respect. The case of Gropius is particularly relevant here, because early in his career he had celebrated craftsmanship (Junghanns 1982, 171). By 1916, however, he was arguing strongly in favor of replacing "all the factors of the old, individual work" (quoted in Whitford 1984, 36). Gropius's master, Peter Behrens, had also warned against the "imitation of handcraftsmanship" on the occasion of his appointment as chief designer of the AEG company in 1907 (Buddensieg 1984, 207). In the early Soviet Union, the art historian Boris Arvatov, echoing the beliefs of the modernist architects, rejected the "individual craft method" in favor of the "scientifically organized," "collective artistic work" (quoted in Lodder 1983, 106–7). Ginzburg carried the idea of the division of labor to its most extreme consequences when arguing that the job of the architect should be decomposed into its constituent tasks to remove individual discretion and intuition. He used work flow diagrams in an attempt to achieve that goal (Ginzburg 1982, 114; Lodder 1983, 118; Cooke 1995, 121, 127).

Hierarchy and unity of command constituted central ideas in scientific management and the modernist architects defended them, especially when addressing the problem of urban planning (Le Corbusier [1923] 1986, 274–75; [1924] 1987; C5 and C6 in table 2.4). The modernist housing projects in Germany during the 1920s speak to the belief in unified artistic management as well as in technocratic planning. The postwar housing shortage generated much artistic activity in Germany thanks to the ambitious building programs of several regional and city governments run by the Social Democratic Party and often supported by a wide spectrum of political forces. Rapid industrialization and urbanization had expanded the demand for affordable housing, while the years of war and rampant inflation had prevented cities from tackling the problem before 1924. The challenge was to build large-scale, low-cost housing settlements as quickly and efficiently as possible. In fact, the tight budgetary constraints forced architects to experiment with new forms, materials, and techniques, including scientific management and assembly methods. The large-scale housing projects in Frankfurt, with architect Ernst May as head of Municipal Housing, and in Berlin, under the direction of Martin Wagner, paved the way for numerous other projects throughout Germany after 1927 (RFGWBW 1929, 92–130; Wingler 1969, 126–27; NGBK 1977, 41–108; Lane 1985, 87–124; Kaes, Jay, and Dimendberg 1994, 454–73).

Simplification and standardization of designs and tasks, including a division of labor, were a cornerstone of both scientific management and modernism (C7 in table 2.4). The designer Theodor Fischer made it clear at the first session of the German Federation of Artistic Workshops in 1907 that "mass production and division of labor must be made to produce quality" (Bayer, Gropius, and Gropius 1975, 11; Campbell 1978, 51 n. 66; Buddensieg 1984, 16). In a

1910 memorandum to AEG's top management, Gropius wrote: "To implement the concept of the industrialization of house construction, the company will repeat individual components in all of its designs and hence facilitate mass production, promising low costs and easy rentability [i.e., profitability]" (quoted in Wingler 1969, 20; see also Gropius 1926, 96). In 1925 the Bauhaus adopted the famous industrial standards, DIN (*Deutsche Industrie-Normen*). Standardization was also a priority for other German architects like Hilberseimer and May (Hays 1992; Hilberseimer 1927, 21–26, 97–98; Lane 1985, 90–103).

Standardization captured the imagination of designers working in related artistic fields as well. Standardized textiles and clothing by Varvara Stepanova, Lyubov' Popova, and Vladimir Tatlin were massively produced at the First State Textile Print Factory in Moscow. In fact, clothing became an important area of research in the early Soviet Union, a development underscored by the creation in 1925 of the Committee on Standard Clothing at the Decorative Institute in Leningrad (Lodder 1983, 145–55, 181–204; Kopp 1985, 10–11; Andel 1990). At the Bauhaus theater, Oskar Schlemmer standardized the characters through costume and mask (Droste 1990, 158–62). Gropius went beyond most modernists to suggest that standardization was not only desirable from a technical point of view but something far more momentous: "Standardization is not an impediment to the development of civilization, but, on the contrary, one of its immediate prerequisites" (Gropius [1936] 1965, 34).

Modernist architects displayed a boundless enthusiasm for the assembly line and Fordism. Gropius, Meyer, Wagner, and Le Corbusier proposed to make houses "by machine tools in a factory, assembled as Ford assembles cars" (Banham [1960] 1980, 222). The leaders of the German prefabricated housing movement, Gropius and Konrad Wachsmann, refined construction methods and collaborated with several industrial firms (Herbert 1984, 52, 70–71, 81, 87–103, 107–59; Kaes, Jay, and Dimendberg 1994, 439–49), as did the French pioneers in this area, Sauvage and Hennebique. Architects May and Wagner founded the "New Economy of Building" movement (Nerdinger 1985, 11–14). Another German architect, Hilberseimer, used Ford's ideas about the spatial decentralization of cities to further his views about modern city planning and suburbanization (Pommer, Spaeth, and Harrington 1988, 92–93), while Wagner wrote about "The teachings of the Automobile-King Henry Ford" (Nerdinger 1985, 16–17). In Russia, Ginzburg read and often quoted from Ford's autobiography, published in Russian in 1924. The Russian modernists predicted that "millions of producers will be making normalized objects for everyday life" (quoted in Bowlt 1988, 240, 254–61), and Lissitzky even proposed that "building norms and construction times must be worked out, so that building can be transferred to mass-production factories and houses ordered from a catalogue" (quoted in Lissitzky-Küppers 1967, 374). Mies van der Rohe ([1924] 1971, 82) wrote about "Industrialized Building," arguing that "Industrial production of all the parts can really be rationalized only in the course of the manufacturing process, and work on the site can be entirely a matter of assembly. . . . This will result in greatly reduced building costs." And Costa argued that "it is vital that industry supports construction, producing, conveniently, all those elements that it requires, with the same degree of perfection that the coachwork of automobiles shows" (quoted in Deckker 2001, 17).

The possibility of economizing on labor through new organizational methods and monetary incentives has already become evident in several of the excerpts quoted above (item C8). As early as 1894 the Spanish architect Soria was observing the "daily economy of time and labor" that could be realized from improved methods and design (Soria y Mata 1894, 7). The German architect Erich Mendelsohn wrote: "For each challenge demands efficiency, clarity, simplicity. Each must be efficient because all labor is too valuable to be wasted senselessly" (quoted in Kaes, Jay, and Dimendberg 1994, 452). Perhaps Behrens was most clear about this cardinal scientific management idea (C8 in table 2.4) when looking for solutions to the housing shortage after World War I: "The Taylor System, therefore, means a most intensive use of individual labor power, which . . . will significantly reduce the number of workers or the length of working time" (Behrens and de Fries 1918, 60). This quotation could easily be found in one of Gilbreth's landmark treatises on bricklaying, yet it comes from an important book in the development of European modernism.

THE "LOST" MESSAGE: FROM IDEOLOGY AND TECHNIQUES TO AESTHETICS

The preceding analysis of the ideological and technical affinities between scientific management and modernism sets the stage for an understanding of the aesthetic elements that the modernist architects and designers perceived in the new realities created by Taylorism and Fordism. Their taste for the machine as a metaphor for aesthetic theory seems to have blended handsomely with an enthusiasm for the new organizational methods pioneered by American engineers. Thus, the modernist architects saw beautiful things and possibilities for artistic expression in the rationalized world of machine production. As the Spanish architect Casto Fernández Shaw put it, "architecture must be modern, like an airplane in which no element is missing or superfluous; well defined, without hesitation, engineered architecture, all of it following a formula or diagram" (quoted in Diéguez Patao 1997, 216–17).

The architects' fascination with the regularity, continuity, and speed of machinery, technology, and mass production represents, therefore, the last affinity between modernism and scientific management, one that the European modernists were the first to articulate (item D1 in table 2.4). The Italian futurist

F. T. Marinetti's most powerful and famous line went as follows: "We affirm that the world's magnificence has been enriched by a new beauty: the beauty of speed. . . . A roaring car . . . is more beautiful than the Victory of Samothrace," in a reference to the imposing Greek sculpture at the Louvre Museum in Paris (Marinetti [1909] 1973, 21). In appropriately less adorned prose, the most accomplished Italian modernist architect, Giuseppe Terragni, made it clear in 1928 what his main source of inspiration was and why: "The house can in a certain way be compared to a machine and must be constructed so that every one of its parts serves a precise purpose. There should be nothing there that is useless or superfluous, because like a machine, this will end up hindering its functioning" (quoted in Etlin 1991, 265). Terragni had found his inspiration in the designs of the futurist Sant'Elia, who declared: "We must invent and fabricate *ex novo* the modern city similar to an immense shipyard, tumultuous, moving, dynamic in every aspect, and the modern house similar to a gigantic machine" (quoted in Etlin 1991, 74). Gropius argued that "the Bauhaus believes the machine to be our modern medium of design," and that "we want an architecture adapted to our world of machines, radios and fast cars . . ." (quoted in Curtis [1982] 1996, 193–94). Mendelsohn agreed: "The machine, till now the pliable tool of lifeless exploitation, has become the constructive element of a new, living organism." (quoted in Curtis [1982] 1996, 187). In 1921 the Mexican muralist David Alfaro Siqueiros drove home this same point in quite emotional terms: "*Let us live our marvelous dynamic age!* Let us love the modern machine which provokes unexpected plastic emotions, the contemporary aspects of our daily lives, the lie of our cities under construction, the sober practical *engineering* of our modern buildings, devoid of architectural complications (immense towers of iron and cement stuck in the ground) . . ." (quoted in Fraser 2000, 37).

The machine became an ideological, technical, and aesthetic frame of reference. As Collins has aptly put it: "The lesson of the machine is . . . reduced to three generalizations: firstly, that a well-stated problem naturally finds its solution; secondly, that since all men have the same biological organization, they all have the same basic needs; and thirdly, that architecture, like machinery, should be a product of competitive selection applied to standards, which, in turn, should be determined by logical analysis and experimentation" ([1965] 1998, 165).

The formulation of a modernist aesthetic meant that the architect could learn from engineers not only forms but a new set of principles, a new vocabulary to approach the process of artistic creation. It is important to realize that the modernists found in scientific management much more than new formal and technological possibilities. The "mechanization" of architecture was supposed to go beyond making building methods more efficient and rationalizing the job of the architect. Yakov Chernikhov, an architect and professor of geometry at the Leningrad Institute of Railroad Transport Engineers and the

Institute of Engineering Economy, explained in an influential 1928 book: "We are gradually uniting artistic construction and machine construction; the boundary dividing them is being erased. A new conception of the beautiful, a new beauty, is being born—the aesthetics of industrial constructivism [which] *is indebted for the concrete definition of its principles mainly to the artistic and technological research of the last decades*" (quoted in Bowlt 1988, 260–61; emphasis added).

European modernism went beyond American scientific management to formulate an aesthetic drawing on a similar ideology and set of techniques. Thus, Ladovsky thought of modernism as the creation of "a scientific statement of architectural principles on the basis of rationalist aesthetics." He further observed: "Architectural rationality is founded on the principle of economy just as technical rationality is. The difference lies in the fact that technical rationality is an economy of labor and material in the creation of a suitable and convenient building, but architectural rationality is the economy of psychic energy in the perception of the spatial and functional properties of the building. It is a *synthesis of these two forms of rationality* into one building" (quoted in Cooke 1995, 98, 178; emphasis added).

As one of the founders of architectural modernism, Gropius made it clear in 1926 that the new architecture, by merging scientific method and aesthetics, added value above and beyond what either engineering or art had achieved separately:

> The new construction procedures must be affirmed from an artistic point of view. The assumption that the industrialization of housing construction entails a decline in aesthetic values is erroneous. On the contrary, the standardization of structural elements will have the wholesome result of lending a common character to new residential buildings and neighborhoods. Monotony is not to be feared as long as the basic demand is met that only the *structural elements* are standardized while the contours of the building so built will vary. Well-manufactured materials and clear, simple design of these mass-produced elements will guarantee the unified "beauty" of the resulting buildings. (quoted in Kaes, Jay, and Dimendberg 1994, 441–42)

Le Corbusier was perhaps the most thoroughly Taylorite of the modernist architects. In 1923 he lamented that "the Engineer's Aesthetic and Architecture are two things that march together and follow one from the other: the one being now at its full height, the other in an unhappy state of retrogression." He was quick to realize that architecture could borrow creatively from engineering so as to revitalize artistic design. "The purpose of construction is TO MAKE THINGS HOLD TOGETHER; of architecture TO MOVE US." "A house is a machine for living in. . . . An armchair is a machine for sitting in, and so on." Le Corbusier longed for a " 'House-Machine,' the mass-production house, healthy (and morally so too) and beautiful in the same way that the working tools and instruments which accompany our existence are beautiful." As a source of aesthetic inspiration, the machine was a "factor of economy, which makes for selection," thus promoting good taste by overcoming the eclecticism of the traditional architectural styles (Le Corbusier [1923] 1986, 1, 4, 19, 95; capitals in original). He proposed that "in order to BUILD: STANDARDIZE to be able to INDUSTRIALIZE AND TAYLORIZE" (quoted in McLeod 1983, 143, capitals in original; Nerdinger 1985, 15).

Le Corbusier and the other standard-bearers of European architectural modernism found their inspiration not in nature but in the rationalized or Taylorized world of machine production. They found in scientific management an aesthetic message emphasizing regularity, continuity, and speed at the expense of symmetry, ornamentation, and solidity. In their eyes, endless repetition and monotony had become beautiful. After reading about scientific management and observing what industrial engineers had accomplished in work rationalization and design, they proceeded to apply method, standardization, and planning to architecture.

What Caused Modernist Architecture?

> On or about December 1910,
> human nature changed.
> —Virginia Woolf (quoted in Bell [1976]
>   1978, 48).

THE RISE OF A MODERNIST ARCHITECTURE rooted in the machine age and in scientific management has preoccupied numerous architectural historians and social scientists. The vast literature on modernism, however, contains surprisingly few detailed analyses of the different causes that may have produced such a distinct and influential architectural movement. What made some architects approach architecture in a method-driven, standardized, and planned fashion? In this chapter I outline the major explanations that have been proposed. I then explore in subsequent chapters the extent to which the explanatory variables put forward in the literature help sort out the origins and spread of modernism in different countries.

Available explanations of architectural modernism make different assumptions about the role of architecture in society, and result in different arguments (see table 3.1). For many historians, architecture is primarily shaped by material and intellectual conditions, and thus modernism in architecture needs to be seen as an outgrowth of machine-based industrialization, of the new forms, materials, techniques, and ideas of the industrial age. Other architectural historians, by contrast, assume that architecture responds to social and political conditions, so that modernism was the result of a concern for social reform in the wake of the dislocation caused by industrialization. Social scientists—especially sociologists—have proposed a third way of looking at architecture, one emphasizing the tastes and preferences of those who pay for it or use it. Their argument is that such an innovation as modernism emerged only when architects enjoyed a measure of autonomy from the immediate pressures of the mass consumption market. In a related argument, other social scientists and some architectural historians have highlighted the patronage of industrial firms and the state as direct causes of architectural modernism. Finally, another group of social scientists assumes that architecture is primarily to be seen as a profession that rests on a claim to some body of abstract knowledge. Modernism in architecture is supposed to be based on the worldview and techniques that stem from an engineering model, one that includes scientific management as a key component. Accordingly, modernism emerged to the extent

TABLE 3.1
Explanations for the Rise of Machine-Age Modernism in Architecture

Main Explanatory Variable	Key Assumptions about Architecture	Argument	Relevant Authors
Industrialization	Architecture is shaped by material and intellectual conditions.	Modernism in architecture was a response to the machine age, to industrialization, enabled by new techniques and materials (glass, steel, cement), and inspired by romanticism and rationalism.	Hitchcock and Johnson [1932] 1995; Pevsner [1936] 1960; Giedion [1941] 1982; [1948] 1969; Hitchcock [1958] 1971; Tafuri 1976; Frampton [1980] 1992. Emphasis on intellectual conditions: Scully [1961] 1974; Collins [1965] 1998; Zevi [1973] 1994; Banham [1960] 1980.
Sociopolitical upheaval	Architecture responds to social and political conditions. Architectural discontinuities occur during periods of intense social and political change.	Modernism in architecture emerged in the wake of industrialization out of a concern for social reform, and benefited from revolutionary politics.	Jencks 1973; Benevolo [1960] 1977; Lodder 1983; Bowler 1991; Bozdoğan 2001.
Class dynamics (rise of the worker-consumer & mass consumption)	Architecture and design are shaped by the tastes and preferences of those who use it and/or pay for it.	Only with a belated rise of the new class of worker-consumers did an autonomous modernist architecture emerge.	Bourdieu 1984, 1996; Adorno 1994, 1997; Gartman 2000.
New sponsors (industrial firms & the state)	Architecture and design are shaped by the tastes and preferences of those who commission it or pay for it (though not necessarily use it).	Modernist architecture emerged only when industrial and state sponsorship made it autonomous from the upper class and from the market.	Campbell 1978; Lane 1985; DiMaggio 1991; Nolan 1994.
Professionalization of architecture linked to engineering	Architecture in the contemporary world is shaped by the way in which it has become a professional activity based on a body of abstract knowledge.	Modernism in architecture emerged and flourished when the engineering model influenced the education and professionalization of architects.	Kadushin 1976; Guillén 1997; Pfammatter 2000.

Sources: Curtis [1982] 1996, 685–92; Larson 1993, 23–34; Guillén 1997.

that engineering influenced the education, training, and professionalization of architects.

It is important to note that the five views outlined in table 3.1 do not necessarily exclude one another. In fact, they complement each other to the extent that, for instance, the availability of new materials and techniques, the social problems engendered by industrialization, and the patronage of industrial firms or the state all encouraged designing and building standardized, functional apartments to make it possible for workers to afford housing in the city. Let us dwell upon the assumptions, logic, and predictions of each of the theoretical perspectives.

INDUSTRIALIZATION

There is no shortage of historians of architecture who strongly believe that industrialization was the single most important factor behind the emergence of modernism. There are two sides to this argument. The first is that industrialization provided new materials and techniques that some pioneering architects adopted to revolutionize design. Historians such as Giedion ([1941] 1982), Hitchcock ([1958] 1971), and Frampton ([1980] 1992) note that industrially produced materials like glass, steel, and cement; novel techniques such as prefabrication and structural engineering; and new transportation technologies like the railways and the automobile made it possible for architects to experiment with new conceptions of form and space, a process that eventually led to the rise of a new style, or at least a new approach to architecture, thanks to the "bewildering multitude of possibilities" that they offered (Giedion [1941] 1982, xli). In this view, technology drove changes in design: "Structural engineering grew out of new methods of calculation and new developments in the manufacture of ferrous metals. . . . All structural parts were conceived as linear elements . . . so that their behavior could be measured and controlled in advance. These forces were guided through beams, trusses, and arches as through a pipe line. Prefabrication and standardization naturally followed this linear procedure" (xxxix–xl).

The thesis that industrialization and "continual technical revolution" gave rise to the various strands of the modern movement in architecture has also been proposed, from a Marxist perspective, by Manfredo Tafuri, for whom "the laws of production thus became part of a new universe of conventions" (1976, 86, 89). According to him, modernist architects, especially those at the Bauhaus, "fulfilled the historic task of selecting from all the contributions of the avant-garde by testing them in terms of the needs of productive reality." He goes on to define architecture as the "programming and planned reorganization of building production and of the city as a productive organism" (98, 100). Tafuri sees the connection between Taylorism and modernism as yet another manifestation of architecture's new mission and outlook (107, 110), and argues that "architecture as ideology of the plan is swept away by the *reality of the plan* when, the level of utopia having been superseded, the plan becomes an operative mechanism" (135).

A second type of influence that industrialization had on architecture involved the new industrial forms, symbols, and motifs that architects sought to emulate and incorporate into their repertoires. Several architectural historians have pointed out that industrialization generated "demonstration effects" with important implications for the evolution of modernist architecture, and these effects were largely of a symbolic nature. Thus, Giedion refers to the "pure beauty" of the machine and of engineering structures, "a beauty [that] was not arbitrary" ([1941] 1982, xl). Industrialization created a cultural Zeitgeist of sorts in the midst of which a new intellectual approach to design emerged (Kern 1983). For instance, Pevsner argued that it was "the conquest of space, the spanning of great distances, the rational coordination of heterogeneous functions that fascinates [modernist] architects" ([1936] 1960, 214). This was perhaps most apparent in the written and built works of Le Corbusier, who found inspiration in the silos, grain elevators, bridges, automobiles, airplanes, and ocean liners that proliferated with industrialization (see chapter 4). He openly displayed his admiration for engineering and his disdain for the academic architecture of the past: "Our engineers are healthy and virile, active and useful, balanced and happy in their work. Our architects are disillusioned and unemployed, boastful or peevish. This is because there will soon be nothing more for them to do. *We no longer have the money* to erect historical souvenirs" ([1923] 1986, 14–15).

Still within the group of historians emphasizing industrialization, there is an important stream of thought that criticizes the emphasis on material conditions over intellectual ones. Peter Collins has perhaps offered the best and most comprehensive analysis of the rise of modernist architecture from an intellectual perspective in his *Changing Ideals in Modern Architecture* ([1965] 1998). He takes issue with Giedion's ([1941] 1982) and Hitchcock's ([1958] 1971) focus on the material conditions created by industrialization, arguing instead that "modern architecture is essentially an ethical art, so that it is only intelligible historically in the light of the ideals of those who designed the buildings" ([1965] 1998, xix). He reviews the influence of various intellectual trends from the eighteenth to the twentieth centuries, which he groups under the labels of romanticism, stylistic revival, functionalism, and rationalism. Vincent Scully has also emphasized the importance of intellectual conditions. He argues that "the forms created by the engineers cannot have arisen simply because new materials became available" (Scully [1961] 1974, 13). He sees modern architecture as the outgrowth of the democratic and industrial revolutions. Other historians (e.g., Zevi ([1973] 1994; Jencks 1973; Banham [1960]

1980; Weston 1996) have subsequently provided further analyses of the various intellectual strands and ideas that coalesced, however discontinuously and haphazardly, into modernism.

The importance of industrialization to the development of modernist architecture is predicated on the assumption that architecture is shaped by the material and intellectual conditions of the age. Historians emphasizing the influence of new materials and techniques tend to relegate intellectual conditions to the background (e.g., Hitchcock and Johnson [1932] 1995; Giedion [1941] 1982; Hitchcock [1958] 1971; Tafuri 1976), while those highlighting the impact of ideas tend to downplay material conditions (Collins [1965] 1998; Banham [1960] 1980). The commonality between the two groups is that forces related to industrialization are emphasized as an explanation.

SOCIOPOLITICAL UPHEAVAL

A second group of historians assumes that architecture is primarily the result of social and political conditions rather than material or intellectual ones. In their view, modernist architecture emerged in response to the social dislocation and the political turmoil of the early twentieth century, in part induced by industrialization. Architects sought to come to terms not with the new aesthetic possibilities offered by the machine age, but with problems such as chaotic urbanization, poor working and living conditions, and alienation. As in the case of the industrialization argument, the view that modernist architecture developed hand in hand with sociopolitical upheaval is double-sided. First, modernist architecture offered solutions to the new social and political problems being faced by industrial societies. Second, change in architectural theorizing and practice was facilitated by the occurrence of social and political discontinuities, which made it easier for a new generation of architects to successfully depart from the past, secure resources, and establish a new style. Conversely, in some countries modernism collapsed when favorable political conditions disappeared (Benevolo [1960] 1977; Jencks 1973; Weston 1996).

What sets apart the proponents of the sociopolitical upheaval thesis from the previous group is the rejection of technological determinism as an explanation of the rise of modernism. Thus, Benevolo explicitly argues that "the movement from [industry] to [architecture] obviously could not be continuous, but was achieved by repeated breaks and at the expense of considerable strife; because the modern movement was, in another sense, a revolutionary experiment, which implied a complete re-examination of the cultural inheritance of the past" ([1960] 1977, x). Likewise, Jencks adopts what he calls a "political bias," and seeks not only to chronicle the different strands of the modern movement but also the "informing political acts and motives of the architects" (1973, 31). Another key difference between the industrialization and the sociopolitical theses is that while the former leads to the argument that modernism would be expected to develop more quickly in the most advanced countries industrially, the latter proposes to look at the *speed* of industrialization rather than its absolute level, because social dislocation and political turmoil tend to be more acute in the wake of rapid transformations.

Much scholarship on modernist architecture highlights the link between political and architectural movements. Many modernist architects developed political associations with movements focused on achieving social and political change: utopian Socialism, Marxist Socialism, Communism, Fascism, or the *Falange* (the Spanish Fascist movement and party). They hoped their designs would improve the lives of the masses thanks to the aesthetic application of industrial technology and design (see chapter 2). In Russia (Lodder 1983), Italy (Bowler 1991), Mexico and Brazil (Fraser 2000), and Turkey (Bozdoğan 2001), modernist architects actively participated in revolutionary politics, and in postrevolutionary state and nation building (see chapters 5 and 6).

It should be noted that some architectural historians have argued that modernism emerged out of the complex interaction among the materials, techniques, forms, symbols, motifs, and sociopolitical problems associated with industrialization. For instance, William Curtis proposes that modernist architecture was seen by its precursors and founders as fulfilling historical, economic, political, and social roles:

> "Modern architecture," it was intimated, should be based directly on new means of construction and should be disciplined by the exigencies of function; its forms should be purged of the paraphernalia of historical reminiscence, its meanings attuned to specifically modern myths and experiences; its moralities should imply some vision of human betterment and its elements should be capable of broad application to certain unprecedented situations arising from the impact upon human life and culture of the machine. ([1982] 1996, 11–12)

CLASS DYNAMICS

A third argument about the rise of modernist architecture proposes class dynamics as the key driver. While it builds on some of the insights of the upheaval thesis, it emphasizes continuous rather than discontinuous sociopolitical conflict and change. Class dynamics are always a prime candidate as a possible cause of developments in the society and the culture. The standard Marxist analysis of art argues that the artist responds, in large measure unconsciously, to the contradictions inherent in capitalist society by producing cultural artifacts that reflect his or her position in the class structure.[1] Building on this insight, Bourdieu (1996) has argued that class position does not automatically translate into artistic production catering to specific tastes because classes are themselves divided into fractions. Thus, the bourgeoisie includes both industrial and cultural fractions whose claim to power and influence rests on different kinds of capital. Moreover, the cultural fraction is itself divided in terms of how close it is to the marketplace, with engineers and managers being relatively close while artists and intellectuals are relatively distant. This distinction is also present in the works of the Frankfurt School of critical sociology, which sees cultural production as divided into two fields, one that is autonomous from the market (art) and another which is dependent on it (the so-called cultural industry). This line of thought is fairly critical of the cultural industry and of modernist art. "Strictly technical artwork comes to ruin. . . . If technique is the quintessence of art's language, it at the same time inescapably liquidates its language" (Adorno 1997, 218).

The theoretical argument that modernist architecture emerged only in countries in which it became an autonomous activity free from the exigencies of the mass consumption market has been explored by Gartman (2000), who compared developments in the United States and Germany. According to him, in the United States the incipient modernism of Sullivan and Wright was thwarted by the strong alliance between the industrial bourgeoisie and the technocracy of engineers and managers that saw an opportunity for higher profits in the development of mass consumption markets. Following the Frankfurt School (Adorno 1994), Gartman explicitly argues that American worker-consumers, in seeking to escape from their experience of alienation in the workplace, turned against rationalist, modernist cultural artifacts when it came to deciding where to live, what home furnishings to buy, and which leisure activities to engage in. Accordingly, American architects and designers had no choice but to cater to the tastes of the working and emerging middle-class consumer for cheap but richly decorated buildings and home furnishings, oftentimes following an eclectic mix of historical styles. Architecture and design thus came to be dependent on a mass consumption market for the kind of unsophisticated cultural artifacts often referred to as kitsch.

Gartman then contrasts the dependence of architects and designers in the United States on the coalition of capitalists, technocrats and consumers, with the architect-designers' autonomous position in the German context of the 1920s, which left them free to pursue an aesthetic based on the machine and attentive to scientific management principles. In Germany the mass consumption market was still in its infancy and the industrial bourgeoisie was wrestling to assert its position vis-à-vis the landed aristocracy. According to Gartman,

---

[1] This section relies heavily on Gartman's (2000) comparison of various class-based explanations of artistic production and consumption.

modernist architects found in the social-democratic state of the Weimar Republic an actor willing to introduce rationalization into the worlds of production and consumption, while the capitalists—divided as they were between the large-scale enterprises and the smaller firms—could not provide such support. As a result of the autonomy awarded to them by the state bureaucrats, the German modernists were able to impose their own ideas about aesthetics, a theme that Lane (1985) has highlighted in her masterful analysis of the rise and fall of modernist architecture during the Weimar Republic and the Third Reich.

NEW SPONSORS

The preceding argument that class dynamics and the architect's autonomy may create the conditions for artistic change suggests a related explanation of modernist architecture, one emphasizing interest and agency. Building on Bourdieu's ([1972] 1977, 1984) concept of the "field," Paul DiMaggio (1979, 1988) has called attention to the systematic and dynamic patterns of interaction among various actors in a recognized social arena as the potential explanation for the spread of practices. Architecture constitutes such a field because various actors—ranging from users and critics to clients, patrons, and architects—enter into contact (and conflict) with one another in ways that may be different across societies and time. It is precisely such spatial and temporal variations that enable the neoinstitutional sociologist to formulate arguments and predictions about the adoption and spread of specific practices (Scott 1995a, 92–112). A similar approach was adopted by White and White ([1965] 1993) in their study of the interaction among the government, painters, dealers, and critics in the field of French painting during the eighteenth and nineteenth centuries.

In his pioneering study of the institutionalization of different models of the art museum, DiMaggio (1991) singles out sponsorship and professionalization as the critical variables in the construction and reconstruction of fields of organized cultural activity. This approach seems germane because the rise of modernist architecture coincided in time with key changes in the relative importance of the upper class, the Church, industrial firms, and the state as patrons of art and architecture. Similarly, the profession of architect started to go through institutional changes in the mid-nineteenth century that could also be invoked as sources of innovation and renewal. Let us examine changes in patronage and in professionalization in turn.

Several important studies of modernist architecture have highlighted the role of the state and of industrial firms as sponsors of modernist architecture, though in a different way than the one proposed by Gartman (2000) and other authors emphasizing class dynamics. Campbell's (1978) study of the German Werkbund stands out as one of the best treatments of the relationship between industrial patrons and modernist architects. Lane (1985) and Nolan (1994) draw attention to social democratic policies in Germany during the 1920s as a crucial element in the rise of modernism. The argument can be summarized as follows. New sponsors such as industrial firms and the state funded modernist building and urban planning projects that emphasized functionality out of a concern for more efficient (i.e., less costly) working and living conditions. The social and economic situation of the 1920s prompted employers and governments—the most progressive ones, anyway—to experiment with new organizational ideas in order to tackle problems such as industrial chaos, declining productivity, and the housing shortage. Traditional patrons of the arts such as the Church or the upper class rarely sponsored the work of modernist architects, with a conspicuous exception being Le Corbusier's villas (see chapter 4).

THE PROFESSIONALIZATION OF ARCHITECTURE

The last view to be considered here assumes that architecture is an organized activity undertaken by professionals who lay claim to some body of abstract knowledge. Thus, changes in architectural theory or practice must bear some relationship with the incorporation of innovations to architecture's underlying knowledge base. This view of professional activity has been developed over the last three decades or so by a number of sociologists, who emphasize that expert knowledge lies at the root of professional dynamics. Professional groups and trends emerge and evolve as the result of specific attempts to establish professional boundaries and to monopolize the production and use of expert knowledge (Abbott 1988; Freidson 1986; Larson 1977).

Although artistic movements do not always draw precise boundaries separating insiders from outsiders (Crane 1989), the modernist architects did succeed at controlling key support structures such as sources of sponsorship and educational institutions, especially in certain countries, a development consistent with a model of cultural production emphasizing exclusivity (Kadushin 1976) and also with one focused on cleavages and conflict within a profession (Bucher and Strauss 1961). Modernist architects established new claims to expertise based on a combination of design and technology, borrowing selectively from both the heritage of architectural theory and practice, and from the new conceptions and techniques emerging from engineering and scientific management (Pfammatter 2000). This happened, of course, in the midst of varying degrees of opposition from architects lacking such an engineering orientation, depending on the country. Even in the world of painting we find an important effect of education and professionalization on the structure of the field, as in the case of French painting during the nineteenth century (White and White [1965] 1993).

The link between engineering and modernist architecture has been made by virtually every major architectural historian. However, only a handful of historians have made explicit the important connection between engineering and the *education* of architects, let alone turned it into the core explanation for the rise of modernist architecture. Peter Collins, with his emphasis on ideas, has explicitly argued that it was events such as the founding of the civil engineering school in France, the beginnings of revivalism, and the publication of the first books on architecture and rational construction "rather than technological innovations which first produced the theory of modern architecture" ([1965] 1998, 29). He repeatedly, if briefly, refers to changes in the education of architects as key to the rise of modernist architecture, noting the influence of engineering on training in some countries (140–41, 185, 190, 193, 221–36). His approach is much closer to the one adopted in this book than, say, that of Hitchcock ([1958] 1971), who does not even refer to key educational experiments of the twentieth century like the Bauhaus.

In spite of his emphasis on sociopolitical conditions, Benevolo also highlights the importance of architectural education: "Modern architecture was born of the technical, social and cultural changes connected with the Industrial Revolution. . . . When the single elements had emerged with sufficient clarify, there arose the need for their mutual integration," which was first achieved by William Morris (see chapter 4). "Once the aim has been specified, there is the problem of finding a method of putting it into practice . . . the crucial point of the whole development . . . achieved . . . in 1919, when Gropius opened the Weimar school [i.e., the Bauhaus]" ([1960] 1977, xi). Neither Collins nor Benevolo, however, studied the effect of architectural education systematically. While they comprehensively reviewed social and intellectual developments, they failed to devote sustained attention to architectural education and its emerging links to engineering. Chapter 7 will provide such a systematic analysis.

COMBINING SPONSORSHIP AND PROFESSIONALIZATION

In the following chapters I will demonstrate that industrialization, sociopolitical upheaval, and class dynamics were in some cases necessary but certainly not sufficient conditions for change in the field of architecture between 1890 and 1940. My proposed explanation draws heavily from the sociological theory of institutions and from the theory of social movements, and emphasizes the roles of both new sponsors and a new set of architects with an engineering background seeking to professionalize architecture. John Campbell has defined institutions as consisting of "formal and informal rules, monitoring and enforcement mechanisms, and systems of meaning that define the context within which individuals, corporations, labor unions, nation-states, and other organizations operate and interact with each other. Institutions are settlements born from struggle and bargaining. They reflect the resources and power of those who made them and, in turn, affect the distribution of resources and power in society" (2004, 1).

From this perspective, an explanation for the emergence of modernist architecture based on the dual context of the rise of new sponsors and of the professionalization of architecture as an activity combining artistic and engineering elements has the virtue of overcoming three important limitations in the explanations most frequently advanced by historians of architecture. First, institutional change is not triggered by "problems" such as sociopolitical upheaval alone because "actors may fail to recognize problems as such for a long time. They may also disagree about how serious a problem is, how to solve it, or whether anything can or should be done about it in the first place" (Campbell 2004, 175). Change does not just "happen." In order for change to take place, problems need to be defined and tackled by "social actors," "agents of change," or "institutional entrepreneurs," frequently against the opposition of others (Zald and Useem 1987; Meyer and Staggenborg 1996). Thus, it is imperative that actors frame and construct problems in a way that captures the imagination of architects, sponsors, and users (Frickel and Gross 2005; McAdam, McCarthy, and Zald 1996). It is also possible that actors socially construct a problem exaggerating its importance or pertinence. From an institutional perspective, however, reality is less important than social construction, for when people "define situations as real, they are real in their consequences" (W. I. Thomas as quoted in Merton 1968, 473).

Second, assuming problems are identified and constructed by some actors as demanding change, the proposed institutional change may put at risk the distribution of resources or power, namely, between architects trained or versed in engineering and those clinging to the notion of architecture as one of the Beaux-Arts, or between old and new sponsors, or perhaps between different types of contractors, some specialized in the use of traditional building materials and techniques, and others in modern, industrial ones (Frickel and Gross 2005; Bucher and Strauss 1961). Third, and as a consequence of the previous point, most theories proposed by architectural historians fail to consider that the likelihood of change depends on whether the actors that mobilize for such change command enough resources to overcome historical inertia, undermine the entrenched power structures in the field or triumph over alternative projects of change. This point has been highlighted by students of organizations and social movements as crucial to any argument about change within a field of activity (DiMaggio 1988; Frickel and Gross 2005; Guillén 1994; Bendix 2001; Campbell 2004, 175–79; McAdam, McCarthy, and Zald 1996; Zald and Useem 1987; Meyer and Staggenborg 1996).

An institutional theory of the emergence of modernist architecture focused on new sponsors and patterns of professionalization overcomes the aforementioned three limitations. As documented in the previous chapter, architects trained or versed in engineering and scientific management defined academic architecture as a problem because of its inability to appreciate the new realities generated by industrialization (new materials and techniques, social dislocation, kitsch art), and its failure to make design available to the masses at low cost. They mobilized resources from industrial companies and the state in an attempt to reorient architectural education and practice. In the next three chapters I will show that their actions were met by the resistance of academic architects, whose power and resource base differed from country to country. In the end, modernist architecture developed more quickly and fully in certain countries than others depending on the outcome of this power struggle.

It is also useful to think about modernist architecture as a social movement. Social movements are "conscious strategic efforts by groups of people to fashion shared understandings of the world and of themselves that legitimate and motivate collective action" (McAdam, McCarthy, and Zald 1996, 6). The success of a social movement depends on the structure of opportunities and constraints faced by a "*group* of actors sufficiently well organized to act on [a] shared definition of the situation" (McAdam, McCarthy and Zald 1996, 8; see also Rochon 1998). Those actors—the modernist architects in this case—emerged as a separate "segment" within the profession with its own, distinctive sense of mission (designing buildings with the user in mind), methodology and techniques (borrowed from engineering), clients (industrial firms and the state), and definition of who qualifies as a true "architect" (Bucher and Strauss 1961; Rao, Monin, and Durand 2003). In several countries the modernist movement generated a reactionary countermovement, and the two opposing factions competed against the other for state favors, business connections, media attention, and the public's approval (Meyer and Staggenborg 1996). Thus, the institutional and social-movement perspectives coincide in noting the importance of sponsorship, resources, professionalization, and power struggles when it comes to understanding change within a field of activity.

This chapter's review of the main arguments regarding the emergence of modernist architecture cross-nationally reveals that previous scholarship has not produced a systematic comparative study with a balanced coverage of the various countries and architects. We now have some important questions to guide our journey around the world following the emergence of modernism. Was modernist architecture the result of industrialization, sociopolitical upheaval, class dynamics, new patterns in sponsorship, or professionalization along an engineering model? Was it perhaps a combination of two or more of these variables? The next three chapters offer in-depth analyses of the rise of modernist architecture in three groups of countries, namely, the industrial pioneers (Britain, France, Germany), the revolutionary late-industrialization cases (Italy, Russia, Spain), and the Latin American countries (Argentina, Brazil, Mexico). In chapter 7, I return to the arguments summarized in table 3.1 to examine the comparative merits of each of them.

CHAPTER FOUR

Industrialization, Technology, and the State: Britain, France, Germany

> Mechanical drudgery cannot be harmonized into art.
> —William Morris ([1888] 1902, 213).

> The great buildings of our time consist of a skeleton, a structure in steel or reinforced concrete.
> —Auguste Perret (quoted in Benevolo [1960] 1977, 327).

> Architecture equals "function × economics."
> —Hannes Meyer (quoted in Curtis [1982] 1996, 199).

IF SHEER INDUSTRIAL GROWTH had been the main driver of modernist architecture, its development should have taken place first and most decisively in Britain and France, the two most advanced European countries during the nineteenth century. A modernist architecture firmly rooted in the machine aesthetic and strongly tied to the world of business, however, actually emerged in Germany, a country whose industry developed relatively late (Benevolo [1960] 1977, 380–81; Curtis [1982] 1996, 99; Gerschenkron 1962). It was there that the first curriculum in modern architecture—the Bauhaus—took shape during the postrevolutionary and chronically unstable period known as the Weimar Republic. The German case illustrates the fact that the rise of modernism was driven by a complex set of forces including not only the availability of new materials and techniques, but also an active role by the state and leading industrial firms that provided funds and institutional legitimacy for educational and building projects. American scientific management was embraced by German officials, industrialists, labor leaders, and architects, unlike in Britain and France. Understanding German developments, however, requires a review of British and French architecture and design practices, which were the leading in the world until the turn of the century, and provided the foundations for the modernist architectural revolution in Germany.

Machine-age modernism did not find fertile soil among British artists, architects, and industrialists. This was the country, though, that produced the early engineering marvels of the Crystal Palace and the Firth of Forth Bridge. While these achievements captured the imagination of architects in Germany, they were met by contempt in Britain, where an aversion "to novelty and artistic adventure" remained the rule (Pevsner 1937, 135).

Towards the end of the long period of Victorian stability, British intellectual elites were characterized by a mentality of cultural conservatism resulting from several influences: "a social philosophy grounded on naturalistic and organicist concepts, the ideals of handwork and craftsmanship, a social reformist attitude, ruralism, nostalgia, and revivalism" (Guillén 1994, 215). Despite the obvious differences in economic development, this mentality paralleled the Spanish mindset at the time, and was completely at odds with the emerging modernist mentality among German architects and designers. Instead of becoming a source of inspiration, the machine and the mechanical were seen as something unnatural and inorganic by the leading Victorian social thinkers, especially Thomas Carlyle and Charles Dickens (Sussman 1968, 233). Although the 1851 Universal Exhibition's Crystal Palace in Hyde Park, London, was received at the time as a mind-boggling demonstration of British industrial prowess (plate 4.1),[1] the long Victorian period of political stability and economic growth on the basis of imperial expansion seemed to create the kind of complacency and aversion to change that would hamper a modernist movement. Tastes and aesthetic inclinations remained anchored in the past, and industrialization, if anything, contributed to the proliferation of mediocre design. For example, the aesthetic quality of the objects displayed at the 1851 Exhibition was "abominable," "incongruous," "rich in atrocity," and "vulgar," as harshly, though rather accurately, assessed by Pevsner ([1936] 1960, 41, 42).

Another important contextual factor in the evolution of British architecture at the turn of the century had to do with the reception given to scientific management during the 1900s and 1910s. Not only did engineers lack clout within the British educational and occupational hierarchy, but they also reacted, at least initially, "with reticence and even open animosity" to Taylorism (Guillén 1994, 214). The publication of the main books by Taylor or the Gilbreths received scant attention. One of the key journals, *The Engineer*, even took issue with *The Principles of Scientific Management*'s main postulates and underlying philosophy: "We do not hesitate to say that Taylorism is inhuman. As far as possible it dehumanizes the man, for it endeavors to remove the only distinction that makes him better than a machine—his intelligence" (quoted in

---

[1] Although the Palace was 1,851 feet long, it was built in just sixteen weeks, thanks to the prefabrication of iron and glass parts (Pevsner [1936] 1960, 133).

Levine 1967, 63). British engineers thought that scientific management was "a too rigorous systematization of method to the exclusion of all other considerations," preferring instead to apply commonsense approaches to management. "We have yet to learn that British works managed on American lines have paid higher dividends than British works managed on British lines" (a 1913 statement quoted in Littler 1982, 95–96). During World War I engineers and their associations and journals did shed many of their reservations towards scientific management, but actual implementation at firms remained rare and piecemeal at best (Whitston 1997a).

Most importantly perhaps, the British state and trade unions were staunchly critical of scientific management, seeing in it a threat to the humanity of workers and managers alike, and to the British way of life. The unions effectively resisted the implementation of the new methods of work, clinging to the traditional definitions and practices associated with craftsmanship and the skilled trades, and effectively shaping, although not always defeating, the introduction of Taylorism (Guillén 1994, 219–20; Whitston 1997b). While the government intervened to increase productivity during the war, it undermined managerial efforts at gaining control over the shop floor by requiring labor participation (Lewchuk 1984). Thus, very few voices in Britain were ready to propagate the gospel of method, standardization, and planning. Guesswork, tradition, and intuition remained pervasive not just in the world of industry but also in architecture.

Ruskin, Morris, and the Arts and Crafts Movement

The story of the origins and stagnation of the modern movement in Britain is dominated by two prominent figures, John Ruskin and William Morris. As an intellectual, social critic, artist, and theorist of architecture, Ruskin played a central role in Britain's artistic ostracism from the new developments taking place in America and Continental Europe at the turn of the century. He was keenly aware of the languishing of British art and architecture, but identified the surrounding economic and social conditions as the root cause, rather than the process of artistic creation itself (Benevolo [1960] 1977, 171). He believed that industry was to blame, and placed his hopes with medievalism and historical styles.

In his *Seven Lamps of Architecture*, Ruskin defined architecture as the "art which so disposes and adorns the edifices raised by man, for whatever uses, that the sight of them may contribute to his mental health, power and pleasure" ([1849] 1891, 7). He argued that the architect had to consider the historical antecedents that bound architecture to primitive societies and to the use of clay, stone, or wood. Ruskin denounced as "deceits" the "suggestion of a mode of structure or support, other than the true one . . . the painting of surfaces to represent some other material than that of which they actually consist . . . [and] the use of cast or machine-made ornaments of any kind" (32). In his view, building in glass and steel was "eternally separated from all good and great things by a gulf which not all the tubular bridges nor engineering of ten thousand nineteenth centuries cast into one great bronze-foreheaded century, will ever over-pass one inch of" (quoted in Pevsner [1936] 1960, 146). He also argued that architecture and building were different things: "Architecture concerns itself only with those characters of an edifice which are above and beyond its common use" (Ruskin [1849] 1891, 8). Clearly, some of Ruskin's theoretical statements were utterly reactionary: his blistering attack on machine-made architectural elements, his criticism of steel and glass, his fondness for ornamentation, or his insistence that architecture is something other than building for common use. In spite of these, one can also find in his writings some of the seeds of the modern movement, especially his emphasis on truthfulness in structure and in the use of materials.

Ruskin's most enduring impact came from being the teacher of the turn-of-the-century generation of British architects and designers, and from believing that design could improve people's lives (Curtis [1982] 1996, 100). His most influential disciple, William Morris, occupies a prominent place in the history of architecture and design as the founder of the Arts and Crafts exhibitions (1888 onwards), and perhaps as the "father of the modern movement" itself (Benevolo [1960] 1977, 181).[2] Although he strived for an art "of the people for the people," his rejection of most machine manufacture ("production by machinery is altogether an evil"), and of the principle of the division of labor in favor of the "production of unique specimens of artistic workmanship," meant that art and architecture would be affordable only to the rich: "cheapness as a rule . . . can only be obtained at the cost of the . . . cheapening of human life and labor" (quoted in Pevsner [1936] 1960, 22–25). Morris was a typical product of the late Victorian era with his disdain, in the face of it, for technological progress (Guillén 1994, 216). He was "at one time or another, an architect, a painter, a poet, a businessman, an interior decorator, a book illuminator, a furniture maker, a lecturer, a weaver, a magazine editor, a novelist, a Socialist campaigner, a translator, an essayist, a printer, and a publisher" (Ackroyd 1996, 90). His influence was to be as wide-ranging as his expertise.

Morris thought of art as "the way in which man expresses joy in his work." In his view, the machine destroyed the "joy in work" (quoted in Benevolo [1960] 1977, 179–80), and "mechanical drudgery cannot be harmonized into art" (Morris [1888] 1902, 213). "When I was young, I think I really succeeded in ignoring modern life altogether," Morris intimated in a letter to one of his illustrators. "And it was of great service to me" (quoted in Ackroyd 1996, 90). His love for the medieval period was only matched by his commitment to

---

[2] William Morris, the artist, designer, and architect, is not to be confused with the homonymous automobile manufacturer.

utopian Socialist ideas (Morris [1888] 1902); the common thread in these seemingly contradictory avocations being his longing for community and justice. As Ackroyd (1996, 92) cogently argues, "his central purpose was to bring the past back into the minds of his contemporaries." He found his inspiration in historical styles, and in the forms of nature. "In a complete Morris room . . . one is in danger of being suffocated with leaves or pressed to death by flowers" (90; see also plate 4.2).

Morris, although interested in historical styles, helped lay the foundations of the modern movement, especially when arguing that "the art of any epoch must of necessity be the expression of its social life" (Morris [1888] 1902, 204–5). As Pevsner ([1936] 1960, 53) has noted, his designs became the paragon of clarity and sobriety, and he emphasized the "logical unity of composition," the "coherence of surfaces," and "simplicity and economy as opposed to wasteful confusion." His ideas about "art for the people," and architecture as embracing "the whole surroundings of the life of man" were reinterpreted by the German pioneers of modernist architecture and industrial design as a call to substitute rationalized methods of production for the principles of individual work, without abandoning the ideal of craftsmanship (Sussman 1968, 104–34; Read 1954, 79–80, 219–25; Banham [1960] 1980, 44–5). In Britain, by contrast, preservationism, historical styles, and "village values" triumphed over the machine aesthetic. As Pevsner has put it, "the Arts and Crafts kept their retrospective attitude, the engineers their indifference to art as such" and "England forfeited her leadership in the shaping of the new style just about 1900" ([1936] 1960, 147, 175).

One of the most gifted British architects of this period, Morris disciple William Lethaby, made it clear in 1910 that he was no fan of the machine-age approach to work: "Human work, I say, not machine-grinding. Machining is no more real work than hand-organ noises are real music" (quoted in Banham [1960] 1980, 46). He also railed against mass production and standardization: "One cannot sufficiently hide away from the ugliness of things made under £4,000" (quoted in Pevsner 1937, 202). Such a devastating attack on the machine and mass production, of course, connoted a profound dissatisfaction with all things "modern."[3] Lethaby was not alone. Architect Walter Crane, also a student of Morris's, shared his disdain for industry and mechanical production, although he asserted that "plain materials and surfaces are infinitely preferable to inorganic or inappropriate ornament" (quoted in Pevsner [1936]

---

[3] It should be noted, however, that Lethaby was in favor of introducing construction and engineering into the architecture curriculum (Powers 1983, 66, 69). He also displayed occasionally some truly modernist thinking: "We confuse ourselves with these unreal and destructive oppositions between the serviceable and the aesthetic, between science and art," and "The house of the future will be designed as a ship is designed, as an organism which has to function properly in all its parts" (Lethaby 1922, 9, 10).

1960, 29). Another leading architect and architectural theorist of this period, Geoffrey Scott, was overtly classicizing in his approach to design and defended the orthodoxy of the academic style unashamedly (Banham [1960] 1980, 48, 65–67; Rybczynski 2004). Richard Norman Shaw relied on historical styles, although he selected the simplest ones (Benevolo [1960] 1977, 186–87). Among the most influential architects of the first third of the twentieth century, only Charles Robert Ashbee and Charles Voysey accepted the machine as a fact of modern life. The former argued that "[m]odern civilization rests on machinery, and no system for the encouragement . . . of the arts can be sound that does not recognize this," while the latter strove for "precise, bold and simple [designs] absolutely consonant with mechanical processes of production," and for "discarding the mass of useless ornaments" (quoted in Pevsner [1936] 1960, 26; Benevolo [1960] 1977, 186; and Pevsner [1936] 1960, 29, respectively; see also Weston 1996, 41).

The Glasgow Movement

Separate from the Arts and Crafts movement, one finds in Scotland another contemporaneous movement that also influenced modernism in Britain and beyond. Charles Rennie Mackintosh, the main exponent of the Glasgow Movement, while modernist in certain respects, is more easily classified as an innovative art nouveau architect. Like many of his British contemporaries, he was heavily influenced by traditional and historical styles, especially Gothic and Scottish baronial architecture (Benevolo [1960] 1977, 278–84; Curtis [1982] 1996, 64–66; for the dissenting view, see Cooper 1977, 20).

Mackintosh anticipated several key modernist themes when arguing and practicing that materials should be used naturally and honestly, and that the façade should be consistent with the arrangement of space inside. However, he championed traditional decoration based on indigenous stylistic elements, and believed that "construction should be decorated, and not decoration constructed" (quoted in Cooper 1977, 11). The Glasgow School of Art building (1897–99, extended 1907–09) is perhaps Mackintosh's finest contribution (plate 4.3). Like Morris, Mackintosh was more influential on the Continent than in Britain. German architects appreciated his pioneering use of steel and glass, and his innovative arrangement of space and light (Pevsner [1936] 1960, 166–75, 180).

Industry and Industrial Design

In spite of being the birthplace of the Industrial Revolution, the machine aesthetic and modernism failed to capture the imagination of British industrialists. The collaboration between British industry and the design community was limited. The Design and Industries Association or DIA (1915), and the British

Institute of Industrial Art (1920) were met by the indifference of manufacturers. DIA's goal was "to harmonize right design and manufacturing efficiency, accepting the machine in its proper place, as a device to be guided and controlled, not merely boycotted," in a veiled reference to Morris (Pevsner 1937, 160). As late as 1931, the British Board of Trade commissioned the Gorell Report, which readily recognized the exhaustion of industrial art in Britain. The Board's attempt in 1934 to promote good industrial design through a Council for Art and Industry failed for lack of support from industry or the state. British managers missed the potential of modernist design for industry, arguing against product standardization and work simplification because consumer tastes and the size of the market in Britain were so different from those in the United States.[4]

Before World War II, British industrial design remained backward. During the mid-1930s Nikolaus Pevsner undertook an extensive survey of artistic design in industries as diverse as metalwork, furniture, textiles, carpets, wallpapers, pottery, glass, silver, jewelry, leather, packaging, printing, and automobiles. His conclusion could not have been gloomier: "I said in the Introduction to this book that 90 per cent of English industrial products are artistically objectionable. That may have sounded an exaggeration at the time. My survey of trades, I am afraid, has shown that it was a mild statement" (Pevsner 1937, 179). Pevsner believed that modernism could not be "un-English" if it had originated in England, and he blamed Britain's artistic backwardness on the "skepticism and steadiness that characterize English politics and English cultural life," on the "attitude of the upper class," which was the "most serious obstacle to its divulgation," and on the majority of manufacturers and industrialists because "their predilection for the bad, the meretricious and the showy is ineradicable" (136, 206, 207).

British architecture continued to be influenced by classicist and revivalist themes in spite of the early, pathbreaking achievements of the Crystal Palace, the Firth of Forth Bridge, and the incipient modernism of Morris and some of his disciples. Architects and designers were reluctant to carry modernist ideas forward. In the area of city planning, developments followed a similar pattern. The Garden City movement, led by Sir Ebenezer Howard, was essentially ruralist and shared with John Ruskin a distaste for the modern metropolis (Benevolo [1960] 1977, 351–58). The once vigorous movement of prefabricated housing collapsed in the 1920s under pressure from the trade unions and the general distaste for industrialized construction methods (Herbert 1984, 20–21, 29–30).

---

[4] See the following British management journals: *System* 41 (1922): 270–71, 54 (1928): 333; *Business* 55 (1929): 91–92, 113; *Industry Illustrated* 1 (4) (1933): xx, 2 (3) (1934): 24–25, 2 (8) (1934): 13, 2 (9) (1934): 13, 14 (3) (1946): 11; *British Management Review* 3 (1938): 5–27. On the pusillanimous attempts at product and process standardization see Stewart (1987, 39–73) and Read (1954, 222–34).

It is revealing to note that English literature and visual arts echoed the dominant antimachine state of mind. Such key works as Aldous Huxley's *Brave New World* ([1932] 1989, 3, 52–5), Charlie Chaplin's *Modern Times* (1936), and George Orwell's *Nineteen Eighty-Four*, (1949; see also [1946] 1968), "satirized scientific methods of mass production and raised . . . fears about the 'massification' of society" (Guillén 1994, 217, 1997). Only a few, isolated voices accepted the machine. For instance, Oscar Wilde actually praised its aesthetic qualities: "All machinery may be beautiful, when it is undecorated even. We cannot but think all good machinery is graceful, also, the line of the strength and the line of the beauty being one" (quoted in Pevsner [1936] 1960, 27). But then, Wilde was not exactly representative of the British intellectual establishment of the time.

Because of some combination of reactionary upper-class culture, utopian anti-industrialism, the prominence of rural "English values," and an anemic scientific management movement, by the 1910s British modernism in architecture and design had fallen behind developments on the Continent, and did not recover from this delay until the mid-1930s with the arrival of some of the exiled architects from across the English Channel, for example, Berthold Lubetkin and Erich Mendelsohn (Curtis [1982] 1996, 331–33; Weston 1996, 177–84). British artistic "retardation" occurred in spite of the fact that this was the pioneer of the industrial revolution and the richest country in the world until just before World War I.

FRANCE: CLASSICISM, TECHNICAL EXCELLENCE, AND THE RISE OF MODERNISM

Together with Britain, France was the most advanced industrial country in nineteenth-century Europe. It also was the "main repository and authorized interpreter" of the tradition of classical architecture (Benevolo [1960] 1977, 320). The École des Beaux-Arts was well established as the world's leading academic and training institution for architects. French architectural practice, resting on the dual pillars of academic classicism and the glorious technical tradition of the engineering *grandes écoles*, evolved into eclecticism towards the end of the nineteenth century (Martin 2001; Moore 1977; Pfammatter 2000). When art nouveau arrived in Paris during the late 1890s from Belgium, Austria, and other European countries, it was met by some resistance, although architects like Héctor Guimard made good of it with contributions such as the main stairway at Galeries Lafayette and the entrances to the Métro subway stations (Curtis [1982] 1996, 58–59). Art nouveau was merely added to the repertoire of styles, without having a more systematic impact, except for perhaps in the field of furnishings. Modernism in architecture took a long time to coalesce in France, and only after the German, Italian, and Russian avant-garde, had shown the way.

Rationalism and the First Departures from Classicism

Before French architects even started to think in modern terms, it was engineer-constructors who took the first few steps away from classicism. Auguste Choisy was perhaps the most prominent of the turn-of-the-century engineers determined to bring some fresh air into architecture. His approach was unquestionably rational, even Cartesian: logic had to impose itself over caprice. In his view, style should always follow the technical means available to the architect: "La question posée, la solution était indiquée" (quoted in Banham [1960] 1980, 23–24). Thus, Choisy's rationalism was heavily indebted to the Gothic: "Everywhere, in the detailing of the forms, we have recognized the spirit of analysis that governs the economy of the whole work . . . in effect, a construction where stone works to the limit of its resistance" (quoted in Banham [1960] 1980, 30). Choisy thought of buildings as "witnesses fixing the way of life and the moral condition of humanity" (quoted in Banham [1960] 1980, 26). He believed in the "total work of art," and in the "all-round designer," a clear classical influence from the Renaissance.

Choisy partially influenced the two key figures in the rather timid French departure from the prevailing eclecticism in architecture: Auguste Perret and Tony Garnier, both educated in the Beaux-Arts tradition. Their ideas were not well received by their compatriots, and they remained isolated during the better part of their careers, which started around the turn of the century and lasted until well into the 1930s. Their basic contribution was to apply classical geometry and clarity to the new building materials so as to achieve structural coherence (Benevolo [1960] 1977, 321).

Auguste Perret's claim to fame is his designs for the apartment building at 25 bis rue Franklin in Paris (1903) and the garage in rue Ponthieu (1905), in which he showed his (partial) adherence to one of modernism's central tenets, that is, that architecture should be truthful and honest in the use of materials (Banham [1960] 1980, 40–41; Benevolo [1960] 1977, 325–26). The visual effect of the rue Franklin building was stunning: "Everything seems to grow lighter and lighter toward the ground, until finally only a few thin members connect the building with the earth" (Giedion [1941] 1982, 331). Moreover, like Horta, he introduced a flexible ground plan for each floor (plate 4.4). The garage in rue Ponthieu was the first ever to display the reinforced concrete frame on the façade, or in his own words, the "première tentative (au monde) de béton armé esthétique" [first attempt in the world at using reinforced concrete aesthetically] (quoted in Giedion [1941] 1982, 331; see plate 4.5). While Perret pioneered so many aspects of modernism, he failed to abandon the idea of symmetry, one of the dogmas of classicism. In 1952 he described his thinking as follows: "The great buildings of our time consist of a skeleton, a structure in steel or reinforced concrete. The framework is to the building what the skeleton is to the animal; as the animal's skeleton, measured, balanced, symmetrical, contains and supports the most various and most variously situated organs, so must the structure of a building be composite, measured, balanced and also symmetrical" (quoted in Benevolo [1960] 1977, 327–28).

Perret applied the same principles of clarity and honesty to all manner of buildings, including factories, churches, theaters (the Théâtre des Champs Élysées in collaboration with Henry van de Velde), schools, and government offices, but without abandoning the formal vocabulary of the classical orders. As Benevolo ([1960] 1977, 329–31) aptly puts it, "with Perret the last cycle of French academic culture was concluded, with incomparable dignity, once and for all." His most lasting contribution was perhaps to promote the acceptance of reinforced concrete as a building material exposed to the eye (Banham [1960] 1980, 43), an area in which other contemporary French architects like Anatole de Baudot and François Hennebique—a key innovator in skeleton construction with continuous reinforcements throughout the building—also excelled (Curtis [1982] 1996, 76; Benevolo [1960] 1977, 322; Giedion [1941] 1982, 325–26; Pfammatter 2000, 187–91; Pevsner [1936] 1960, 144).

Tony Garnier's name is closely associated with his project, *Une Cité Industrielle*, originally formulated in 1904 but not published until 1918 (plate 4.6). It was partly put into practice with the large-scale works at Lyon, France's second largest city, between 1904 and 1914, and included residential complexes, a stadium, and a hospital center (Banham [1960] 1980, 35–43; Jullian 1989). His benefactor was the mayor of Lyon, Edouard Herriot, a strong supporter of Taylorism (McLeod 1983, 138). In his sparse writings Garnier analyzed the importance of hygienic or sanitary factors like light, air, ventilation, and vegetation. He also theorized about the need for space between buildings, and for a careful choice of orientation. His most important contributions were perhaps his rejection of symmetry as a principle of architecture and city planning, and his ideas about the rationalization of life in the city, although he clung to the use of classicist ornaments. The abandonment of symmetry was a pragmatic decision dictated by the impracticability of remodeling the entire city of Lyon from scratch. Instead of symmetry, he used indefinite repetition in order to obtain regularity, a distinctively modernist solution (Benevolo [1960] 1977, 331–41). He had a deeper theoretical belief in the need to rationalize the use of space, allocating separate areas to housing, utilities, manufacturing, transportation, sport, and health. This idea later became a central thesis of modernist city planning (Banham [1960] 1980, 36).

By 1900 French rationalism in architecture produced an alternative to the eclecticism of the past, but links between architects and industry were slow to develop until the 1920s. While a long tradition of time-and-motion research existed in France during the nineteenth century (Rabinbach 1990, 244–53), there are no documented links between the human engineers and architects like Choisy, Perret, or Garnier. In the meantime, developments in Germany would far outstrip what British and French architects and designers had accomplished. France did eventually jump on the train of modernist architecture thanks to Le Corbusier, whom I will analyze after considering the contributions of German architects to the rise of modernism.

GERMANY: TECHNOLOGY, BIG BUSINESS, AND THE STATE

Modernism flourished the most and developed the closest links to industry in Germany. The German modernists proposed new approaches to industrial and artistic work, and contributed decisively to the development of standardized mass production in the context of a country trying to catch up industrially with Britain and the United States. While they emulated American engineers and constructors in seeking to design functional buildings, they went far beyond in terms of symbolizing the modern world of machines. The German intellectuals and designers saw in the forces of industrialization and modernity an opportunity to combine traditional values with the wonders of mass production (Maier 1970). Two key debates in contemporary German history, the *Streit um die Technik* (debate about technology) and *Technik und Kultur* (technology and culture), date back to the turn of the century, and reached a climax during the Weimar Republic of 1919–33, a period haunted by "military defeat, failed revolutions, successful counterrevolution, a divided Left, an embittered Right, and Germany's famous illiberalism" (Herf 1984, 19). The achievements of Peter Behrens, the Werkbund, and the Bauhaus all need to be understood against the backdrop of a vibrant, but troubled, country, struggling to find its place in a part of the world caught up in the crosscurrents of authoritarianism and democracy, socialism and capitalism, and tradition and modernity.

Unlike in Britain, the German intellectual, governmental, business, and labor elites afforded scientific management a most favorable reception. German engineers were keenly interested, and engineering was a well-organized, powerful profession (Gispen 1989, 1990). Most importantly, the flow of ideas from America to Germany started early on, at the time systematic management was emerging. By the time Taylor published his famous books in the early 1900s and 1910s, Germany was ready to listen. In 1907 the journal, *Werkstattstechnik* (Workshop Techniques), was founded to foster the adoption of better workshop management practices. In a typical statement, one engineer exclaimed: "Just observe the reaction when you mention the word 'American' in a technical context! 'American conditions,' 'American work methods,' 'American manufacturing systems, '*Watchwords*' whose resonance suffices to intoxicate the majority of our minds" (quoted in Kocka 1969, 358). Against this backdrop, the ideas of Taylor, Münsterberg, and Ford were received most enthusiastically in both industrial and artistic circles.

Peter Behrens and the AEG

It should be no surprise that the first successful attempt at applying modernist aesthetic-philosophical ideals in industry took place at the electrical conglomerate AEG, one of the most Taylorite of German firms (Guillén 1994, 100–102). In 1907 this 32,000-worker company appointed as its chief architect and designer Peter Behrens, who promised to work towards the "most intimate union possible between art and industry." Behrens combined a vigorous nationalism with an enthusiasm for engineering science ("the engineer is the hero of our age"). He made crucial contributions in several areas: product standardization and design, printed publicity materials, and design of factory buildings, among them his famous 1908 *Turbinenfabrik* (Turbine Hall, plate 4.7). He also worked for the steel giant Mannesmann (Buddensieg 1984, 207–8, 213, 219; Anderson 2000). Behrens's studio became an attraction to young architects. The most important modernist architects—Le Corbusier, Mies van der Rohe, and Gropius—spent months, even years working with Behrens before World War I.

From Werkstätten to Werkbund

Important as it was, the collaboration between modernist designers and such firms as AEG was only one exponent of a much wider trend. Following the aesthetic and design principles of the Arts and Crafts movement, the *Deutsche Werkstätten* (German Artistic Workshops) were incorporated in 1913. They were preceded by Werkstätten in Dresden, Munich, and Vienna. By 1919 they had established several joint activities with firms and adopted the principles of standardization and mass production, especially of furniture (Wichmann 1992). In 1907 a group of twelve industrialists and twelve designers—architect Hermann Muthesius among them—founded the *Deutscher Werkbund* (German Federation of Artistic Workshops) to attract funds to industrial design activities (Fischer 1975; Campbell 1978; Whitford 1984, 20–21). By 1914 the Werkbund had nearly 1,900 members.[5] Muthesius ([1914] 1971, 29) was convinced that "the existence of efficient large-scale business concerns with reliable good taste is the prerequisite of any export." He was once quoted as saying that the rather daunting goal of the Werkbund was no less than to revive the applied arts "from the sofa cushion to urban planning" (Campbell 1978, 3). He proposed a *Maschinenstil* (machine style) in which objects and buildings are "produced according to the economic nature of the age," "with a severe and almost scientific *Sachlichkeit* [objectivity], with abstinence from all outward decoration, and with shapes completely dictated by the purposes which they are meant to serve," so as to arrive at "a neat elegance which arises

---

[5] *Jahrbuch des Deutschen Werkbundes* 1914, 88.

from suitability and . . . conciseness" (quoted in Pevsner [1936] 1960, 32–33). "We admire a fine surgical instrument," he argued, "because of its elegance, a vehicle because of its pleasing lightness, a wrought-iron bridge soaring over a river because of its bold use of material. . . . In the muscularity of those slim parts we confirm the triumph of technology which has risen to the limits of mastering of materials" (quoted in Weston 1996, 48). He was in many ways reacting to his perception of art nouveau as being "a sham modernity express-ing itself extravagantly in whimsical artificiality" (quoted in Etlin 1991, 53).

The best architects of the time (Behrens, Muthesius, Gropius, Mies van der Rohe, Taut) joined the Werkbund. Throughout the 1910s, the most important contribution of the workshops was to "introduce the idea of standardization as a virtue, and of abstract form as the basis of the aesthetics of product design," notions which would have momentous implications (Banham [1960] 1980, 72; Buddensieg 1984, 46). The Werkbund Yearbooks for 1913 and 1914 in-cluded several pictures of battleships and grain silos to illustrate the principles of functionality and abstract form.[6]

The Avant-Garde and the Bauhaus

The early German experiments in modernist design were firmly rooted in the English Arts and Crafts tradition of utilitarianism and honesty in the use of materials. During the 1920s German modernism flourished in the midst of a flurry of artistic activity. The painters of the *Neue Sachlichkeit* (New Objectiv-ity) and of the *Magische Realismus* movements were using industrial motifs in many of their paintings. They were directly influenced by Giorgio de Chirico, Pablo Picasso, and Ferdinand Léger (who served in the French army's engi-neer corps during the war). German novelists, poets, and moviemakers por-trayed working life in the machine age: Berthold Brecht ("The Impact of the Cities," [1925–28] 1979), and Fritz Lang (*Metropolis*, 1927).[7]

In the field of architecture, the Werkbund tradition was combined with avant-garde notions by the Bauhaus during the 1920s. A school of art and ar-chitecture at the Republic's new capital city of Weimar, the Bauhaus became the most important movement of modernist industrial design. It was founded

[6] See *Jahrbuch des Deutschen Werkbundes*, 1913 and 1914.

[7] Despite the creative outpouring for modernism, there were some dissenting voices in the Ger-man artistic community. Behne and Lüders were perhaps the most outspoken critics of the mech-anization of art and the standardization of life (Nerdinger 1985, 22–23; Campbell 1978, 123; Kaes, Jay, and Dimendberg 1993, 468–69). In the mid-1920s some architects warned that stan-dardization and "the industrialization of building" would bring about higher unemployment (Lane 1985, 135). For instance, the Werkbund's first director was Theodor Fischer, a professor of archi-tecture. In his speech at the first annual meeting, he emphasized the need for "quality work," and expressed doubts about mass production and the division of labor (Eckstein 1958, 39). The vast majority of German designers, however, adopted a decisively modernist stand.

in 1919 by Walter Gropius, a staunch believer in standardization and scientific management methods (Gropius 1927, [1936] 1965), who was well acquainted with industrial developments in America, where he visited the Taylor Society and Ford's automobile factories (Nerdinger 1985, 20). The new school was the result of the merger of the Academy of Fine Arts and the School of Applied Arts founded in 1906 at Weimar by Belgian art nouveau pioneer Henry Van de Velde. Gropius's main goals were to train designers in the various crafts and to have all kinds of artists collaborate to create a "the new building of the future that will bring all into one simple integrated creation: architecture, painting, and sculpture rising to heaven out of the hands of a million craftsmen, the crystal symbol of the new faith of the future" (quoted in Curtis [1982] 1996, 184; Gropius [1926] 1971). The Bauhaus offered a unified curriculum taught by a superstar faculty, including over the years the architects Walter Gropius, Josef Albers, Hannes Meyer, and Ludwig Mies van der Rohe; the painters Paul Klee, Johannes Itten, and Wassily Kandinsky; and the designers László Moholy-Nagy, Lyonel Feininger, Marcel Breuer, and Oskar Schlemmer (see plates 4.8 and 4.9). The Circle of Friends of the Bauhaus included such celebrities as Peter Behrens, Marc Chagall, Albert Einstein, Oskar Kokoschka, and Arnold Schönberg.[8] The German avant-garde architects, designers, painters, and musicians discovered that art or music freed from a harmonic principle could evoke aesthetic emotion (Zevi [1973] 1994, 22, 33).

The Bauhaus made lasting contributions to each and every area of modern design, including architecture, painting, sculpture, furniture, product design, wallpaper, graphic design, typography, pottery, clothing, photography, music, and the performing arts. A distinctive programmatic feature of the Bauhaus was its desire to establish close ties to industry. In 1935 Gropius explained: "I endeavored to secure practical commissions for the Bauhaus, in which both masters and students would put their work to a test. . . . The demonstration of all kinds of new models made in our workshops, which we were able to show in practical use in the building, so thoroughly convinced manufacturers that they entered into royalty contracts with the Bauhaus" (quoted in Benevolo [1960] 1977, 415). Over the years Gropius and his assistants collaborated with many firms: Waggonfabrik of the Prussian State Railways, Hannoversche Papierfabriken, I-G Farben, Adler-Automobilwerke, Junkers, Mannesmann, Ruppelwerk, and Siemens, among others. The Bauhaus designers signed lucrative contracts with several firms for the construction of worker housing quarters (e.g., Junkers), with I-G Farben on advertising and product presentation, and with various lamp, furniture, and wallpaper companies.

When the Thuringian regional government cut its support for the Bauhaus in 1924, the school moved to Dessau, the home of major coal-mining operations and of the Junkers aircraft and engineering works, a key Bauhaus customer

[8] See "Kreis der Freunde des Bauhauses" in Bauhaus-Archiv Schrank 58 GS 9/10.

(Erfurth 1985; Jablonowski 1983). The Dessau Bauhaus emphasized architecture and played a key role in the rise of the *Internationale Architektur* movement, especially since the arrival in 1927 of Hannes Meyer, who became the Bauhaus director after Gropius's departure a year later. Meyer was more radical than Gropius regarding the utilitarian aspects of design. For him, architecture was "function × economics" (Curtis [1982] 1996, 199). His efforts were stymied by the increasingly hostile political environment. The school later moved to Berlin—where Mies van der Rohe became a most controversial director because of his accommodating attitude towards the National Socialists (Hochman 1989, 95–101). In 1933 the Bauhaus was shut down by the Nazis, who also expropriated the Junkers works from its owner, the engineer Hugo Junkers (Erfurth 1985; Jablonowski 1983).

Among the Bauhaus architects, two of them deserve special attention, given the originality of their ideas and their subsequent impact worldwide: Gropius and Mies van der Rohe. Gropius first made a name for himself with the Fagus Shoe Last Factory of 1911–13, featuring its famous glazed corners (plate 4.10). He worked for several years with Behrens. In the 1913 Werkbund yearbook, Gropius extolled the AEG factories ("monuments of sovereign strength, commanding their surroundings with truly classical grandeur"), and compared the "compelling monumentality" of the American grain silos and factories to the buildings of ancient Egypt (Curtis [1982] 1996, 103). He was also one of the leaders of the prefabricated housing movement in Germany, which refined construction methods and collaborated with several firms such as Carl Kästner, Wöhr, Deutsche Schiffs- und Maschinebau, Stahlhaus-Baugesellschaft (founded by Vereinigte Stahlwerke, one of Germany's largest firms), Hirsch Kupfer- und Messingwerke (associated with AEG), and Christoph und Unmack, Europe's largest manufacturer of prefabricated wooden buildings, at which one of Gropius's collaborators, Wachsmann, became chief designer (Herbert 1984, 52, 70–71, 81, 87–103, 107–59). His goals as an artist went beyond architecture to include the production of "practical designs for present-day goods" that could be mass-produced (Buddensieg 1984, 18; Scheidig [1966] 1967).

Perhaps the most purely modernist of all modernist architects was Ludwig Mies van der Rohe, who worked in Behrens's studio from 1908 to 1911. He emphasized simple forms, straight lines, and industrial technique. His most influential and immortal statement was, simply enough, "less is more." Over the course of a long career in Germany and the United States, Mies designed some of the architectural landmarks of the twentieth century. In his view, "Architecture [is] the will of the epoch translated into space" (quoted in Hochman 1989, 51). His first major contribution was the project for a Concrete Office Building (1922–23), which he described as "a house of work . . . of organization, of clarity, of economy. . . . The maximum effect with the minimum expenditure of means. The materials are concrete, iron, glass" (quoted in Curtis

[1982] 1996, 190; Mies Van der Rohe [1924] 1971). His apartment building at the Weissenhofsiedlung housing project outside of Stuttgart (1927) became the model for other worker housing projects throughout the world (plate 4.11, Kirsch [1927] 1989). Mies's distinctive style crystallized in the famous Pavilion at the Barcelona exhibition of 1929, the result, according to Curtis ([1982] 1996, 307), of the combination of the principles he would later apply to public buildings and monuments ("symmetry, frontality and axiality"), and to residences ("asymmetry, fluidity and interlocking volumes"). Some of his best known works date to the postwar years: the Lake Shore Drive Apartment Houses in Chicago (1949–51), and the Seagram Building in New York City (1954–58), a fine example of aesthetic purity (Larson 1993, 272n.89).

It is important to keep in mind that the Bauhaus emerged out of an environment shaped by the political and ideological agendas of a rather broad coalition of German political and social forces intent on pursuing the promise of modernity. Two key ingredients were scientific management and Fordism, which lay at the core of the vigorous movement of industrial rationalization (*Rationaliesierung*) that started toward the end of World War I and gained speed during the 1920s. "German industrial rationalization represented a synthesis of a series of ideas about technical progress, a corporatist version of capitalism, and the combination of mass-production techniques with mass-consumption markets. It embodied a corporatist response to economic and political liberalism. Industrial rationalization appealed to many groups in Weimar Germany: industrial, intellectual, and artistic elites as well as social democratic politicians and labor union leaders" (Guillén 1994, 100).

Not surprisingly, the most important proponents of this approach to the reorganization of economic production, distribution, and consumption came from AEG, the firm that had made it possible for Behrens to explore new architectural possibilities. Walther Rathenau became the President of AEG in 1915 after the death of his father. His brief stint in the government, where he improved raw material supplies during World War I, gave him the opportunity to apply some of his ideas and to learn about the potential of business-government collaboration. His best-selling books helped popularize ideas about scientific management and Fordism. The engineer Wichard von Moellendorff, also from AEG, was another best-selling author and indefatigable apostle of scientific management. Like Rathenau, he believed in a state-led implementation of rationalized methods of production throughout industry (Guillén 1994, 100–102).

The incipient collaboration between government and industry that started during World War I became a hallmark of the Weimar Republic's effort to reorganize and revive the German economy during the 1920s. The state created in 1921 the best funded and most influential scientific management promotion agency of any country, the *Reichskuratorium für Wirtschaftlichkeit* (National Board of Efficiency), best known by the acronym RKW. Its first president was Carl Friedrich von Siemens, president of the large electrical equipment company, and, like AEG's Rathenau, a second-generation business leader. His successor at the RKW was Carl Köttgen, also from Siemens, who presided over Germany's most important professional society of engineers, the Verein Deutscher Ingenieure or VDI (Guillén 1994, 113–16). The Bauhaus collaborated assiduously with several RKW organizations, especially with the one concerned with the building and housing industries, of which Gropius was vice-president (Nerdinger 1985). Many of the firms with which the Bauhaus collaborated over the years (especially Junkers, Mannesmann, Siemens, and certain AEG and Vereiningte Stahlwerke subsidiaries) were among the earliest and most ardent supporters of scientific management in Germany (Guillén 1994, 119–20).

The modernist architects actively campaigned for the diffusion of scientific management in the construction industry and beyond. In so doing, they became effective propagators of the new ideas and methods of production. Such leading architects as Behrens, Gropius, Hilberseimer, May, Mendelsohn, Taut, and Wagner collaborated with, and held important positions in, scientific management organizations like the National Society for Research into Efficiency in Construction and Housing, the Research Society for Economical Construction Business, the German Committee for Economical Construction, or the Committee for the Promotion of Clay and Building Methods.[9]

Industry and the state were joined by the dominant social democratic labor unions during the Weimar Republic in their support of scientific management and Fordism, a development that made it even more ideologically reassuring for the largely left-leaning modernist artists and architects to turn to scientific management as a source of inspiration. Labor leaders and intellectuals endorsed Taylorism as early as 1914. For example, Wilhelm Eggert wrote in the official journal of the Free Unions, the largest labor confederation, that "humanity has based many achievements, as well as the whole culture, on the principle of division of labor. . . . Taylorite work methods may bring about struggles, and may represent a further stage in the way towards Socialism" (quoted in Stollberg 1981, 88). The very idea of founding the RKW came from the ministers of Labor and of the Economy, both of whom were former labor leaders. One could read in *Der Arbeiter-Rat* (Workers' Council) in 1920 that "we need the Taylor System; we need it as much as our daily bread" (quoted in Stollberg 1981, 83).

German socialists thought that under democratic conditions Taylorism and Fordism could actually help the working class. Gustav Bauer—a labor unionist, member of the Social Democratic Party, Reichsminister for Labor, and later

[9] See Behrens and de Fries 1918, 60–61; Wingler 1969, 126–27; Conrans 1970, 29, 96; Bayer, Gropius, and Gropius 1975; Buddensieg 1984, 18, 124–37, 207–8, 213, 219; Whitford 1984, 20–21, 36, 143–46, 181; Nerdinger 1985, 11–14; Pommer, Spaeth, and Harrington 1988, 83, 92–93; Kaes, Jay, and Dimendberg 1994, 452, 457, 461.

Chancellor of the Reich—explained in early 1919 that, "in the capitalistic economic order, Taylorism stood in opposition of the worker. Labor feared that the capitalist, and not itself, would be the beneficiary of the new method of work. Now that the democratization of Germany has ensured an ample economic influence of labor, these objections are not only futile but also obscure the fact of the possibilities offered by rationalization" (quoted in Stollberg 1981, 85). In 1925 the Free Unions adopted an official position of acceptance and even enthusiasm towards Taylorism and Fordism: "Not lower wages and longer working times in connection with technical backwardness, but higher wages, shorter working times, rational production methods, and economic organization guarantee the economic rise and the competitiveness of Germany in the world market."[10] Only the relatively marginalized Christian and Communist unions pointed out the shortcomings and dangers of scientific management (Guillén 1994, 109–13; see also Fromm 1984, 98–104).

Expressionism

Werkbund and Bauhaus were not the only modernist trends in Germany. Another important artistic and architectural development was expressionism, which also emphasized rationality and functionality, although it was infused with a lyricism mostly lacking from streamlined modernism. Among many others, Gropius and Mies van der Rohe went through expressionist periods at the beginning of their careers. As Curtis ([1982] 1996, 103) has cogently argued, in the context of industrial design, expressionism refers to "an attitude in which sobriety and stability were eschewed in favor of restless, dynamic and highly emotive forms." Expressionism descends from art nouveau and represents an individualist and subjective creative effort. The first great German expressionist architect was Bruno Taut, also affiliated with the Werkbund. His buildings stand in stark contrast with those of Behrens and Muthesius in their utopian exaltation of mystical motifs and geometrical forms like triangles and spheres evoking mountains and the celestial bodies, as evident in the Steel Industry Pavilion in Leipzig (1913) and the Glass Pavilion in Cologne (1914). Taut looked for the poetic side of industrialization, and found in glass the material with the greatest expressive potential (106–7).

Perhaps the finest German expressionist architect was Erich Mendelsohn, the designer of such an exhilarating building as the Einstein Tower in Potsdam (1920–24): "An axial plan, with overlapping curved forms in high tension rising to a crescendo in the tower-telescope" (Curtis [1982] 1996, 187); a building

---

[10] From the Proceedings of the Twelfth Congress of the Unions of Germany (1925), as reproduced in Stollberg (1981, 181). Similar viewpoints were adopted at the Thirteenth Congress of 1928, and in the Free Unions' report, "Gegenwartsaufgaben deutscher Wirtschaftspolitik," addressed to the national government. See Hoff 1978, 182; Hinrichs and Peter 1976, 89.

"bristling with protuberances and undulations, [that] bursts out of the earth like a volcano in eruption" (Zevi [1973] 1994, 190; see plate 4.12). Thus, he was interested in depicting the dynamic aspects of nature by dramatizing the formal tensions in the building. His maxim was "function plus dynamics is the challenge" (quoted in Curtis [1982] 1996, 188). Mendelsohn designed factories, film studios, cinemas, crematoria, and numerous department stores.

Whether expressionist or not, the German contributions to the rise of a modernist aesthetic in architecture and design were crucial. Behrens's studio, the Werkbund, and the Bauhaus became models to imitate, especially because of their strong ties to the state and to business, the two most important patrons of architecture in the twentieth century. German developments were watched in Italy and Russia, where the modern movement in architecture was more fragmented and full of contradictions, but vibrant and evocative (see chapter 5).

BACK TO FRANCE: LE CORBUSIER'S MANY ROLES

While modernism in design was flourishing in Germany, the early achievements of Perret and Garnier led to a dead end in France. It was Charles Édouard Jeanneret (Le Corbusier) who belatedly succeeded in aligning French architecture and design with the modernist movement and served as a bridge between the world of industry and scientific management on the one hand, and that of architecture on the other. As analyzed in chapter 2, he was well versed in Taylorism and Fordism. He became the driving force behind the international modernist movement and helped spread it to Spain, Latin America, India, Northern Africa, and elsewhere.

As a child, Le Corbusier was exposed to geometry and to new research then in vogue in his native Switzerland on prehistoric lake dwellings, which he liked for their simple geometry, functional and economical use of wood, and elevated design on trunk supports above the surface of the lake (Vogt 1998). After moving to Paris, he read about American mass production, Fordism, and Taylorism. He was also influenced by French rationalism, Parisian Cubism, German modernism, Italian futurism, and Russian constructivism (Curtis [1982] 1996). For him the most important principle was that of planning. "The Plan must rule," he asserted (McLeod 1985, 110; Le Corbusier and Jeanneret [1935] 1967, 91). He worked at the studios of Perret and Behrens. Together with a Cubist painter, Amedée Ozenfant, Le Corbusier founded the purist movement in 1919, publishing the influential review *L'Esprit Nouveau* (Benevolo [1960] 1977, 435–49; Curtis [1982] 1996, 163–68). Ferdinand Léger was also active in the purist movement. Fascinated by the mechanical and Le Corbusier's ideas, Léger conceived of art as "assembly work" of various elements. Purism advocated the "Law of Mechanical Selection," which "establishes that objects tend toward a type that is determined by the evolution of forms between the ideal of maximum utility, and the satisfaction of the necessities of economical manufacture" (quoted in Banham [1960] 1980, 211).

Although French businesses did not embrace Taylorism until after World War I, Le Corbusier and other French architects of his generation grew up in a milieu in which American management techniques were widely discussed and gaining in acceptance (Merkle 1980, 136–38; Devinat 1927, vi). Le Corbusier read Taylor's books while fighting in the trenches of World War I. During the 1920s French industrialists became "mesmerized by the Fordist spectacle, and dazzled by the image of American productive efficiency" (Van Casteele-Schweitzer 1987, 73). Both employers and workers, as well as their unions, saw in Taylorism and Fordism the way of the future, but seemed to be reticent about adopting the recommended techniques and practices. As Merkle (1980, 136–37) argues, Taylorism impregnated the French technical elites but did not reform management practice on the shop floor. The Conference of French Organization, the first Taylorite association, was created in 1920, and merged with the Center of Administrative Studies (founded around Henri Fayol, the classic French theorist of administration) to form the National Committee of French Organization in 1926. In France, Taylorism made greater inroads into government-run activities such as shipyards, gun powder, and the postal system, and into services like insurance, banking, and commerce, than into manufacturing, where it was met by resistance from managers and workers alike (Merkle 1980, 136–66).

By the early 1920s the young Jeanneret had decided to move away from painting and focus on architecture, and adopted the name of Le Corbusier.[11] He published what many regarded as the best manifestos on modernist architecture and city planning: *Towards a New Architecture* and *The City of To-Morrow and Its Planning* (Le Corbusier [1923] 1986, [1924] 1987). These books contain myriad references to American industrial architecture and design, engineering, mass production, and Taylorism (see chapter 2). His most inspiring ideas were the 1914 *Dom-ino* system (widely used throughout the world to this day),[12] the 1920 *Maison Citrohan* (a "machine for living," named after the Citroën automobile), *l'unité d'habitation* (the "habitation unit," an idea dating back to 1907), and *les maisons en série* (the "serial houses"). He also started at this time to influence other architects in France, including Rob. Mallet-Stevens, commonly referred to as France's leading art deco designer, later turned modernist: "We will build simply and cleanly, the edifices will be

[11] "A conflation of 'Le Corbesier,' an ancestral name, and of 'Corbeau' or 'Crow,' a nickname" (Curtis [1982] 1996, 168).

[12] "A structural unit consisting of three horizontal slabs, smooth below and above, each of the upper two supported on square sectional posts of concrete, the lower level lifted from the ground on squat concrete blocks . . . [with] concrete stairs connecting the levels" (Curtis [1982] 1996, 84). Essentially, it is an application of the cantilever principle (165). Originally formulated in 1914 in collaboration with Max Dubois, it was not published until the early 1920s.

suited to their functions. . . . The new architecture will reestablish the reign of reason" (quoted in Pinchon 1990, 13). Mallet-Stevens built modernist shops, factories, flats, office buildings, and private homes, mostly in and around Paris.

Le Corbusier also excelled as an effective organizer and propagator. He founded three organizations: the Society of Industrial Enterprises and Studies (SEIE), the Association of Builders for an Architectural Renewal (ASCORAL), and the Builders' Workshop (ATBAT), which had a "works management" section (Brooks 1987, 117–18; CGP 1987). Although these organizations were not entirely successful at achieving the goal of articulating a modernist movement in design and architecture linked to French industry, Le Corbusier established contacts with, and worked for, many industrial firms. The two most important connections were with Aeroplanes Voisin, and with Ernest Mercier, the managing director of France's largest utility, and later of Compagnie Français des Petroles. Mercier was the key figure in the technocratic-corporatist *Redressment Français* movement (McLeod 1983, 141–42; CGP 1987, 400). Gabriel Voisin pioneered both prefabricated housing and urban planning, as well as airplane construction and automobile manufacturing.

Where Le Corbusier led, other French architects and city planners followed. Henri Sauvage and his collaborators designed prefabricated, low-cost, concrete, terraced apartment houses, department stores, and large garages (Etlin 1991, 82–85; Minnaert 1994, 2:280, 312, 325–26, 464). A corporatist town planning movement called "municipal Taylorism" emerged during the 1920s under the leadership of Henri Sellier (the secretary of HBM, Habitations à Bon Marché, a low-cost housing organization), Maxim Leroy (a professor and town planner), Georges Benoit-Lévy (president of the French Garden City Association), and Louis Renault, the automobile manufacturer (Banham [1960] 1980, 220–63; McLeod 1983, 137, 145; Frampton 2001, 116–17). The French modernist movement, however, failed to establish links to industry comparable to those of the German and Italian movements, in spite of Le Corbusier's efforts and flirtations with industrialists, labor leaders, and even the Vichy government, in which he held a temporary position for eighteen months (McLeod 1985, 74–75, 384–405).[13]

Le Corbusier's influence and organizing activities extended far beyond France. He was one of the driving forces behind the founding in 1928 of the International Congress of Modern Architecture or CIAM, which articulated the international modern movement and spread the principles of modernist architecture to Russia, Spain, Brazil, India, and many other countries (Mumford 2000). Le Corbusier invited the director of the International Institute for the Scientific Management of Work, Paul Devinat, to join CIAM. In return, he was invited to attend the Fourth Congress of the Scientific Management of

[13] Auguste Perret also collaborated with Vichy, but joined the Resistance soon afterwards.

Work in Paris in 1929, where he presented a paper on "Household Economics and Economic Construction" (CGP 1987, 400). While his enthusiasm for Taylorism and Fordism waned after the 1929 crash, his theories and built works were thoroughly influenced by American production methods (Bacon 2001, 102–5; CGP 1987, 400).

Like Choisy, Le Corbusier had a rare ability to generate enthusiasm for modern architecture in writing and in lecturing. Besides being an organizer and propagator, he was an accomplished architect and city planner, both in theory and in practice, and an effective consultant to business firms. His most important theoretical contributions had to do with the creation of a new architectural vocabulary based on the machine aesthetic and scientific management, and with the elevation of regularity, exactitude, and efficiency as the main principles of architecture. His designs were unmistakable—buildings erected on slender pilotis or cylindrical, smooth reinforced-concrete pillars or stilts high above ground (like the prehistoric lake dwellings), with terraces replacing the sloping roof; the pilotis positioned inside the house so that the floor continues overhanging until reaching the façade; an inside plan free from the constraints of load-bearing walls, with windows running along the façade, the flexible ground plan of Horta and Perret that Le Corbusier named the "free plan" (Vogt 1998, 6; Benevolo [1960] 1977, 440, 444–45; Curtis [1982] 1996, 176; Blake [1960] 1996).[14]

Thus, Le Corbusier effectively blended the French tradition of reinforced concrete building with the aesthetic of the avant-garde and the machine age. The Villa Savoye of 1929–31 (plate 4.13) is perhaps the most stunning example of the new approach. In a 1929 lecture, he described the design as follows: "The house is a box in the air, pierced all around, without interruption, by a long window. . . . From the interior of the vestibule, a gentle ramp leads up, almost without noticing it, to the first floor. . . . [The] different rooms adjoin each other radially from a suspended garden which is there like a distributor of light. . . . It is onto the suspended garden that the sliding walls of glass of the salon and several other rooms are opened in all freedom. . . . Poetry, lyricism, produced by technology" (quoted in Benton 1984, ix). The Villa was a fine exemplification of the five points or principles that Le Corbusier outlined in 1926, which could be rephrased as "the 'free' plan, the 'free' façade, the pilotis that leave the ground 'free' under the building, the roof garden that implies the 'free' use of the top of the building, and even the strip window, insofar as it offers further evidence that the façade is 'free' of structural elements" (Zevi [1973] 1994, 12; Le Corbusier and Jeanneret [1926] 1971, 99–101). The entire design revolves around the imagery of the machine: "The scale of the house derives not only from Vitruvian man, but from what one must call the

[14] Benton (1984, x) has aptly described the pilotis as "a Platonic device to lift living away from the soil."

Vitruvian automobile: the ground floor dimensions match the turning circle of a large car" (Benton 1984, xi).

This necessarily brief review of the British, French, and German pioneers and founders of modernist architecture reveals the importance of the state and big business as key patrons of the new architecture. It also points out that modernist architecture was born with a moral mission in mind, namely, to improve life in the city and the factory, frequently on the basis of Taylorite and Fordist ideas. This endeavor resonated with historical circumstances to a greater extent in Germany than in either Britain or France, mostly because industrialization was more recent in Germany and had led to more social dislocation and political upheaval. As the next chapter will show, the social, political, and economic convulsions felt in Russia, Italy, and Spain at different points between the late 1910s and the late 1930s also created a milieu favorable to the rise of modernist architecture.

Backwardness and Revolution: Italy, Russia, Spain

> The new architecture is the architecture
> of cold calculation . . . boldness and
> simplicity.
> —Antonio Sant'Elia (quoted in Curtis
>   [1982] 1996, 109).

> One of the most urgent needs of our time
> is the rational organization of objects,
> their functional justification. And this is
> the rejection of everything that is
> superfluous.
> —Yakov Chernikhov (quoted in Bowlt
>   1988, 259).

> Capitalists!!! Here you have a new
> architecture!!! Good, beautiful, and
> cheap!!!
> —Casto Fernández Shaw (quoted in
>   Bohigas 1998, 31).

THE PREVIOUS CHAPTER contrasted German modernism's renewal of architecture and design with the gradual, timid, and contradictory developments in Britain, the pioneer of the industrial revolution, and France, another early manufacturing powerhouse. This occurred in spite of the fact that British and French architects and designers were the first to hit upon some of the most important modernist ideas, including the notion of the "total work of art," the desire for architecture to be honest and truthful in the use of materials, and the notion of architecture as a moral enterprise aimed at improving living conditions. The comparison of these three cases suggested that industrialization per se was not directly associated with modernism in architecture. I now turn to the dynamics leading to the (fleeting) triumph of the modernist movement in three relatively backward European countries during periods of acute social and political upheaval: the late 1910s and the 1920s in Italy and Russia, and the late 1930s in Spain. As in Germany, a totalitarian regime eradicated modernism in the Soviet Union during the 1930s, while the Italian Fascists and the Spanish authoritarian nationalists shattered it during the late 1930s and early 1940s, respectively.

The avant-garde flourished in Italy during the early years of the twentieth century. Late industrial development around Turin and Milan inspired attempts to create an Italian modern movement in the arts that would become a part of the international style and contribute to the formation of a national Italian school. The anarchic state of the arts during the 1910s provided fertile soil for the spread of futurist ideas. Architectural futurism, however, was mostly a theoretical movement. During the 1920s architects and designers produced a more coherent approach to architecture based on the machine aesthetic and rationalist principles, although other tendencies combining modernist and classical themes were also important. As in Germany, architects collaborated with large firms interested in new manufacturing methods such as Taylorism and Fordism and produced dozens of important modernist public buildings and residences. As in France, the early roots of Italian modernist architecture go back to the mid-nineteenth century.

The Beginnings: Structural Construction and Art Nouveau

The origins of Italian modernism are to be found in early developments in structural construction and in the arrival of art nouveau. The break with the eclecticism of the nineteenth century, however, did not come easy. As the architect and critic Alfredo Melani complained in 1890, "ours is an architecture suffocated by art, with inspiration stifled under the inordinate weight of stylistic erudition and under the invalid authority of a doctrinaire scholasticism" (quoted in Etlin 1991, 6).

Italian architects, however, had long been interested in applying new methods of structural construction to architecture. During the 1850s Alessandro Antonelli formulated the idea that the building should be supported by pillars, with walls merely covering and separating space. His Mole Antonelliana in Turin, designed in 1862 but not completed until 1889, was described by contemporaries as a "formidable stairway to the sky" (see plate 5.1). It was originally conceived as a synagogue, and later turned into a monument to King Vittorio Emanuele II after the local Jewish community declined to pump more money into the massive project (Etlin 1991, 14–21). This building, compared by some to the Eiffel Tower, captured the imagination of several of the architects who eventually became the leaders of Italian modernism.

Art nouveau or *arte nuova* appeared on the Italian scene in 1902 at the First International Exposition of Modern Decorative Art, also in Turin, which attracted architects and designers from all over Europe. Melani showed his enthusiasm: "A step forward has been made. The rigorism of styles is out of season; and the public will get used to a new art that wants to provide it with new emotions and new pleasures" (quoted in Etlin 1991, 21). Turin was a probable birthplace for Italian modernism, as it was not burdened by the past to the extent other Italian cities, especially Rome, were, and it was a major center of industrial activity, home to thriving manufacturing industries. The art exhibited in 1902 ranged from luxury items to functional and affordable objects, as in the words of one contemporary, "art must be in everything and for everybody" (quoted in Etlin 1991, 29). While the Exposition generated much criticism for lacking a clear sense of local identity, it did stir the sleepy world of Italian architecture and design, inviting architects to experiment with new forms and techniques.

Industrial Growth, Taylorism, and Futurism

Although relatively backward, Italian industry developed quite rapidly at the turn of the century, especially in the northern manufacturing enclaves of Turin and Milan, where firms in the assembly industries were located: FIAT and Alfa Romeo in automobiles; Pirelli in tires, cables, and other rubber products; and Olivetti in machinery and typewriters. The first attempts at introducing Taylorism and other rationalized production methods took place in the early 1900s, and later during and after World War I. It was not until the beginning of the Fascist period, however, that an infrastructure for the diffusion of scientific management was put in place. A National Institution for the Scientific Management of Work was founded in 1926 by the employers' confederation (Confindustria), which joined forces with engineering associations, the Ministry of National Economy, and some industrial firms like FIAT and Olivetti, both patrons of modernist architecture (Buselli, Finzi, and Predrocco 1976, 51–52; Sapelli 1976, 160; Pedrocco 1976, 13; Castronovo 1977, 113–15, 245–48). Italian Fascism, a self-proclaimed regime of "soldiers and producers," was somewhat reactionary but embraced non-zero-sum solutions to economic and social problems, especially Taylorism and Fordism (Buselli, Finzi, and Predrocco 1976, 40–44; Lyttleton 1976). While there is some debate in the literature as to whether the Fascist regime succeed at reigning in the labor movement, the relative weakness of the unions during the 1920s facilitated the introduction of scientific management (Sapelli 1976, 159; Lyttleton 1976, 139–43). And although Mussolini personally endorsed scientific management (Buselli, Finzi, and Predrocco 1976, 101–2), his regime hesitated when confronted with the question of how to organize work and placate labor unrest, alternating between Taylorite and organic-corporatist approaches, just as Hitler did (Guillén 1994, 121–26). In fact, considerable debate and discussion had met the new American methods of production since the early 1910s (Pedrocco 1976, 6–10).

It was against this backdrop of industrial growth and revolutionary politics that the first avant-garde movements emerged and developed in Italy. Futurism was launched in 1909 as a literary movement by F. T. Marinetti, whose political agenda was geared towards nationalism, violence, war, and destruction. In that same year Mario Morasso published his novel, *Il nuovo aspetto meccanico del mondo*, in which the automobile is the protagonist. Futurism later invaded other artistic areas such as music, painting (e.g., Chirico), and, above all, architecture (Banham [1960] 1980, 98–137). The movement quickly established ties to Fascism. Marinetti was a Fascist candidate in 1919, and a member of the central committee of the Fasci di Combattimento. Mussolini also endorsed futurism in 1919. But during the 1920s their positions began to diverge, as Marinetti proved too much of an anarchist, and Mussolini too accommodating to the monarchy and the Church (Bowler 1991, 786–88). In general, the Fascist regime was remarkably eclectic, organic, and corporatist not only in theory but also in practice, awarding architectural commissions to many different kinds of architects, ranging from modernist to vernacular and neoclassic (Etlin 1991, 387–90).

Italian architecture evolved more quickly in the heavily industrial cities of Milan and Turin, that is, far from the center of political and artistic power in Rome. A new, modernist style crystalized in Milan in the Nuove Tendenze of 1914, which included architects Mario Chiattone and Antonio Sant'Elia, who later became a futurist (Banham [1960] 1980, 127–37; Etlin 1991, 53–100; Benevolo [1960] 1977, 396–97). "We must invent and rebuild ex novo our modern city like an immense and tumultuous shipyard, active, mobile, and everywhere dynamic, and the modern building like a gigantic machine. . . . [T]he new architecture is the architecture of cold calculation . . . boldness and simplicity," Sant'Elia wrote in his *Messagio* or manifesto of 1914 (quoted in Curtis [1982] 1996, 109). "The Futurist house must be like a gigantic machine" (Sant'Elia [1914] 1973, 170). In this view, the new architecture had to "treasure every resource of science and technics, satisfying in an elegant manner all requirements issuing from our customs and our spirit . . . determining new forms, new lines, a new harmony of profiles and volumes, an architecture that has its raison d'être only in the special conditions of modern life and its aesthetic values corresponding to our sensibility" (quoted in Etlin 1991, 71). Sant'Elia entered the annals of modernist architecture with his project, *La Città Nuova* (see plate 5.2). His designs, however, almost never came to fruition, but his drawings of concrete-frame, terraced apartment buildings with external elevator towers inspired many a modernist architect (Etlin 1991, 80–88).[1] Mario Chiattone, a contemporary of Sant'Elia's, although never a card-carrying futurist, was perhaps even more influential thanks to his geometrical designs for public and apartment buildings (Etlin 1991, 97–99).

---

[1] Sant'Elia's monument to the fallen during World War I, in his native town of Como, was finished posthumously. He was among those who died in the war.

An important aspect of futurism, as captured by Sant'Elia himself after agreeing to become a member of the movement, was the idea that art and architecture should only last enough so that its contemporaries could enjoy it: "HOUSES WILL NOT LAST AS LONG AS WE. EACH GENERATION WILL HAVE TO BUILD ITS OWN CITY. This constant renewal of the architectural setting will contribute to the victory of FUTURISM, that already is affirming itself with WORDS IN FREEDOM, PLASTIC DYNAMISM, MUSIC WITHOUT STAFF, AND THE ART OF NOISES" (quoted by Etlin 1991, 96). Fittingly, Futurism waned as an architectural movement with the death of Sant'Elia and Umberto Boccioni during World War I (Etlin 1991, 97).

Rationalist Architecture

The spirit of avant-garde, machine-age design was most successfully carried into the 1920s and 1930s by the movement of Gruppo 7 of *architettura razionale*. Sant'Elia and Chiattone's ideas were developed by the rationalist architects—Luigi Figini, Gino Pollini, Adalberto Libera, Enrico Griffini, and Giuseppe Terragni, among others—who founded an organization in 1928 (MIAR), and staged several important exhibitions in the late 1920s and early 1930s. They were also influenced by Gropius and Le Corbusier. The term *razionale* was liberally derived from the German *sachlich* (objective); the label was a success. The rationalists were interested in low-cost housing and furniture design, urban planning, prefabricated construction, factory architecture, and standardization (Etlin 1991, 226–29, 239). "We do not claim to create a style, but from the constant application of reality, the perfect correspondence of the building to its aims, . . . style must inevitably result," they asserted in 1926 (quoted in Benevolo [1960] 1977, 564).

The rationalists, however, differed from the futurists in their desire to avoid a "break with tradition" so as to reach a "close association between logic and rationality" (quoted in Frampton [1980] 1992, 203). They also advocated an "Italian aesthetic" that departed from the mainstream modernist theory rejecting symmetry: "The classical foundations that are in us require if not an absolute symmetry, then at least a play of compensation that balances the different parts" (quoted in Etlin 1991, 251). In fact, Italian modernist architecture during the 1920s included another trend even more firmly rooted in the vernacular and focused on producing a truly Italian modernist style, the Novecento movement, whose followers did not expose the structural frame of buildings. The "decorative" version of the Novecento made extensive use of neoclassical motifs like pediments and niches, while the "geometrical" strand emphasized "thick profiles, rounded edges, and modeled lines" (Etlin 1991, 165–224, 367). The rationalists, however, prevailed, and were able to set the terms of architectural debates after World War I. Still, several of them followed a "contextualist" approach emphasizing the importance of taking into account the immediate surroundings of the building being designed, as in Adalberto Libera's Postal Center located in the vicinity of the Pyramid of Cestius (c. 12 BC) in Rome, which Le Corbusier famously described as "Roman, but burdened with a modern formalism" (quoted in Etlin 1991, 294).

The rationalists produced several cardinal examples of modernist architecture: the Casa Elettrica by Figini and Pollini (1930); the Novocomum apartment building (1929, popularly known as the Transatlantico) and the Casa del Fascio, both in Como, north of Milan (1933–36; see plate 5.3), designed by Italy's most accomplished modernist architect, Terragni (Zevi 1980; Etlin 1991, 439–62; Schumacher 1992); and the apartment buildings and houses in Ostia Lido by Libera (1933), whose cantilevered balconies "with the concrete ribs exposed below epitomized in a single image the architecture of the machine age" (Etlin 1991, 297; see plate 5.4). Another important architect was Giuseppe Pagano, designer of the building of the Università Bocconi in Milan, Italy's foremost business school (1936–42), where professors lectured about scientific management.

It was precisely during the late 1920s and early 1930s that Taylorism and other methods of scientific management were adopted by some of the largest Italian firms. A number of scientific management journals appeared around this time (Pedrocco 1976, 14 n. 26), and automobile production expanded rapidly after the introduction of Fordist methods at FIAT (Bigazzi 1987). The Turin-based automobile firm had first experimented with American methods in the first decade of the twentieth century, and had gained direct experience through its engine plant located in New York State (Bigazzi 1987, 80). An internal report of 1919 argued in favor of standardizing products, removing "lazy or slow workers," and making them as "interchangeable as the gear in a machine" (quoted in Bigazzi 1987, 81). Similar developments took place at Olivetti's typewriter assembly operations (Olivetti 1976, 119–24).

As in Germany and the Soviet Union, Italian modernist designers were enlisted by the firms most inclined to use scientific management methods. For example, Figini and Pollini designed several factory and office buildings for the electrical machinery firm Olivetti (Frampton 1992, 208), and collaborated with Bauhaus graduate Xanti Schawinsky to design the famous Olivetti Studio 42 typewriter (Weston 1996, 172). Architect and engineer Giacomo Mattè-Trucco worked primarily for FIAT, where he witnessed and contributed to the efforts at work rationalization. He designed the Lingotto Factory in Turin (1916–23), partially modeled after the Ford plant at Highland Park. "The engine and body 'grew' from floor to floor in two separate areas of the building until they flowed together, on the fifth floor, for the final assembly line. From here each vehicle was sent up to the test track on the roof" (Bigazzi 1987, 81; Castronovo 1977, 48; Pozzetto 1975; see plate 3.5). It is important to note, however, that at Lingotto assembly proceeded from the bottom to the top of the building, in the opposite direction than at Ford, which made it impossible to benefit from the force of gravity to slide parts and subassemblies along the assembly line.

Italian architectural modernism was not only the result of highly novel aesthetic trends in literature and the arts, and of sociopolitical upheaval, but also the outcome of industry and mechanization. In fact, the most important modernist buildings were designed by architects from Turin or Milan, the two main centers of Italian industry. Also important was the fact that in Italy qualified architects were trained at engineering schools until the creation of the first Higher School of Architecture in 1920 (see chapter 7). The long rationalist tradition in Italian architecture, emphasizing structural elements, no doubt facilitated the development of modernist architecture, but industry, engineering, and scientific management exerted a key influence, especially in the context of a revolutionary political regime intent on promoting manufacturing activity (Etlin 1991, 8–9, 14–19, 53–100, 111–28, 154–57).

RUSSIA AND THE EARLY SOVIET UNION: REVOLUTION, THE AVANT-GARDE,
AND CONSTRUCTIVISM

Russian and Italian architecture evolved similarly from the mid-nineteenth century onward. Although the architectural landscape under the last tsars was dominated by a combination of classicist and vernacular elements, the seeds of a rationalist, engineering-based architecture were already present at the turn of the century. Unlike in Germany, the Russian route to modernism was swift and fragmented. Myriad avant-garde movements were spurred by the Bolshevik revolution, and architecture quickly became one important aspect of the new social and economic system. As in Germany, a modernist school of architecture was founded, and the aspirations and dreams of its teachers and students succumbed to totalitarianism in the 1930s.

Modernism Unbound

Modernism became the dominant approach to artistic design and architecture in Russia and the early Soviet Union, though the movement included a variety of trends and groups often at odds with each other (Bowlt 1988; Gray 1986; Guggenheim Museum 1992). St. Petersburg and Moscow had become important centers of the European avant-garde by the 1910s, with such towering figures as Kazimir Malevich, Vladimir Tatlin, and Wassily Kandinsky (Cooke 1995, 14–16). Meanwhile, the Russian arts and crafts movement was already experimenting with the artistic possibilities of mass production (Lodder 1983, 74). Revolution and civil war offered artists and designers experience in political agitation and in the management of artistic enterprises, as well as an exposure to revolutionary ideology. A Fine Art Department (IZO) was created within the Narkompros (People's Commissariat for Enlightenment, 1917) to formulate an artistic policy for the new Communist society. Narkompros promoted an utilitarian, scientific, and productivist version of art (Lodder 1983). An antagonism emerged early in the development of the Russian modern movement between material utility as the highest technical principle, and the need to "express the new political ideas in emotional terms" (Benevolo [1960] 1977, 556). In 1917 revolutionary artists created the Proletkult group to promote art inspired by collectivist principles (Kopp 1985, 10). In 1919, the Communists and Futurists Movement (Komfut) was created to emulate the Italian futurists. This group included writer Boris Kushner, literary critic Osip Brik, poet Vladimir Mayakovsky, and politician and philosopher Aleksandr Bogdanov, who were true believers in Taylorism and standardization. Komfut's theories prepared the ground for constructivism, the most successful Russian modernist movement of the 1920s (Bowlt 1988, 166–67).

The revolution created new needs and opportunities calling for experimentation with American production methods. Although initially opposed to Taylorism for its exploitative character, Lenin reversed his position after coming to power and witnessing the results obtained by German rationalization measures during the war. Scientific management came in handy to address the reigning chaos in Soviet industry and labor relations. As Leon Trotsky, the Commissar of War and reorganizer of the Red Army, observed, Taylorism was "on the one hand . . . a refined form of exploitation of the labor force, the most merciless. . . . On the other hand . . . a system of wise expenditure of human strength participating in production. . . . This side of Taylorism the socialist manager ought to make his own" (quoted in Merkle 1980, 119). "Communist Americanism," in the words of a Soviet Taylorite leaflet, became the slogan of the time (quoted in Baumgarten 1924, 111–12).

The new regime created or supported a number of scientific management organizations—the Central Institute of Labor, SovNOT, and the Time League—which helped incorporate rural workers into the nascent state-owned industries. Russian engineers were enthusiastic even before the Revolution, and they were joined by American engineers brought to Russia by the Soviet planning agencies. While there was much criticism and opposition to Taylorism, even within the Communist Party, research on new production and work methods, incentive systems, and organization in general flourished during the late 1910s and 1920s. State-run firms adopted the techniques of scientific management, if only to be able to meet the Plan's production targets (Merkle 1980; Dobb 1966, 188–89, 258–59; Bendix 2001, 207–8, 236–44; Traub 1978; Lieberstein 1975; Bailes 1977; Ebbinghaus 1975).

Many of the Soviet architects and designers endorsed scientific management or applied its principles and techniques. The modernist poet Alexei Gastev— dubbed the "Ovid of engineers, miners, and metal workers" and "the bard of scientific management"—was the founding director of the Central Institute of

Labor. In 1924 he proclaimed his trinity of heroes as follows: "Taylor was an inventor, Gilbreth was an inventor, Ford was an inventor" (quoted in Bailes 1977, 384). Gastev was praised by the Russian futurists, and even by Vladimir Mayakovsky for his machine-age poems (Bailes 1977; Traub 1978). Reportedly, a working group of constructivist architects operated at the Institute for some time during the 1920s (Bowlt 1988, 242). Architect Vladimir Krinsky joined the Time League. Such architects as Ginzburg and the Vesnin brothers also endorsed or used scientific management in their projects (Lodder 1983, 93, 254; Kopp 1985, 136; Bowlt 1988, 43; Senkevitch 1990).

Perhaps the first important Russian modernist architectural design was Vladimir Tatlin's Monument to the Third Communist International of 1919 (see plate 5.6), which was meant to exemplify the dynamic combination of "purely artistic forms with utilitarian intentions," and to serve agitation and propaganda purposes (quoted in Cooke 1995, 29; Lodder 1983, 55–67). The interplay between form and utility in Tatlin's work became a constant theme of the Russian modernist movement in architecture. His ideas were further developed by the research and discussion organization known as the Institute of Artistic Culture (INKhUK). Founded in 1921, it was briefly directed by Kandinsky before his departure for Germany in December of the same year to join the Bauhaus (see chapter 4). The next director was Osip Brik, a theorist of "art into production" (Cooke 1995, 29). The Institute subsequently became a focal point of constructivist architecture.

Rationalism/Formalism versus Constructivism

The Soviet Union's distinctive contribution to architectural modernism was constructivism, a movement that quickly gained sway over other avant-garde trends (Bowlt 1988, 204–61). In the late 1910s the Russian modernist movement in architecture was divided into two distinct camps, although both believed in the importance of applying scientific principles to art and design. The formalists or rationalists of the Association of New Architects (ASNOVA), included Vladimir Krinsky, El Lissitzky (see plate 5.7), and Nikolai Ladovsky, a fan of Münsterberg's industrial psychology (see chapters 1 and 2; Senkevitch 1983). They saw architecture as an expression of abstract form, the result of composition based on certain predetermined rules. They followed Kandinsky's emphasis on composition and psychological perception: "A work of art consists of two elements: the inner and the outer. The inner element . . . is the emotion of the artist's soul which . . . evokes a corresponding emotional vibration in the other person, the perceptor . . . emotion—feeling—work of art—feeling—Emotion" (quoted in Bowlt 1988, 19; see also Senkevitch 1983).

The constructivists believed in quite the opposite concept, namely, that architecture emerged from the utility of its parts aggregated by the process of construction (Cooke 1995, 88; Lodder 1983, 83–94, 1984). The First Working

Group of Constructivists, of which Aleksei Gan was a member, was formed at the INKhUK in 1921. They also founded the Union of Contemporary Architects (OSA, 1925), a group that included Aleksei Gan, Moisei Ginzburg, Ivan Leonidov, and the Vesnin brothers, Leonid and Viktor (Lodder 1983, 78–83, 94–144). Ginzburg explained that constructivism was "above all . . . the creation of a materialist working method which would make impossible in principle the dualism between social content and form, and which would guarantee us the creation of an integral, unified and holistic architectural system" (quoted in Cooke 1995, 89). OSA's Fedor Yalovkin summarized the main point of disagreement with the rationalists or formalists:

> The principal difference . . . consists in their very aim, i.e. for the constructivists (the OSA), the social role of architecture is essentially as one of the instruments for the building of socialism by means of the collectivization of life, by means of the rationalization of labor, by means of the utilization of scientific data and so on. . . . [The formalists'] pathetic ejaculations about art are reminiscent of antediluvian searches for a god; for we believe that what is needed is not the invention of an art . . . but work on the organization of architecture, proceeding from the data of economics, science and technology. (quoted in Curtis [1982] 1996, 208)

In an intensely revolutionary context, Ginzburg and the Vesnin brothers, armed with their constructivist approach, quickly dominated the Left Front for the Arts, Lef (Kopp 1985, 22). The elitist group formed around the arts journal *Lef* (1923–25)—including Kushner, Mayakovsky, and Brik—also promoted a utilitarian conception of art and scientific research into art (10). A good example of their work is Ginzburg's Narkomfin Communal House in Moscow (see plate 5.8), a building heavily influenced by Le Corbusier, who visited the Soviet Union frequently during the 1920s.

The constructivists were keen supporters of the application of engineering and scientific management concepts and techniques to architecture and building (Lodder 1983, 90–94; 106–7). They proposed the ideals of the "artist-constructor," and the "artist-engineer," and argued for a functionalist and engineering-oriented approach to design, prefabricated housing, standardization, modular coordination, efficient building methods, new materials, and industrial production. The constructivists designed and built factories, entire industrial complexes, government agencies, youth hostels, high-rise apartment blocks, settlements, worker canteens, Communist Party headquarters, railway stations, and electrical power systems. Yakov Chernikhov was perhaps the most successful designer of industrial buildings and large production complexes. A professor at the Leningrad Institute of Railroad Transport Engineers and Academy of Transport, he also headed a department at the Institute of Engineering Economy. He was somewhat isolated from the Moscow group of constructivists, but arrived independently at a very similar belief in the machine as the metaphor and the method for design in architecture. "The mechanization of movement and building in life peculiar to our time, the intense development of industrial production and of technology in general have radically changed our way of life and generated new needs, new habits, and new tastes. One of the most urgent needs of our time is the rational organization of objects, their functional justification. And this is the rejection of everything that is superfluous." He added that rational construction was "gradually uniting artistic construction and machine construction" (quoted in Bowlt 1988, 259–60; see also Cooke 1995, 113–15).

Rationalism/formalism and constructivism, however, did not nearly exhaust the outburst of modernist design in the early Soviet Union. Many are the architects who cannot be effectively classified under either rubric. For example, Konstantin Melnikov's modernism rejected both the extreme formalist proposals and the revolution in method advocated by the constructivists. He entered the history of modern architecture with his Soviet Pavilion at the Exposition des Arts Décoratifs in Paris (1925), and the Tram Workers' Club in Moscow of 1927–28 with its distinctive cantilevered auditoria (see plate 5.9). Unlike the formalists and the constructivists, Melnikov was more interested in practice than in theory, and built more than most other modernist architects (Cooke 1995, 91–92, 132–45).

Educating the New Architect: The VKhUTEMAS

As in Weimar Germany, Soviet modernism extended into the training of architects and designers with the creation of a state-sponsored school. The Moscow Higher State Artistic and Technical Workshops (VKhUTEMAS) were the Soviet equivalent of the Bauhaus. They were founded in 1920 by a decree signed by Lenin himself. The goal was to train "highly qualified master artists for industry." Their immediate antecedent was the productional art movement at the Fine Art Department (IZO) in 1918. The Soviet leadership thought at this time that new industrial design would improve product quality and the USSR's position on the "international exchange market." As in Germany, there clearly was a coherent governmental attempt to improve production methods through good design (Lodder 1983, 113). The workshops had an average of 1,500 enrolled students throughout the 1920s.

Unlike the Bauhaus, however, the VKhUTEMAS did not have a unified curriculum. Rather, separate faculties were set up for painting, sculpture, textiles, ceramics, graphics, woodwork, metalwork, and architecture, among others. Sculpture, textiles, and ceramics were quite traditional in their approach. Only woodwork and metalwork were explicitly oriented towards modernist design for mass production (Lodder 1983, 115–18). The architecture faculty was dominated by the rationalists/formalists, especially Ladovsky and Krinsky, although some of the architectural workshops taught historicist and constructivist approaches. The constructivists eventually controlled the basic course, and the wood and metalworking faculties (Cooke 1995, 163–64; Lodder 1983, 118–22).

The VKhUTEMAS were less successful than the Bauhaus at developing links to industry. The furniture designs, for example, were never mass-produced (Lodder 1983, 130–40, 155–59). Textiles and clothing by Stepanova, Popova, and Tatlin were the only designs of the workshops massively produced, at the First State Textile Print Factory in Moscow. In fact, clothing became an important area of research, a development underscored by the creation in 1925 of the Committee on Standard Clothing at the Decorative Institute in Leningrad. As at the Bauhaus, typography, poster design, and photomontage also flourished at the workshops (Lodder 1983, 145–55, 181–204; Kopp 1985, 10–11; Andel 1990). The constructivists' attempts at entering the field of practical industrial design were not successful either, mostly because of the sorry state of Soviet industry after years of revolution and war (Kopp 1985, 27–28, 70–71; Lodder 1983). Still, Soviet modernism in architecture and design contributed a wide array of ideas and methods until it was brutally repressed and effectively uprooted during the Stalinist purges of the 1930s.

SPAIN: BACKWARDNESS, EXPRESSIONISM, AND A MUTED MODERNISM

Spain represents a third case of brief architectural revolution in the midst of sociopolitical upheaval. Summarizing the evolution of Spanish architecture between 1890 and 1940 is a complicated task. Spain (and especially Catalonia) harbored the rise of various modern tendencies in design that combined elements of art nouveau, modernism, and expressionism. Although there clearly was a break with the classical tradition and with regional styles, Spanish *modernismo* "did not follow the methodological revision proclaimed in Europe by the modern movement" (Bohigas 1998, 28). Moreover, machine-age modernism came to Spain in full force only during the mid- to late 1930s, and was discontinued in the aftermath of the Civil War of 1936–39. Modernist designs of roofed marketplaces, railway stations, hospitals, clinics, and other public buildings were somewhat common in Spain. Architects learned and applied the new techniques based on the use of cement, glass, and steel. However, they continued to combine "moderate," "vague," "testimonial," or "hesitant" modernist features with purely academic ones, without embracing the radically new modernist aesthetic (Pizza 1997, 32, 40–41, 49, 95, 96, 104; Bohigas 1998, 36).

It is important to distinguish among three generations of Spanish architects active during this period: the Catalan "modernists," whose works fall more properly within the art nouveau trend (Freixa 1986, 13); the so-called 1925 generation of Madrid-based architects, more in tune with European modernism

(Diéguez Patao 1997); and the younger generation of architects who became fully integrated with the international modernist movement (Bohigas 1998).

Catalan Modernisme

Catalonia and, to a lesser extent, other parts of Spain fostered an arts and crafts movement similar to the English and German ones of the late nineteenth century. The movement's greatest achievements were the architectural works of the so-called Catalan "modernists," Antoni Gaudí being perhaps the most widely known. As in England, during the 1910s Catalan and Spanish modernisms evolved into an extremely revivalist, nostalgic, and baroquely monumentalist movement called Noucentisme, that is, the antithesis of the machine-age modernism then developing in Continental Europe. This "modernist" movement in and around Barcelona developed after the growth of light manufacturing at the turn of the century had slowed down.

Programmatically, the Catalan modernists combined a strong arts and crafts influence, an eclectic Gothic revival, a panoply of decorative arts elements, a taste for the forms of the natural world, an anti-mechanistic ideology, and an inclination towards social revisionism (Freixa 1986, 38–39; Bohigas 1973, 1998, 45; Solà-Morales 1992). For example, Cipriano Montolíu—the founder in 1912 of the Garden City Civic Society, a fan of John Ruskin's social philosophy, and a blistering critic of Frederick Taylor's scientific management— "theorized against the practical-utilitarian component of Catalan *modernisme*, and in favor of its utopian exaltation of nature" (Guillén 1994, 168; Freixa 1986, 38). According to Montolíu, Taylor's method could not deliver what it promised. Scientific management capitalized on the advantages deriving from "firing workers, cutting wages, and other customary coercive means," while it disdained the possibility of "sharing profits equitably." In his view, Taylor proposed to deprive the worker of "all personal initiative . . . , subjecting him or her to the higher precision allowed by the stopwatch and the slide rule," a process which might ultimately "destroy the human being as a personality, as a free individual and as a rational and sensitive person." In sum, the application of the Taylor system would "ominously reveal the great harms and dangers behind some of the methods that [Taylor] so eagerly recommends" (Montolíu [1915] 1916, 9, 20, 46).

During the 1910s and 1920s, Catalonia's business, political, and cultural elites were deeply concerned with the problem of labor unrest. They felt, however, that science and method could not provide a complete solution, and were eager to explore the human aspects of the worker. Thus, in 1908 the provincial government of Barcelona founded the Social Museum (Museo Social), aimed at "the improvement of the moral and material situation of the popular classes," advising workers, and gathering relevant information (Estivill and Tomàs 1978, 45). In 1912 a quite effective Employment Bureau (Bolsa de

Trabajo) was created because of rising unemployment. A crucial institution was the Training Secretariat (Secretariado del Aprendizaje), founded in 1914 to improve the matching of work aspirants to jobs by means of the examination of their mental and physical aptitudes. The Training Secretariat had the political backing of the Mancomunitat (the autonomous administration of the four Catalan provinces, created in 1914), although it lacked funding (Tomàs and Estivill 1979, 21–25). In 1917 the Training Secretariat was transformed into the more effective Institute for Vocational Guidance (Institut d'Orientació Professional, IOP), which helped local firms introduce group incentives, profit-sharing, welfare schemes, and worker participation so as to "perfect production and achieve social peace."[2] The Institute comprised three sections: statistical, anthropometric, and psychometric. It was staffed by prominent economists, pedagogues, physicians, and psychiatrists of moderate Catalan regionalist convictions, including Montolíu, the Taylor antagonist (Guillén 1994, 156–60).

A private National Committee for Scientific Organization of Labor (Comité Nacional de Organización Científica del Trabajo, CNOCT) was created in 1928. The Committee was strongly backed by the Catalan employer association Fomento del Trabajo Nacional, and several engineering associations, but its resources were meager (it could only organize a few lectures and publish a journal). Its message was mixed, praising scientific management on the one hand, but embracing professional and vocational education as well as the upgrading of worker skills on the other. Before 1930 few, if any, Spanish firms adopted scientific management in a coherent way (Tomàs and Estivill 1979, 39–43; Guillén 1994, 172–74).

In part as a result of the backward industrial structure, modernism in Catalonia was a mixture of romantic nostalgia and a resolution to address the reality of an emerging, if rather pusillanimous, industrial society. It drew ideas and techniques from the experience of local metal manufacturers and engineers, as well as upon the Mediterranean tradition of brick building. In the 1910s, Gropius was favorably impressed by Catalan industrial design when he visited Josep Puig i Cadafalch (also an architect and president of the Catalan regional government in 1917–24). He was, however, no modernist in the European, machine-age sense. He collaborated with the anti-Taylorite Montolíu in the diffusion of the ideas of the English Garden City movement, and was flatly opposed to the use of a grid plan—which he called "showy American"—as the organizing principle of urban planning (Solá-Morales 1990, 38; Termes 1990, 94). Puig i Cadafalch was in fact quite skeptical of the value and beauty of architectural engineering (Jardí 1975, 39). His Casarramona yarn factory of 1911–13 was filled with superfluous ornamentation, although it hinted at a rational organization of the space (plate 5.11). Not surprisingly, the Catalan

[2] *Anals de l'Institut d'Orientació Professional* 1 no. 2 (1920): 64–69; 2 no. 2 (1921): 79–82.

"modernist" workshops never replaced the principles of craftsmanship with mass production techniques (Mackay 1989, 32, 34). After World War I, Catalan and Spanish industrial architecture failed to join the European modernist mainstream (58–59).

The Catalan modernists did complete a number of industrial buildings, hospitals, healthcare centers, and wine cellars of importance. The leading wine cellar designer, architect Cèsar Martinell Brunet, campaigned for rational, economical, and simplified construction methods, and also made contributions to the design of the isolation, circulation, and fermentation systems used in the production of wines (Villalón and Plasencia 1992, 60–61). Industrial architecture was taught at the Barcelona School of Industrial Engineering. After World War I, however, Catalan and Spanish industrial architecture failed to join the new rationalism of Behrens, Gropius, and Le Corbusier, as is evident in one of the finest buildings of this period, Antoni Puig i Gairalt's Myrurgia Cosmetics factory of 1928–30, "a classic, anti-avant-garde, timidly reactionary [building] in its ornamentation, moldings, and in the composition of the façades, although it contains new approaches like Perret's, some art deco ornaments, and a taste for an open and optimistic architecture" (Bohigas 1998, 50; see also Pizza 1997, 156). An influential architect, Josep Domènech i Estapà, thought that mechanical forms should be adorned to make them more beautiful (Freixa 1986, 76–77), a proposal that avant-garde modernism would reject outright. He also attacked engineers for "dismissing the proportions and laws of good taste" (quoted in Bonet Correa, Lorenzo Fornies, and Miranda Regojo 1985, 57). Another key architect, Félix Cardellach, wrote that the new "technical architecture" of Behrens's AEG Turbinenfabrik aroused in him a "strange sensation which is not . . . the feeling of admiration evoked by the usual architectural style" (Cardellach y Avilés 1916, 108). He was critical of architecture in metal, especially Eiffel's (Bonet Correa, Lorenzo Fornies, and Miranda Regojo 1985, 60).

Antoni Gaudí figures prominently among Catalan modernists not only because of the popularity that his works have achieved over the years, but also because he struck a delicate balance between modernism and expressionism that enabled both the avant-gardists and the conservatives to admire him and his buildings. In fact, Gaudí is considered to be, with Charles Rennie Mackintosh and Erich Mendelsohn, one the greatest expressionist architects of all time (Zevi [1973] 1994, 190; Scully [1961] 1974, 23; Pevsner [1936] 1960, 116, 172). "The richness of Gaudí's art lies in the reconciliation of the fantastic and the practical, the subjective and the scientific, the spiritual and the material" (Curtis [1982] 1996, 60), or in the "delight in the arbitrary curve" and in the "keen interest in the possibilities of materials" (Pevsner [1936] 1960, 115). He "combined the sure instinct of a sound constructor with an adventurous sculptural imagination" (Giedion [1941] 1982, 874). Thus, it is important to distinguish between two Gaudís. First, there is Gaudí-the-avant-garde-modernist, who understood that "the volume of a building is not constrained but is part of a larger cosmic space," and attempted to design each building as a total work of art (Bohigas 1998, 168). Gaudí's free plan inspired some of the leading European modernists, especially Le Corbusier (Marzá 1997; Monteys 1997). Second, as a good expressionist, however, Gaudí also understood the sculptural potential of cement and reinforced concrete (Gaudí [1878] 2002, 6), and pursued the biological, organic, and whimsical aspects of form and space. Although he favored prefabrication, he intended not to "produce repeated industrial types," but to use it as "a sculptural rather than architectural technique" (Bassegoda Nonell 1992, 148).

Gaudí was heavily influenced by art nouveau and by Ruskin's cult of natural motifs (see plate 5.10; Sweeney and Sert 1960). Like the anti-Taylorite Montolíu, Gaudí was well versed in Ruskin's social philosophy, and probably shared his views about the organization of work. For example, he lamented the effect of machine production on architecture: "Modern industry is about labor economy. The use of machines has reduced the cost of manufactured goods, but has tended to increase the cost of labor [relatively speaking]. This trend has affected all industries, and construction has suffered from it. Relative to ancient building practices, the reduction in the importance of labor has complicated construction methods from a procedural point of view so as to simplify work tasks" (Gaudí [1878–83] 2002, 130). Moreover, he looked down on engineers: "The architect is the human constructor, building for the person who works, gets married, seeks entertainment, prays. . . . The engineer constructs for beasts or for machines: roads, which are only indirectly for the people" (Gaudí [n.d.] 2002, 126).

Gaudí's expressionist leanings went against the homogeneity of the rationalist, avant-garde modernism emerging in Europe at the time. Later Spanish architects would emphasize either the modernism or the expressionism in Gaudí, and thus become true believers or "marginal" players in the modern movement, respectively. Gaudí's influence is also clear in Gropius, who, after seeing him at work, wrote: "I was still too immature to understand his unique daring and inventiveness as a structural engineer" (quoted in Isaacs 1991, 21).

Much of Gaudí's work was sponsored by Eusebio (Count) Güell, a second-generation tycoon with interests in a wide array of industries (Rodrigo Alharilla 2000; Güell 2001). Güell was a key figure in the conservative and somewhat reactionary Catalan political party known as the Lliga, which later transformed itself into Acció Catalana, more nationalist in leaning. Architect Puig i Cadafalch and noted anti-Taylorite Cipriano Montolíu also participated in this political movement, which emphasized social harmony and humanism while despising technocratic solutions to social problems (Ucelay-Da Cal 1997). Gaudí's lack of interest in social issues (Bohigas 1998, 174; Van Hensbergen 2001) parallels other art nouveau architects, who, with the only exception of Van de Velde, did not see architecture and design as moral activities geared towards the improvement of life and the amelioration of social problems. This omission became also a feature of architectural expressionism during the 1920s and '30s.

As in Victorian Britain, the stabilization of political and social conservatism in both Catalonia and Spain during the 1910s and 1920s contributed to the decline of the modernist movement (Freixa 1986, 107). The leading Spanish intellectual magazine of the 1920s and 1930s, *Revista de Occidente* (Review of the Western World), contained little debate over modernism.[3] Its founder, the philosopher and essayist José Ortega y Gasset, achieved worldwide celebrity with his antitechnical stand in the influential book *The Revolt of the Masses* and in other of his essays on art, industry, and culture. In articulating his view, Ortega y Gasset stood on the shoulders of an entrenched tradition of anti-industrialism dating back to the writers of the 1898 generation—Unamuno, Azorín, Valle-Inclán, and Baroja—if not earlier. Ortega was not against art for art's sake, and he observed that "each era must have a congenital [architectural] style" (quoted in Diéguez Patao 1997, 18, 21). However, he railed against technical fixes to labor problems in industry and endorsed the human relations approach to the organization of work, the nemesis of scientific management (Ortega y Gasset [1954] 1983, 28; Guillén 1994, 189–90, 1996). He liked to lecture people that "if you do not have a history, start building it right now" (quoted in Gutiérrez 1998a, 22). Likewise, Catalonia's most influential intellectual at the time, Eugeni d'Ors, ridiculed Le Corbusier's "machine for living" (Bohigas 1998, 14). More often than not, Spanish intellectuals and artists criticized European modernism (García Hernández 1997; Isac 1997), although a few, like poet Federico García Lorca and painter Salvador Dalí, aligned themselves with Le Corbusier's purism (Lahuerta 1997).

Perhaps the most persuasive evidence of the difference between Spanish and European modernisms is to be found at the 1929 International Exhibition in Barcelona, whose main buildings were designed by Puig i Cadafalch and other Catalan architects in an eclectic, revivalist, and in some cases Brunelleschian, that is, baroquely monumentalist, fashion. These stood in sharp contrast with the masterful German pavilion, designed by Mies van der Rohe, which has been recently reconstructed in its original location (Bohigas 1998, 67–73).

Until the late 1920s, Catalan and Spanish modernism deviated considerably from the European movement, although some engineers had designed many noteworthy industrial buildings using the new materials of the age (reinforced

[3] Only a handful of articles in *Revista de Occidente*, including one by Le Corbusier, furthered modernist points of view: 20 (1928): 157–93; 32 (1931): 308–13; 37 (1932): 48–352; 50 (1935): 1–55, 308–17. But there were also strongly anti-modernist articles: 35 (1932): 1–42, 121–66, 241–77.

concrete, glass, steel). Stylistically, however, industrial architecture was beset by huge variations in style, with ornaments still playing a key role (Sobrino 1996). Lluís Muncunill's textile and electrical factories, warehouses, stores, wine cellars, country estates, churches, and public buildings in and around Terrassa, an industrial town just outside Barcelona, amounted to perhaps the single most important attempt to create a machine-age modernism that could have placed Spain within the European mainstream, but did not depart significantly from the historicist, vernacular, and expressionist parameters set by Gaudí (Freixa 1986, 99, 120, 1996; Oller i Foixench and Rodulfo i Giménez 2002). Also worth noting are the manifold activities of engineer, urban planner, and entrepreneur Arturo Soria y Mata. He founded the Ciudad Lineal in Madrid and the Compañía Madrileña de Urbanización (1894). Although influenced by Howard's ruralism, Soria believed in rational and utilitarian urban planning (Benevolo [1960] 1977, 358–61).

The 1925 Generation

The first truly revolutionary break with architectural tradition in Spain occurred at the hands of several architects trained at the Madrid School of Architecture during the mid-1920s. They were the first to discuss and help diffuse the ideas of the Werkbund, the futurists, the Bauhaus, and Le Corbusier. This movement was a direct response to the eclecticism and confusion that had characterized Spanish architectural education and practice. Although receptive to the latest trends in Europe, in no way did the Madrid architects aim at applying all of modernism's aesthetic, technical, and social postulates. The philosophy of the Generation of 1925 amounted to a "diffused rationalism" of sorts. Intellectually, the Madrid architects inherited the tradition of liberalism and rationalism of the Institución Libre de Enseñanza, founded in 1876 to foster intellectual, scientific, and technical life and activities in a markedly decadent country. The Institución emphasized study trips around Madrid as part of the curriculum, thus enabling future architects to learn about popular architecture, which has always been utilitarian, that is, focused on the user's needs, and rational and economical in the use of materials and elements (Diéguez Patao 1997, 19, 34, 42–55). Using the resources available at new institutions like the Residencia de Estudiantes during the 1920s (a residential college attended by such celebrities as Federico García Lorca, Salvador Dalí, and Luis Buñuel), the recently graduated architects arranged for visits by Gropius, Le Corbusier, Mendelsohn, Stravinsky, Bergson, Valéry, Einstein, and Keynes, among others. At the height of their enthusiasm for machine-age modernism, the Madrid architects argued for "function against form, comfort against luxury," while their literary colleagues, in an ostensibly inquisitorial fashion, declared themselves being in favor of "burning alive any architect who is not an admirer of Le Corbusier" (Diéguez Patao 1997, 53, 59).

Two of the generation's architects proved especially influential: Casto Fernández Shaw and Fernando García Mercadal. Fernández Shaw stunned Madrid with his Petróleos Porto Pi gasoline station (1927; see plate 5.12), a fine example of the machine aesthetic that borrowed motifs from both airplanes and ships. The architect explained: "The dispensers for gasoline, petroleum, oil, water, pressure air . . . the fire extinguishers 'decorate' the facility. The automobiles, the loudspeaker, the lights will give it life" (quoted in Diéguez Patao 1997, 211; Pizza 1997, 291; Bohigas 1998, 32; Ucha Donate 1980, 159–62). In 1928 he proclaimed:

> Capitalists!!! Here you have a new architecture!!! Good, beautiful, and cheap!!!
> The hangar at Orly [Airport] is as classical as the Parthenon.
> Tectonic architecture is not designed with a pencil but with a sliding rule.
> Our individualist temperament is the enemy of the "mass-produced house."
> We all want custom-made shoes, and, naturally, we are shoeless. (quoted in Bohigas 1998, 31)

García Mercadal—who studied in Rome, traveled extensively around Europe, and met Behrens and Mies van der Rohe—also gained notoriety with an audacious building, the library-museum he designed in Saragossa, a city dominated by baroque architecture, to mark the centenary of Francisco de Goya's death (built 1926–28). Contemporaries brutally criticized this architectural masterpiece for being "simple, monotonous and oppressive" (Pizza 1997, 119; Bohigas 1998, 34; Diéguez Patao 1997, 156–59).

When Fernández Shaw was asked in 1928 who was in opposition to machine-age modernist architecture in Spain, he replied: "Established architects, who would have to dispense with corbels, vases, garlands, and so on. . . . Architects who are beginning to work with clients, out of fear of losing them if we propose audacious designs. Recently graduated architects who have not yet contributed to avant-garde exhibits." He also blamed the public for its belief that the architect's mission was to design a house "with a beautiful façade and that will not fall down" (quoted in Diéguez Patao 1997, 60, 63). Another noted architect observed in 1930 that "in Spain architecture does not exist; there are no architects, just confectioners" (J. Manuel Aizpurúa as quoted in Diéguez Patao 1997, 64–65). Spanish architects continued to be absent from the European scene. For instance, a Spanish competition on "minimum existence housing" projects attracted many "confused" and "disoriented" entries. None of those preselected by the Spanish jury to represent the country were chosen by Ernest May to be part of the exhibit at the second CIAM congress of 1929 (Diéguez Patao 1997, 149).

Unfortunately, the backlash against these early experiments in rational and functional modernism retarded its development in Spain until the proclamation of the Republic in 1931. The so-called "marginal rationalists" and the outright reactionary Spanish architects of the 1920s rebelled against machine-age modernism, many of them by emphasizing the expressionist solution that Gaudí had foreshadowed (Bohigas 1998, 174). One of them, Pere Benavent, put it delicately: "Neither eighteenth-century archeology, nor 1920s archeology! Only simple and pure architecture, the one that springs from our immortal spirit!" In this way, many Spanish architects abandoned the activist social and political agenda of the European modern movement, and succumbed to the more conformist and conservative themes of expressionism (Bohigas 1998, 143, 173–74).

The Fleeting Triumph of Modernism during the Republic of 1931–39

Catalonia retook the initiative from Madrid during the 1930s, thanks primarily to the efforts of an aristocrat and Socialist Party member, Josep Lluís Sert, a disciple of Le Corbusier, who helped organize a movement of modernist architects with direct links to the international style, first in Catalonia (GATC-PAC, 1928), and later in the rest of Spain (GATEPAC, 1930). "Architecture should both obey utilitarian requirements and satisfy the aspirations of our highest intellectual needs. . . . We must dispense with all superfluous ornamentation. . . . We must refrain from imitating past styles, and bring architecture back to its natural expression, closely linked to the technical, social and economic conditions of the present" (quoted in Freixa 1997, 12–13; Mumford 2000, 66–73).[4]

Although Sert was influenced by Gaudí (Sweeney and Sert 1960), he took part in a totally different Catalan political movement, the technocratic and social-democratic Unió Socialista de Catalunya, led by a group of industrial engineers (Ucelay-Da Cal 1997). He designed several landmark buildings before going into exile in 1939 to eventually become dean of Harvard University's Graduate School of Design.[5] The key event was perhaps the creation of a truly autonomous government in Catalonia in 1932 after the ousting of the king and the proclamation of the Spanish Republic a year earlier. The Catalan government, now backed by leftist political forces as opposed to the conservative ones that ruled in the 1920s, embraced rationalism and modernism in its

[4] See also GATEPAC's magazine, *AC*, which contains dozens of articles on the application of the principles of standardization and economizing to architecture, urban planning, and furniture design (reprinted as *AC/GATEPAC 1931–1937* [Barcelona: Gustavo Gili, 1975]).

[5] While at Harvard, Sert redefined the campus with such notable buildings as Holyoke Center (1958–65), Peabody Terrace (1963), and the Science Center (1973). He also designed important buildings for Boston University and the Massachusetts Institute of Technology.

public works, urban planning, and architectural policies. It even proposed to apply to architecture the "rational principles of work" (Bohigas 1998, 200). Sert's first major accomplishment was the Casa Bloc of 1931–36 (see plate 5.13), a 200-apartment complex in Barcelona, with separate residential, commercial, and recreational areas, the first in all of Spain "absolutely subscribing [to] the new rationalist language" (Bohigas 1998, 91; Pizza 1997, 160–61). Architectural historians single out his Antituberculosis Central Clinic of 1934 as the most important building of this period. Sert's last contribution before going into exile was the Spanish Republic's pavilion at the 1937 International Exhibit in Paris, a fine building of Corbusian conception, which housed Pablo Picasso's *Guernica*, Alexander Calder's *Fountain of Mercury*, and Joan Miró's mural *The Catalan Peasant and the Revolution* (Freixa 1997). It is only ironic to note that it was the Spanish pavilion that carried the banner of avant-garde modernism at the Exhibit, confronted by the classicist and reactionary buildings designed by Albert Speer (Germany), Marcelo Piacentini (Italy), and Boris Iofan (Soviet Union).

The modernist architects and designers of the 1930s introduced the latest achievements of the international architectural style. Their influence in Spain, however, waned quickly because of the premature death of some of their leaders and because most of the others were forced into exile in the wake of the Civil War of 1936–39, delaying for several decades the transformation of architectural and artistic work. Unrelated to the group led by Sert, but certainly modernist in aesthetic and technique, were the two designers who pioneered the architectural use of reinforced concrete in Spain—Antonio Flórez and Eduardo Torroja. However, they were not influential enough to create a school of followers before the war (Flores 1989, 111–31; Giner de los Ríos [1952] 1980, 69–79, 135–38; Bonet 1999; on Torroja, see Fernández Ordóñez, Antonio, and Navarro Vera 1999; Pizza 1997, 284–86, 302–3).

On balance, modernist architecture in the avant-garde, European sense, did start to develop in Spain before 1940, but the Civil War and economic backwardness prevented the seeds planted during the 1930s from growing. In their canonical book, *The International Style*, Hitchcock and Johnson ([1932] 1995, 174) only mention one building in Spain, the Nautical Clubhouse at San Sebastián (Donostia), which evokes the shapes and rational efficiency of a vessel, although it is expressionist more than modernist in going beyond the strictly functional. It was erected in 1928–29 by two Basque architects—J. Manuel Aizpurúa and Joaquín Labayen—who failed to make any other major contributions.[6]

[6] Aizpurúa, a member of the Falange, the Spanish Fascist Party, was executed during the first weeks of the civil war.

As French cultural sociologist Pierre Bourdieu (1984, 56) once pointed out, "aesthetic intolerance can be terribly violent." Italian, Russian, and Spanish avant-garde modernism lasted only as long as favorable political conditions and sympathetic state bureaucrats willing to fund architectural projects did. The totalitarian regimes of Hitler and Stalin were no fans of the avant-garde or of modernism in architecture, and repressed both quite brutally during the 1930s. Hitler took good notice of the Socialist and Communist affiliations of many of the leading modernist artists and architects, while Stalin detested their allegedly bourgeois origins. Also important was the desire of these totalitarian regimes to exert power and discipline over such an important policy area as architecture and building, an ironic testament to the success of the modernists at transforming architecture. Perhaps better than anybody else, the Nazis and the Stalinists saw in architecture a powerful political tool. Not negligible also was the fact that Hitler—a frustrated artist—was a fan of grandiose classical designs, and regarded modernism and the avant-garde as subversive, decadent, "degenerate art" (*entartete Kunst*). The Nazis shut down both the Werkbund and the Bauhaus (Barron 1991; Herf 1984; Hochman 1989, 311–12; Lane 1985). Meanwhile, in the Soviet Union the party leadership began to favor "socialist realism" in art after suppressing the avant-garde because of its alleged elitism and bourgeois character and sending many architects and designers to the Gulag, including Gan, who perished there. At roughly the same time, the early Soviet institutions created to foster scientific management were dismantled in favor of the indigenous Stakhanovite system of wage differentials and piecework (Kopp 1985, 154–57; Golomstock 1990; Lieberstein 1975).

The relationship between Italian Fascism and modernism was more complex. Fascism was initially enthusiastic about modernism, but it refused to adopt futurism or rationalism as the official style of the regime (Bowler 1991, 786–88; Etlin 1991, 475). It is important to note, however, that several of the most prominent architects were enthusiastic about Fascism, mainly because of its revolutionary rhetoric. Terragni, Libera, and Pagano (a Fascist Party member since 1920), for instance, did not hesitate to praise Fascism and to participate in the extensive architectural and urban planning projects sponsored by the regime—railway stations, post offices, exhibit halls, workers' clubs, Fascist Party headquarters (Etlin 1991, 379, 385). Italian futurists and rationalists, especially Pagano, joined the Fascist anti-Semitic campaign (which was characteristically ambiguous in theory and in practice) as a way to protect their own standing within the regime, claiming that avant-garde painting and modernist architecture were not invented by Jews. The racial overtones, however, were evident. And yet many of the same rationalist architects who supported Fascism and benefited from official commissions, joined the Resistance during the last years of the regime, especially after the German occupation of late

1943. As a result, many of them were arrested and deported to concentration camps. Several perished at Mauthausen, including Pagano (Ciucci 1989; Etlin 1991, 378, 569–97; De Matteis 2001).

As in Germany and the Soviet Union during the early 1930s, the incipient Spanish machine-age modernism of the late 1930s was brutally uprooted after the victory of the authoritarian rebel nationalists in the Civil War of 1936–39. Dozens of prominent architects went into exile: twenty-two to Mexico, seven to Venezuela, three each to France and Colombia, two to Chile, and one each to Cuba, the Domingo Republic, the USSR, Poland, and the United States (Sert). About a hundred of those who stayed but had leftist or separatist political affiliations were forbidden from practicing as architects, including García Mercadal and Puig i Cadafalch, among others (GATEPAC 2001; Bohigas 1998, 201–6; Diéguez Patao 1997).

Sociopolitical upheaval and revolution did provide artists and architects an opportunity to change the course of architectural history in Italy, Russia, and Spain. Revolutionary political regimes, however, rarely last long, and, if they do, consolidation frequently leads to a reformulation, or even abandonment, of their original ideology and goals. Thus, it is not surprising to see that the rise of modernist architecture in Italy, Russia, and Spain in the wake of revolutionary events proved to be a fleeting phenomenon. While the previous chapter demonstrated that industrialization per se did not produce modernism in Britain and France, this chapter serves as a stark reminder that sociopolitical unrest and revolution are not universally linked to modernist architecture either.

Ironically, the totalitarian/authoritarian suppression of modernism helped spread it throughout the world, as architects and designers left Germany, Italy, Spain, the Soviet Union, and other Eastern European countries for Britain, Latin America, and the United States. The exiles were able to capitalize on the visibility they had achieved by making such conspicuous enemies in their home countries. Most of them wound up at elite American universities: Gropius, Wagner, and Sert eventually took up teaching positions at Harvard; Mies van der Rohe at the Illinois Institute of Technology; and Albers at Yale.[7] Mendelsohn was to be influential in Britain, and Meyer first in the USSR and later in Mexico. Several Latin American architects, however, had shifted towards modernism before the arrival of the European refugees, the subject of the next chapter.

---

[7] Hochman (1989, 218–24) documents that Mies van der Rohe's relationship with the Nazi regime was more complicated than his eventual exile in the United States might suggest. He signed the August 1934 proclamation inviting the German people to confirm Chancellor Hitler as Führer in the wake of President Hindenburg's death, actively sought to obtain architectural commissions from the Nazi regime, collaborated in the organization of several official exhibitions, and was fascinated by Hitler's enthusiasm for architecture. Mies, however, was not alone in feeling that leaving Germany would be an act of cowardice. In fact, only about a third of the most noted German Bauhaus teachers or students included in Neumann's (1993) book left Germany. Mies went into exile in 1937.

Modernism without Modernity: Mexico, Brazil, Argentina

> A house . . . will be a tool, just as the automobile is becoming a tool.
> —Juan O'Gorman (quoted in Burian 1997, 129).

> Down with absurd decoration and on with logical construction!
> —Gregori Warchavchik ([1925] 1965, 265).

> Standardization turns architecture into an ignoble undertaking and not an art . . . it turns the architect into a trafficant or commissioner as opposed to an artist.
> —Ángel Guido (quoted in Gutiérrez 1984a, 152).

DURING THE NINETEENTH and early twentieth centuries the various Latin American countries borrowed from Europe both the ideal of the oligarchical republic, and the architectural eclecticism and monumentalism that still characterizes the Paseo (Boulevard) de la Reforma in Mexico City, the Avenida Central of Rio de Janeiro, and the Avenida de Mayo in Buenos Aires. French classicism appealed to the europhile landed elites that ruled Mexico, Brazil, and Argentina for about one hundred years after independence in the 1820s (Gutiérrez and Viñuales 1998, 162–65). Modernism in architecture only developed after dramatic turning points, that is, in the wake of revolution and counterrevolution, the shift from upper-class rule to mass politics, the introduction of nationalist economic development programs, and, in some cases, the instauration of authoritarian regimes seeking legitimacy through public works.

The rise of a modernist architecture in Latin America within only a few years of its appearance in Europe was something of an improbable event given the region's relative backwardness. Like Spain during the 1930s, Mexico, Brazil, and Argentina are instances of "modernism without modernity,"[1] in a

---

[1] I owe this expression to Ramón Gutiérrez (1998a, 20). This chapter draws heavily from Guillén (2004).

region in which, with perhaps the exception of Argentina, labor has always been so plentiful and cheap that Taylorized methods of production are not economically attractive, a unique part of the world whose intellectual and cultural life was at the time well ahead of economic and technological realities. The modernist materials par excellence—glass, steel, reinforced concrete— were not available in industrial quantities anywhere in Latin America before the 1930s. Moreover, to the present day about 60 percent of all dwellings are erected by their own occupants, and no more than 10 percent are designed by architects (Eliash and San Martín 1998, 53). Just as the classicism of turn-of-the-century Latin American architecture was implemented by the Europe-anizing tastes of elite architects, the rise of modernist architecture had to do with the persuasions and perseverance of a distinctively elite group of local architects influenced by European trends, with a few touches of indigenous influence (Bullrich 1969). The arrival of exiled modernist architects from Fascist and Communist Europe during the 1930s and 1940s contributed to the diffusion of modernism. The Latin American modernists, while elitist, shared with their European counterparts a belief in social progress through good design.

This chapter focuses on the three most dynamic countries in the region— Mexico, Brazil, and Argentina—in order of historical development of a modernist architecture. The Mexican Revolution of 1910–17 and its subsequent institutionalization eventually brought to power a group of reform-minded technocrats that saw in modernist architecture a way to improve public services and lifestyles. In Brazil, Getúlio Vargas's ideas about a "new state" (*Estado Novo*) paved the road to modernism after 1930. In Argentina the process was more protracted and modernism in architecture lacked vigor as a movement, although political change started to occur as early as 1916 with the election victory of the Radical Party, followed by the military coup of 1930, and Juan Domingo Perón's election to the presidency in 1946. Contacts with engineers and scientific managers proved important to the development of modernist architecture in Mexico and Brazil, but not in Argentina.

MEXICO: REVOLUTION AND ARCHITECTURE

In the thirty years following the Revolution of 1910–17, a staggering number of buildings were constructed in Mexico, including single-family homes, apartment complexes, government agencies, hospitals, movie theaters, and schools (Myers 1952). While the new regime promoted a modernist style with a certain touch of indigenous sensitivity in an attempt to turn Mexico into one of the "progressive" countries of the world, many architects still subscribed to the more nationalistic neocolonial and neo-pre-Hispanic styles, based on the rich architectural legacies of the Olmecs, Teotihuacans, Toltecs, Aztecs, Mayas, and Spaniards (Cetto 1961; Méndez-Vigatá 1997, 61). The Mexican revolutionaries themselves were not in agreement as to what kind of architecture was best fit to achieve their social and economic goals. In fact, the Mexican revolution was notorious for the "absence of an ideology," to paraphrase the Nobel Laureate poet Octavio Paz ([1987] 1993, 143). Sure enough, the postrevolutionary presidents pursued quite different policies, in some cases veering towards the right. In *The Labyrinth of Solitude*, Paz (1961) describes twentieth-century Mexico as an attempt to combine its glorious and mythical past with a yearning for modernity. This ambivalence is perhaps best captured in the work of Diego Rivera, whose murals extol the past as well as the present, the countryside and the city, the cosmopolitan and the native, the indigenous/Hispanic heritages and the revolution. After all, the Mexican revolution was "on the one hand . . . a resurrection: the Mexican past, Indian civilization, popular art, the buried spiritual reality of a people; on the other, it was a renovation, or more exactly, a *novation*, in the juridical sense and in the figurative one of a thoroughgoing beginning" (Paz [1987] 1993, 145).

The Muralists and Architecture

Architects of diverse political persuasions were enlisted by the revolutionary Mexican state, in some cases to improve working and living conditions, yet in others to glorify the revolution and the regime. Several laws were passed to promote "cheap housing," "economical housing," and "workers' housing" (Gutiérrez 1998a). By far the most activist agency was the Ministry of Education because of its control over architectural and artistic education, and also because free mass and secular schooling was at the top of the revolutionaries' agenda given the 72 percent illiteracy rate as of 1921 (Meyer 1991, 208). The goal of expanding educational opportunity required the construction of hundreds of schools throughout the country. The first activist Minister of Education was José Vasconcelos (1920–24), who had spent many years in exile in the United States. He was a traditionalist with a taste for neocolonial art and architecture, and a staunch critic of all things American or modern: "Mexico had a university before Boston, and libraries, museums, newspapers and a theater before New York and Philadelphia." "To build is the duty of each epoch, and buildings shall be the glory of the new government. . . . We did not want schools of the Swiss type . . . nor schools of the Chicago type [a veiled reference to modernism]. . . . In architecture, too, we should find inspiration in our glorious past" (quoted in Méndez-Vigatá 1997, 66, 67; see also Fraser 2000, 23–32; Vasconcelos 1963).

Vasconcelos made a momentous decision early on, which was to sponsor the muralists—Diego Rivera, José Clemente Orozco, and David Alfaro Siqueiros among others—to use public façades to glorify things Mexican, the revolution, and the regime's educational policies. This move had several important implications. First, it helped highlight the need to identify and incorporate the local dimension to art and architecture. In 1923 the Manifesto of the Union of Workers, Technicians, Painters, and Sculptors (signed by Rivera and Orozco, among others) proclaimed that "the popular art of Mexico is the most important and the healthiest of spiritual manifestations and its native tradition the best of all traditions. . . . We proclaim that all forms of aesthetic expression which are foreign or contrary to popular feeling are bourgeois and should be eliminated" (quoted in Meyer 1991, 209). Still, the leading muralists were influenced by "foreign" trends, with each of them being different in the relative emphasis afforded to various European influences, including fauvism, cubism, surrealism, expressionism, futurism, and constructivism. Second, the privileged treatment of the muralists had the effect of imposing certain constraints on architects, especially the requirement to build vast wall surfaces in cement and not glass, and the added emphasis on ornamentation.[2]

But perhaps the most important effect of the state's sponsorship of the muralists was the architectural tastes they came to propound. Rivera, while an admirer of colonial buildings, did not agree with Vasconcelos's promotion of neocolonial and Californian architecture, and displayed an interest in the functional aspects of modernist architecture. Moreover, as director of the Central School of Plastic Arts in 1929–30, Rivera pushed very hard to introduce reforms, presenting architecture as a useful social endeavor geared towards the design of honest or sincere buildings (López Rangel 1986, 15–19, 24–26). The muralists furthered a conception of art as a public enterprise at the service of the government, following the great examples of Byzantium, Egypt, Teotihuacán, and the Quattrocento (Paz [1987] 1993, 147), and in parallel with contemporaneous developments in Italy and the Soviet Union. Rivera was also adamant that architecture should advance the cause of the poor: "In the social domain, what are the accomplishments of the organized college of professional architects? With the millions they have earned, what have they done about the dwellings of the factory workers, the miners and the tenant workers at the landed estates? What have they done to humanize the rooms inhabited by the poor?" (quoted in López Rangel 1986, 29).

Architectural Eclecticism during the 1920s

Vasconcelos and other government officials sponsored architects such as Carlos Obregón Santacilia, a great-grandson of President Benito Juárez, who designed schools in neocolonial style, various government buildings in art deco,

---

[2] It is revealing to note that the architects trained in the Beaux-Arts tradition admired Rivera. See the journal of the Society of Mexican Architects, *El Arquitecto: Revista de Arquitectura y Artes Mexicanas* 2 (5) (1925): 1–40, 2 (8) (1926): 3–36. These two issues were almost entirely devoted to an analysis of Rivera's murals and to full-page photographs of them.

and the Monument to the Revolution in Mexico City in a mix of California and vernacular (Mijares Bracho 1997; Fraser 2000, 32–34). Other important architects of this early period included José Villagrán García, the architect of the neocolonial National Stadium of 1929 (Méndez-Vigatá 1997, 66, 67), and Adamo Boari, a personal friend of technocratic dictator Porfirio Díaz, who designed several "revival" public buildings during the 1910s and 1920s.[3]

It was during the presidency of Plutarco Elías Calles (1924–28) that modernism surfaced in Mexico. Both Obregón Santacilia and Villagrán García started to design some modernist buildings, while continuing to build in neocolonial and even neoclassical styles. Villagrán García's gradual evolution towards modernism was key because of his prominent teaching position at the National University. As Méndez-Vigatá (1997, 77) has pointed out, he remained an eclectic architect, mixing Beaux-Arts elements (aesthetic proportions, optical corrections) with the influences of modernism (the concepts of utility and honesty in architecture). In 1927 Obregón Santalicia wrote forcefully about the need for the "Mexican architect to join the international architectural movement" (quoted in López Rangel 1986, 17). These two architects designed a now famous modernist house in the San Miguel neighborhood of Mexico City, praised by Rivera because its "beauty was based on the economy of material and maximum utility . . . even the electricity counter played a decorative role" (quoted in López Rangel 1986, 18).

It was also during the 1920s that Mexican engineers reasserted their role as technocrats in the new regime (Lorey 1990). "The individual that holds the key to the future is the Engineer. Illustrious is the Engineer, and grandiose are his accomplishments. It is through the Engineer . . . that the Creator is shaping the fate of humanity."[4] Without citing Viollet-le-Duc, some engineers suggested that Mexican architects learned from Gothic architecture so as to arrive at a logical and balanced design of the various parts of the building. They argued very strongly for a collaboration between architects and engineers.[5] The engineering profession in Mexico, while not as mesmerized by Taylorism and Fordism as in certain European countries or in Brazil, was keenly aware of the need to incorporate scientific methods of organization, and its opinion leaders firmly believed in that the engineer should be trained not only in technical subjects but also in economic and organizational ones.[6] By the early 1930s, engineers and like-minded architects had seized the initiative in urban planning, proposing to put workers' needs ahead of any other

[3] On one of Boari's designs, the New National Theater, see *El Arquitecto: Revista de Arquitectura y Artes Mexicanas* 2 (1) (1924): 3ff.

[4] See the editorial in the inaugural issue of the journal of the National School of Engineering, *Ingeniería* 1 (1927): 5.

[5] *Ingeniería* 6 (1932): 375, 8 (1934): 93.

[6] See the journal of the Association of Engineers and Architects of Mexico, *Revista Mexicana de Ingeniería y Arquitectura* 1 (1923): 46–50, 374–84, 9 (1931): 234–57, 14 (1936): 450–53.

consideration. They were influenced by the ideas of German exile architect Hannes Meyer (Davis 2004).

A Mexican Modernism during the 1930s

Several Mexican architects, though trained in the fine-arts tradition, eventually embraced a more technical approach to design. The truly revolutionary architect in Mexico was Juan O'Gorman, a devotee of Le Corbusier's functionalism (Luna Arroyo 1973, 94). O'Gorman's ideas were embraced by the governments of the 1930s, especially that of legendary president Lázaro Cárdenas (1934–40). O'Gorman founded the Union of Architects in the Fight for Socialism (1937–41). He was a personal friend of Leon Trotsky, who had left the USSR for exile in Mexico after losing the succession battle to Stalin. Drawing his inspiration from muralist Diego Rivera, O'Gorman found a way to resolve the perennial conflict between the past and the present by incorporating pre-Hispanic motifs (Luna Arroyo 1973). A painter and muralist as well as architect, he was forceful in his commitment to modernism: "We should not forget that men are only rational animals, and to proceed through any medium that is not the one of maximum efficiency through minimum effort, is not to proceed rationally." And in a manner reminiscent of Le Corbusier, whom he read assiduously, he proclaimed, "A house . . . will be a tool, just as the automobile is becoming a tool" (quoted in Burian 1997, 127, 129). He worked for both Obregón Santacilia and Villagrán García, and was instrumental in the creation of the School of Engineering and Architecture at the National Polytechnic Institute.

As chief architect of the Department of School Construction of the Ministry of Education, O'Gorman designed more than thirty "inexpensive schools, economically built, with durable materials, and as efficient as possible in spending the pueblo's [people's] money" (quoted in Burian 1997, 130; see also Luna Arroyo 1973, 65, 117–18). He proposed to build schools at much lower cost than the neocolonial ones constructed during the Vasconcelos period, mostly by "eliminating all architectural style and executing constructions technically" (quoted in Fraser 2000, 47). O'Gorman also designed workers' housing, apartment buildings, and artistic studios, among them the famous contiguous though separate quarters for his personal friends Diego Rivera and Frida Kahlo (1931–32; plate 6.1), with their zigzagging roofs and external helicoidal stairway. Reflecting on his early years as an architect, he explained that "I didn't do architecture; I engineered buildings, using the same mental process by which one makes a dam, a bridge, a road, engineering works" (quoted in Fraser 2000, 46).

Though less strident in his remarks, Juan Segura was also a key architect in Mexican modernism. His Ermita Building in Mexico City (1930–31; plate 6.2) consisted of commercial space, a movie theatre, and apartments, and was built before Le Corbusier's multifunctional concept was made famous by his *unité de habitation*. Segura had to use structural steel creatively so as to be able to build apartments above the ceiling of the theater. Like most other contemporary Mexican architects, he used ornaments more profusely than the modernist dogma would permit, and was thus often classified as belonging to the art deco movement (Toca Fernández 1997). Francisco Serrano was another early designer of movie theaters and affordable apartments, albeit more purely rationalist than Segura, perhaps because of his educational background in engineering.[7] Enrique Yáñez was equally rationalist in his designs for various hospitals and healthcare centers. Another singular exponent was Enrique de la Mora, whose apartment building on Calle Strasburgo in Mexico City (1934) is the paradigmatic space-saving building that looks like an ocean liner, a design reminiscent of Le Corbusier and Terragni. Like the other modernist architects, Mario Pani designed hotels, apartment buildings, conservatories, hospitals, and clinics before 1940. His fame, though, is mostly due to his President Alemán Urban Housing Project in Mexico City (1949), a thoroughly Corbusian design with L-shaped apartment blocs leaving open spaces between them, separate areas for social services and commercial use, and throughways for automobiles and pedestrians (Noelle Merles 1997). Like the good modernist that he was, he showed his commitment to housing the masses: "We must build for all of them. Plan! Build! Plan well! Build now!" (quoted in Eggener 2000, 38; and in Smith 1967, 176).

It is imperative to point out that Mexican "modernist" architecture deviated from the European mainstream in several respects, including the addition of murals, the use of indigenous motifs and materials, the organic design of the building so as to match its surroundings, and the overall emphasis on aesthetics rather than utility. Some architects—for example, Luis Barragán—were adamant in producing a peculiarly Mexican architecture using adobe, stucco, cobblestones, and unfinished wood, although they remained firmly modernist: "It has been a mistake to abandon the shelter of walls for the inclemency of large areas of glass" (Barragán, quoted in Smith 1967, 54; see also Barragán Foundation 2002).

Even O'Gorman eventually joined this "mexicanization" trend. After designing purely functionalist buildings and extolling the virtues of efficiency methods and "industrial prefabrication" during most of the 1930s, he too acknowledged the need for adding aesthetic fantasy to the purely mechanical principles of functionalism. He thought of Antoni Gaudí as the best integrator of modernist functionalism and aesthetic whimsy, and ultimately rejected Le

---

[7] See Serrano's article in *Revista Mexicana de Ingeniería y Arquitectura* 17 (1939): 274–76, and photographs of his Edificio-Jardín Avenida Martí in Mexico City, used by La Tolteca Portland cement company in some of its advertisements (on the back cover of the July 1933 issue). The development was owned by a company called Rentas Baratas (Low Rents).

Corbusier's radical functionalism in favor of Wright's organicism (Eggener 1999; Fraser 2000, 41, 84–85; Smith 1967, 18). In the late 1930s he decided to temporarily abandon architecture to devote himself to painting. He returned to design in the 1950s, embracing Wright's organic view of an architecture firmly rooted in its surroundings, with abundant vernacular elements, especially in the coloring and ornamentation (murals, reliefs, sculptures) of the façade, as for instance in the library at the National Autonomous University of Mexico (1950–52; Cetto 1961). The campus included an Olympic Stadium, which Rivera decorated with one of his powerful sculptural murals, and praised for its functionalism and effective integration with its surroundings, although he disliked many of the buildings for their intrusive character (López Rangel 1986, 123–24).

The debate between the "internationalist" architects wishing to follow the purest modernism, and the "nationalists" who yearned for a modern architecture adapted to Mexican realities and surroundings raged well into the 1950s, with the latter ultimately gaining the upper hand. Rivera animated the debate with articles denouncing the neglect of things Mexican by those he saw as blindly following Le Corbusier without realizing that even the world's most vocal promoter of modernism had proposed an architecture blended with the landscape (López Rangel 1986, 41–44, 113). Still, this "mexicanized modernism" produced a rational architecture that sought to cater to the needs of the population, promote the (shifting) goals of the revolution, and enhance the regime's domestic and international stature.[8]

BRAZIL: A DISTILLED MODERNISM

Brazilian architects produced perhaps the most refined modernist designs in the entire world, including the Casa Modernista in São Paulo (1927), the Ministry of Education and Health in Rio de Janeiro (1937–43), and Brasília, the new capital city. Despite the influence of European modernism—especially Le Corbusier—most of the Brazilian modernist buildings were designed and executed by a relatively small group of brilliant, locally trained architects such as Lúcio Costa and Oscar Niemeyer, who became international celebrities. They were directly influenced by engineering and applied the ideas of method, standardization, and planning to their designs.

---

[8] The pages of the journal of the Society of Mexican Architects are filled with declarations in favor of a national style rooted in building tradition and local materials. See, in particular, *El Arquitecto: Revista de Arquitectura y Artes Mexicanas* 1 (1) (1923): 1, 2 (1) (1924): 1–2. Even engineers argued for a truly national style: *Revista Mexicana de Ingeniería y Arquitectura* 6 (1928): 396–405.

Brazilian architectural modernism begins in the mid-1920s with Russian emigré Gregori Warchavchik, who arrived in São Paulo in 1923 hired by the Companhia Construtora de Santos. This firm had been founded by civil engineer and entrepreneur Roberto Simonsen, Brazil's pioneer in the implementation of scientific management and its most important advocate into the 1930s (Urwick 1956, 271–75). In 1925 Warchavchik published in the daily *Correio da Manhã* his manifesto, "Apropos of Modern Architecture," alluding to the main themes of European machine-age modernism: "If we observe the machines of our times: motor cars, steamers, locomotives, etc., we find in them, along with rationality of construction, a beauty of forms and line. . . . A house is a machine the technical perfection of which ensures, for instance, a rational distribution of light, heat, cold and hot water, etc. . . ." (Warchavchik [1925] 1965, 264–65). He defended the figure of the "engineer-builder" against that of the "architect-decorator." He wrote that "tradition is a sutile poison," and "Down with absurd decoration and on with logical construction!" (quoted in Gutiérrez and Viñuales 1998, 126 and Warchavchik [1925] 1965, 265, respectively; see also Ficher and Milan Acayaba 1982; Benevolo [1960] 1977, 748).

His Casa Modernista of 1927 was the first modernist building in all of Latin America (see plate 6.3). A Brazilian newspaper referred to it as a "rational house, comfortable, purely utilitarian, full of air, light, joy" (quoted in Ferraz 1965, 27). This simple, clean, geometrical design anticipated the direction that key Brazilian architects would take in the 1930s and 1940s. Warchavchik had worked with Piacentini in Italy and Mendelsohn in Germany prior to moving to São Paulo, Brazil's industrial and commercial center. However, he could not implement his most innovative ideas about prefabrication and standardization due to the lack of specialized contractors in Brazil. Moreover, he could not use reinforced concrete, but instead built in brick and then covered it with cement (Fraser 2000, 166), an egregious though perhaps unavoidable departure from the principle of architectural honesty in the use of materials. Warchavik taught or collaborated with other younger Brazilian architects, and was named by Le Corbusier as the South American representative of CIAM, thus exerting an important influence on subsequent developments.

Brazil experienced in 1930 a revolution of sorts at the hands of Getúlio Vargas, the creator of the Italian-inspired, corporatist *Estado Novo*. Although architectural and building activity was basically put on hold for a few years, the new regime promoted industrialization and the rationalization of work. Brazilian engineers had started to discuss Taylorism in the 1920s, but it was not until the 1930s that the first systematic attempts at implementation took place. The Vargas regime was enthusiastic about scientific management as a tool to achieve not just economic growth in the private sector but also improved practices in the public administration. Experiments with Taylorism proliferated, and links developed between industrialists and modernist designers.[9]

In 1935 the regime organized a competition for one of its landmark projects, the Ministry of Health and Education in the country's capital, Rio de Janeiro. A team of young Brazilian architects led by Lúcio Costa and Oscar Niemeyer, and also including Jorge Moreira and Affonso Eduardo Reidy, won with a stunningly modernist design. Le Corbusier—who had first visited Brazil in 1929—was invited to provide advice before construction began, and made important contributions to its design. When the building was finished in 1943 after six years of work, the result could not be more impressive: a large bloc of reinforced concrete built on 30-feet-high pilotis, sun breakers (*quebra sol* or *brise-soleil*) on the north side and glass on the south side (Rio being in the Southern Hemisphere), and a rooftop garden. The design occupied an entire city block, leaving room for a plaza. The building itself included separate areas for civil servants and for the public (see plate 6.4; Ficher and Milan Acayaba 1982; Fraser 2000, 150–64; Bullrich 1969, 22–24; Deckker 2001). Art historians have labeled it the "first realization of a building type of which Le Corbusier had been thinking for some time—the Cartesian skyscraper for administrative purposes" (Benevolo [1960] 1977, 750). American contemporaries were so taken by it that the Museum of Modern Art in New York decided to dispatch a delegation to visit the building. The catalogue of MoMA's 1943 exhibition, *Brazil Builds*, put it succinctly: "While Federal classic in Washington, Royal Academy archaeology in London, and Nazi classic in Munich are still triumphant . . . Rio can boast of the most beautiful government building in the Western hemisphere" (Goodwin 1943, 92).

The Ministry building was just the first of what would be a long series of outstanding modernist designs by Brazilian architects. At around the same time, Marcelo and Milton Roberto designed the ABI building (Associação Brasileira de Imprensa), also in Rio. When it was finished in 1936 it became the first Brazilian office building made of reinforced concrete and with sun breakers (Xavier, Britto, and Nobre 1991, 40). In 1937 Marcelo and Mauricio Roberto won the competition for the Santos Dumont Airport terminal in Rio, a building dominated by two-story high pilotis, which was completed in 1944. Meanwhile, Costa and Niemeyer designed several other landmark buildings and projects, together or individually. Most fatefully, Niemeyer received several commissions from the Mayor of Belo Horizonte, Juscelino Kubitschek, later to become the president who would make the commitment to build Brasília. On the shores of an artificial lake outside Belo Horizonte, Niemeyer

[9] See Saenz Leme 1978; Guzzo Decca 1987; ROC 1932; Urwick 1956, 256–58, 271–78; Weinstein 1990. See also the official journal of the Brazilian Institute for the Scientific Management of Work, *IDORT* 3 (26) (February 1934): 32–35, 40–42, 3 (31) (May 1934): 145–8, 3 (34) (October 1934): 217–25, 233–37, 3 (35) (November 1934): 252–58, 3 (36) (December 1934): 276–79.

designed a number of buildings to promote tourism and entertainment activities, thus giving architecture its most characteristic modernist function, that is, to encourage development (Fraser 2000, 184–89).

Unlike in Mexico, the Brazilian government's building priorities did not include affordable housing for workers. Still, some architects devoted much of their careers to housing of various kinds, always emphasizing simple designs, functionalism, durable materials, and the comforts of modern appliances. These included Oswaldo Bratke, Bruno Levi (an Italian émigré and disciple of Piacentini's), and Affonso Eduardo Reidy.

Brasília

If Brazilian modernism first acquired international fame with the Ministry of Education and Health Building in Rio, the design and construction of Brasília, the new capital city meant to help colonize the country's vast interior and usher in a new era of progress, demonstrated to the world the intellectual maturity of Brazilian modernist architecture. It was supposed to be, in the words of President Kubitschek, the "anticipation of the future," the incarnation of the "national will" to develop Brazil's economy and territory, the "point of convergence of all the interests of the nation" (quoted in Durand 1991, 76). As historian Jonathan Glancey has put it, this was "an epoch-making stride in the evolution of modern architecture . . . the dream of CIAM [Le Corbusier's International Congress of Modern Architecture], of the Athens Charter, of *Vers une architecture*, of the Russian Constructivists, the Viennese moderns, the Weimar pioneers [i.e., the Bauhaus], the German diaspora, the English Garden City enthusiasts, the American skyscraper builders" (quoted in Fraser 2000, 213). It was certainly a vast exercise in architectural and urban planning, in spite of the fact that several of the architects involved in it claimed that they were not engaged in "social architecture" (Holston 1989).

The brightest Brazilian architects of the modernist generation participated in myriad aspects of the project. Lúcio Costa supplied the overall pilot plan in 1956, a thoroughly Corbusian arrangement, with separate areas for housing, work, recreation, and traffic. "As a city dominated by its system of highways for cars, and shaped like an aeroplane, it neatly combines two key images of modernity" (Fraser 2000, 225). In fact, the pilot plan contains multiple references to the automobile (Costa 1991). Costa's design for the residential areas consisted of communal superblocks (*superquadras*) that emphasized collective life rather than private property and intended to avoid "any undue and undesired stratification of society" (quoted in Holston 1989, 76; Costa 1991, 28–30). This approach was heavily indebted to both Le Corbusier's *unité de habitation* and the Russian constructivists' communal house or *dom-kommuna* (Holston 1989, 74–77).

Between 1957 and 1964 Oscar Niemeyer designed the most prominent buildings at the core of the new city, including the Cathedral, the Senate, the House of Representatives, the Presidential Palace, the Supreme Court, the National Theater, and the various ministries. These projects shared something in common, namely, a simplification of Le Corbusier's structural and functional elements, an "extreme parsimony of constructional detail" (Benevolo [1960] 1977, 760). Niemeyer's buildings in Brasília stand out for their audacious combination of modern technology and free shapes, especially curves: "the motif of the sickle-shaped marble screens for the Presidential Palace, of the scrolled wall for the nearby chapel, of the convex dome for the Senate and the concave one for the House of Representatives, of the ring of moulded pillars for the Cathedral" (Benevolo [1960] 1977, 760). Niemeyer achieved virtually surrealist visual effects by challenging conventional architectural composition, by using "structural acrobatics" (Pevsner [1936] 1960, 217), with the help of the engineer Joachim Cardoso (see plate 6.5). In the end, Niemeyer's modernism seems to have deviated from the lemmas of "form follows function" and "less is more." His realization that Brazil was still a backward country freed him from the constraint of having to reflect existing realities and relationships, inviting him to focus instead on formal and technical innovation, to experiment with "forms of surprise and emotion" (quoted in Holsten 1989, 92; Niemeyer 2000).

As a true symbol and myth, Brasília has also aroused intense criticism, being blamed for its supposedly dehumanizing features, and for bankrupting the country. Moreover, some have claimed that Brasília did not accomplish the stated goal of its designers and planners: it actually became five cities in one, four of them not planned, and it failed to instill new living and social habits (Holston 1989; Gutiérrez 1998a, 27; Fraser 2000, 240–41; Ludwig 1980). At any rate, Brasília offers a unique interpretation of modernism, and does not cease to impress even to this day, especially when taking into account that it was planned, built, and officially inaugurated within a mere four years.

By the end of the 1950s modernism had spread throughout Brazil, from the South (São Paulo, Rio, Belo Horizonte), to the Northeast (Recife, Salvador) and the interior (Brasília). No other Latin American country had witnessed such an outburst of modernist creativity and construction, affecting so many different cities and achieving such international stature. And yet Brazilian modernism was also shaped by such mundane local factors as the climate and the availability of materials, although the influence of the styles of the past was much less marked than in Mexico. Like Brazil, Argentina was not burdened by the architectural achievements of ancient civilizations, and yet modernism did not take hold there.

ARGENTINA: THE LAND OF ECLECTICISM

Until 1916, some would argue 1930, Argentina was a liberal republic ruled by a landed oligarchy. It was one of the ten richest countries in the world thanks to staggering exports of agricultural commodities and livestock. The ruling elite imported the best European architecture, mostly following neoclassical and historicist patterns, in an attempt to emulate its counterparts in the Old World, giving Buenos Aires, the various provincial capitals, the fashionable summer resorts, and the country estates a distinctively European outlook (Ortiz et al. 1968; Bullrich 1963). Dozens of luxurious apartment and office buildings, residential mansions, hotels, theaters, government buildings, financial institutions, and railway stations were built under French academic and historicist influence.

Visiting Buenos Aires in 1909, writer Anatole France was stunned by the National Congress building, designed by the Italian architect Victor Meano, which he described as "a mix containing Italian salad, with Greek, Roman and French ingredients. . . . On top of the Louvre colonnade they put the Parthenon; on the Parthenon they managed to place the Pantheon, and then they sprinkled the cake with allegories, statues, balustrades, and terraces. This reminds one of the confusing construction of the Tower of Babel" (quoted in Gutiérrez and Viñuales 1998, 122). The Congress dominates the background of the exquisitely seignorial Avenida de Mayo of 1882–94, modeled after the Boulevard Hausmann in Paris.

There was, to be sure, another side to the Argentine built environment. Much of the infrastructure required to sustain the foreign trade boom was extremely functional in design and outlook. Myriad grain silos, railway halls, harbor facilities, bridges, and marketplaces were built between 1880 and 1910 (Gazaneo and Scarone 1984; Liernur 2000). Art deco was followed at railway stations and apartment buildings (De Paula and Gómez 1984). But, like in the United States, the world of engineering and production was far apart from the world of architecture, and Argentine architects did not manage to bridge the gap between the two, although several tried very hard. Moreover, scientific management and Fordism were not debated or implemented widely until the 1940s. Efforts at work rationalization were random and episodic rather than systematic, in sharp contrast with developments in Brazil and Mexico (James 1981; Kabat 1999; Dorfman 1995; Liernur 2000, 170).

Between Academicism and Nationalism

A unique aspect of Argentine architecture during the first half of the century was the attempt by several prominent academic architects—true believers in the aesthetic and technical superiority of cosmpolitan, Parisian architecture—to arrive at a national style. Perhaps the clearest exponent of academicism in Argentina was Alejandro Christophersen, a Paris-trained architect born in Spain of Norwegian parents. In 1901 he founded the School of Architecture at the University of Buenos Aries, which he modeled after the École des Beaux-Arts. He most famously designed in 1906 the residences of the Anchorena family, nowadays the Ministry of Foreign Affairs, in the most splendid French neoclassicist style with some ornamental touches of art nouveau. The complex includes three separate living quarters around a *cour d'honneur* (see plate 6.6). Christophersen designed dozens of urban and rural residences, churches, hotels, and bank offices. In the 1910s and '20s he toyed with the idea of a national architecture, which he sought to find in the revival of neocolonialism and the so called "mission style." He wrote articles and books on this subject, extolling Ruskin's ideas about workmanship (Crispiani 1999).

Another attempt at renovation came from the Argentine disciples of the Catalan modernists (see chapter 5). Julián García Núñez studied in Barcelona with Gaudí and Domènech i Montaner. He returned to Argentina in 1903 and introduced a combination of Catalan *modernisme* (mostly art nouveau) with the more linear German *Jugendstil*. He designed hospitals, residences, offices, and churches. Other younger architects—Martín Noel, Ángel Guido—continued in this tradition of combining several strands of protomodern European trends well into the 1920s and 1930s, with the innovation of attempting to merge them with vernacular styles, including pre-Columbian, colonial, and Californian influences (Liernur 2000, 114–38). In fact, Noel pioneered the "Nationalist Restoration" movement, advocating the Spanish colonial he saw in Bolivia and Peru as the main source of architectural ideas for all of Latin America, including Argentina. He argued that "the nationalist ideal, based on an intimate relationship between history and architecture, far from detracting from a local art . . . would become . . . a unified and balanced aesthetic" (quoted in Gutiérrez 1984a, 151).

Like Noel, Guido developed a taste for the vernacular while doing restoration work. In 1927 he characterized Le Corbusier as "confusing, capricious, and superficial," and asserted that "standardization turns architecture into an ignoble undertaking and not an art; in other words, it turns the architect into a trafficant or commissioner as opposed to an artist" (quoted in Gutiérrez 1984a, 152). Even foreign-born engineers-turned-architects who moved to Argentina—like Hungary's Juan Kronfuss—embraced the attempt to produce a national style rooted in local traditions and accomplishments (De Paula 1984; Liernur 2000, 143–52).

A Frustrated Modernism

Christophersen engaged during the late 1920s in a rather heated debate with the Argentine modernists, especially with architect Alberto Prebisch, who had graduated from the Buenos Aires School of Architecture in 1921 (Christophersen [1927] 1999; Prebisch 1927). While on a European tour, Prebisch came to the realization that he had learned all there was to be learned about academic architecture. He came in touch with the Parisian avant-garde, and with the writings of Le Corbusier. Upon his return to Argentina in 1924 he won the competition for the Sugar City in his native province of Tucumán, in the northern part of the country, one of the poorest. Inspired by Garnier's industrial city (see chapter 4), Prebisch also included motifs from colonial arquitecture, although the design was eminently modernist in conception and execution (CEDODAL 1999, 59–72). He also designed marketplaces and hospitals with the same sober, measured approach to the incorporation of neocolonial influences so as to make modernism more congruent with its surroundings (Rodríguez Leirado 2001). In 1933–34 Prebisch traveled to the United States, where he absorbed Wright's organicist architecture, and saw firsthand the achievements of industrial engineering and town planning. His subsequent designs marked a milestone in Argentine architecture, including the Obelisk (1936) and the Gran Rex movie theater (1937), located within a couple of hundred yards from each other at the heart of a remodeled downtown Buenos Aires. The Rex was a landmark in the simplication of design, and in the use of glass to provide for continuity between the street and the foyer inside. Ample though slender staircases connect the various levels, providing a sense of visual continuity across them (see plate 6.7).

While Prebisch was somewhat eclectic in his combination of academic, colonial, and rationalist themes, other Argentine architects pursued a more firmly modernist path starting in the late 1920s. Antonio Ubaldo Vilar stunned his contemporaries with his technically impeccable though aesthetically dull Banco Popular Argentino of 1926. Vilar collaborated on many projects with the office of Sánchez, Lagos y de la Torre, which designed the Kavanagh skyscraper in Buenos Aries (1934), at the time the tallest reinforced concrete structure in the world (Gutiérrez 1998a, 22; see plate 6.8). Vilar was also active in the area of low-cost industrialized housing, and in the design of rational service stations for the Argentine Automobile Club (Ortiz and Gutiérrez 1973, 18). But most of the modernist apartment buildings were designed not for the working class or the poor, but for the affluent (Liernur 2000, 196–207; CEDODAL 1999, 56–57).

More concerned with aesthetics was Spanish-born Antonio Bonet, a former student of Sert's and member in the GATCPAC (see chapter 5). After spending two years with Le Corbusier, he moved to Buenos Aires just before the start of World War II. He was a cofounder, with Jorge Ferrari Hardoy (who also worked for Corbu) and others, of the Grupo Austral (1938–41), Argentina's avant-garde modernist group. His most important designs were several summer resorts in Uruguay and Argentina. After getting frustrated with President Perón's anachronistic views of architecture, he decided to accept commissions in Spain, beginning in 1949. Together with Juan Kurchan and Hardoy, Bonet designed in 1939 the famous steel-and-leather B.K.F. butterfly-shaped chair, which was widely publicized in design magazines around the world and became part of MoMA's permanent collection. Another key modernist architect was Mario Roberto Álvarez, a follower of Mies van der Rohe's simplified designs, who gave careful attention to the functions of the building and the mechanical equipment in it.

While these and other architects were struggling to introduce some of the most important principles of modernism, the Argentine government promoted a variety of styles. General Perón, who ruled as President between 1946 and 1955, animated nationalist fervor by commissioning buildings in a neocolonial style, while turning to neoclassical for the buildings signaling major accomplishments of his regime, for example, the Banco de la Nación Argentina, the Banco Hipotecario (National Mortgage Bank), and, most importantly, the Fundación Eva Perón (plate 6.9). He only reached a veiled modernism in the case of minor public buildings. Architecturally, the Perón years were in fact a continuation of the 1930s and early 1940s in that most public buildings were historicist and neoclassical, in what has been referred to by historians as "imperial architecture" for its attempt to present the Argentine state in the most grandiose and monumental way (Ortiz 1984, 192; Gutiérrez 1984b; Gorelik 1987). The president of the Central Society of Architects, Bartolomé Repetto, put it succinctly in 1941: "We are taken by the unstoppable and all-powerful certainty that our homeland is destined to grandeur and splendor" (quoted by Ortiz and Gutiérrez 1973, 24).

By the late 1940s, and despite the achievements of the 1930s, modernism in Argentina appeared to be "isolated and in crisis" (Bullrich 1963, 23). Architects searched for their roots and attempted to shape modernism to local needs. For instance, members of the Grupo Austral declared in 1939 that "the architect, using the facile and superficial motifs of modernism, has created a new academy, sheltering the mediocre, producing the 'modern style.' . . . Functional architecture, with its aesthetic prejudices and puerile intransigence, arrived at intellectual and dehumanizing solutions because it misinterpreted the idea of the 'machine for living' and ignored individual psychology" (quoted in Bullrich 1963, 23). In fact, the mainstream of Argentine architecture reacted against international influences, especially against machine-age modernism (Ortiz and Gutiérrez 1973; Sonderéguer 1986).

It is perhaps ironic that the yearning for an architecture rooted in local tradition was felt so strongly in Argentina, a country in which the pre-Columbian and colonial architectural legacies were much more limited than in Brazil or, especially, Mexico. Argentina was certainly open to foreign influences ranging from neoclassicism to art nouveau to modernism, but in the end it proved to be much less welcoming to modernism than either Mexico or Brazil, mostly because of the pusillanimous role of the state as a sponsor and the lack of interest in engineering, scientific management, and Fordism. Argentine architecture has been characterized by a multiplicity of styles for well over a hundred years, precisely the kind of eclecticism that modernism was supposed to surmount. While several of the leading Argentine architects worked for Le Corbusier or were heavily influenced by him, Argentina was no fertile soil for modernism. When he visited in 1929, Le Corbusier described Buenos Aires as the "most inhuman city I have seen . . . a city without hope" (quoted in Baliero and Katzenstein 1984). Twenty-five years later, the city had become even more so.

As in Central and Southern Europe, Latin American architectural modernism was the result of a complex combination of forces operating in a context characterized by industrial underdevelopment and rapid sociopolitical change, most intensely felt in Mexico and Brazil.[10] As a result, the state was by far the most important sponsor of modernist architecture. Similarly, engineering and scientific management played more of a role in Mexico and Brazil than in Argentina. As the next chapter will demonstrate, the common thread that linked most of the modernist architects to each other in Europe and Latin America was an exposure to machine-age techniques and motifs due to their training in engineering as well as architecture.

[10] It should be noted, however, that modernism tended to emerge in the most developed and urban enclaves of each country (Mexico City, São Paulo, Rio, Buenos Aires).

Sponsorship, Professionalization, and Modernist Architecture

> The difference between a technical
> architect and an academic or artistic
> architect will be made perfectly clear.
> The technician is useful to the majority
> and the academic useful to the
> minority. . . . An architecture which
> serves humanity, or an architecture
> which serves money.
> —Juan O'Gorman (quoted in Fraser
> 2000, 52).

THE PIONEERING MODERNIST ARCHITECTS not only formulated a new aesthetic order based on rationalized machine production but also provided the institutional template for the reconstruction of the organizational field of architecture in their respective home countries and beyond. The rise of modernism occurred first and most decisively in Germany, Russia/Soviet Union, and Italy, with France joining this vanguard of countries during the 1920s. Spain and Latin America witnessed some isolated outbursts of modernism, but it was only in Brazil, and partially Mexico, that the movement gained momentum. In Britain and the United States modernism only diffused after its major postulates and institutional blueprints had been developed in Continental Europe. Thus, the pioneering of an architecture consistent with the machine age shifted from France and Britain to Germany, Russia and Italy, and later from Continental Europe back to the United States, where the crucial influence of engineering and scientific management had first developed.

The fact that by 1940 modernism had flourished after reinterpreting scientific management only in some European or Latin American countries invites a comparative analysis of the contextual and institutional variables that may account for the differences. I will first review the impact of industrialization, sociopolitical upheaval, and class dynamics as important contextual factors. After concluding that these variables, while important in certain countries, do not account for all of the cross-national differences, I will turn to a neoinstitutional analysis of the architecture field in each society to better grasp the emergence of the modernist aesthetic and its subsequent diffusion as a result of new sponsors and patterns of professionalization, mainly having to do with the education of architects. Table 7.1 summarizes the cross-national evidence

TABLE 7.1
A Cross-National Comparison of the Rise of Machine-Age Modernist Architecture

	Britain	France	Germany	Italy	Russia	Spain	Mexico	Brazil	Argentina	U.S.A.
Industrialization	Pioneer of the Industrial Revolution, though not of mass production.	Early industrial growth.	Late, but successful industrialization.	Late industrialization in the North.	Relative laggard, except in certain locations.	Laggard.	Laggard.	Laggard.	Laggard.	Most advanced country in mass production.
Sociopolitical upheaval	No: Victorian and Edwardian stability.	No: Relative stability since the 1870 Commune.	Yes: Defeat, revolution (1918), and inflation.	Yes: Fascist Revolution of 1922.	Yes: Bolshevik Revolution of 1917.	Yes: Social revolution, 1936–39.	Yes: Revolution of 1910–17, and socially progressive state.	Yes: Vargas's Estado Novo of 1930.	No: Haphazard transition to mass politics, 1916–46.	No: Constitutional stability; neutralized labor unrest.
Class dynamics (rise of the worker-consumer & mass consumption)	Early, which thwarted modernism in favor of kitsch.	Relatively early: 1920s.	Late: 1930s and '50s.	Late: 1950s.	Late: 1950s.	Late: 1960s.	Late: 1950s.	Late: 1950s.	Late: 1950s.	Relatively early, which thwarted modernism in favor of kitsch.

TABLE 7.1 (Continued)

	Britain	France	Germany	Italy	Russia	Spain	Mexico	Brazil	Argentina	U.S.A.
New sponsors (industrial firms & the state)	Did not play a role.	Played a role, but belatedly.	Strong role.	Strong role.	Strong role.	Weak role, except late 1930s.	Strong role of the state, not of firms.	Strong role of the state.	Weak role.	Weak role until 1930s.
Professionalization of architecture linked to engineering	No: Weak link; belated adoption of Beaux-Arts.	No: Clash between Beaux-Arts & technical traditions.	Yes: Strong and long-standing link to engineering.	Yes: Strong and long-standing link to engineering.	Yes: Linked to engineering.	No: Strong Beaux-Arts influence.	Yes: Initially based on Beaux-Arts, but influenced by engineering since late 1920s or early 1930s.		No: Strong Beaux-Arts influence.	Yes initially, but Beaux-Arts influence, 1910s–20s.
Strength of the scientific management movement	Weak until 1940s.	Intermediate.	Strong.	Strong.	Strong.	Weak until 1940s.	Intermediate.	Strong.	Weak.	Strong: pioneer.
Outcome: Modernist architecture	Late and timid: 1940s.	Early beginnings, but late consolidation.	Early pioneer; heyday in the 1920s.	Early pioneer; heyday in the 1930s.	Early pioneer; heyday in the 1920s.	Late and short-lived: 1933–39.	Relatively early for its region: late 1920s.	Relatively early for its region: 1930s.	Late, timid, and short-lived: late 1930s.	Early pioneer, but late heyday in the 1930s.

presented in the preceding chapters, and serves as a guideline to the comparative arguments presented below.

THE HISTORICAL CONTEXT OF MODERNISM

As outlined in chapter 3, the bulk of the scholarship on the rise of modernist architecture emphasizes one of three variables: industrialization, sociopolitical upheaval, or class dynamics. The analysis of the rise of modernism in Europe and Latin America in the preceding chapters indicates that industrialization had ambiguous effects on the rise of a modernist aesthetic, while sociopolitical crises and class dynamics help make sense of many but not all historical instances of emergence of a modernist architecture. Let us review each causal factor in turn.

Industrialization

It seems clear that modernism did not necessarily emerge from the most developed or industrialized countries in Europe or the Americas; nor did it necessarily fail in the poorer areas. Table 7.2 displays several indicators of economic development, industrialization, and urbanization between 1890 and 1939. Among the countries with a relatively high level of development, as measured by per capita income, architectural modernism emerged as a vigorous movement in some of them (Germany, Italy, and later, France) but not in others (United Kingdom, United States, Argentina). Some of the relatively poorer countries of Europe (Russia) and Latin America (Brazil, Mexico) saw modernism emerge earlier and more strongly than others (Spain). There is also a lack of correlation between economic development and machine-age modernism when examining specific industries. The two quintessential modernist industries that captured the imagination of the modernist architects—railways and automobiles—were much more developed in the United States and United Kingdom than in France, Germany, Italy, or the Soviet Union. In Latin America, railways and automobiles were more pervasive in Argentina than in either Mexico or Brazil, but it was the latter two countries that embraced modernism more strongly.

Previous scholarship highlights the importance of the new materials of the industrial age to the rise of modernist architecture. However, production of the two key materials used by modernist architects—steel and cement—also fails to correlate with the rise of modernism (table 7.2). Per capita production of steel and cement was comparatively low in countries in which modernism succeeded early on (e.g., Italy, Russia, Brazil, Mexico), and relatively high in others in which modernism stalled as a movement (Britain). As mentioned in chapter 6, architects in Brazil were constrained by the lack of cement, but this

TABLE 7.2
Economic Development, Industrialization, and Urbanization, 1890–1939

	1890	1900	1910	1920	1929	1939
Per capita income (Khamis-Geary 1990 dollars)						
Argentina	2152	2756	3822	3473	4367	4148
Brazil	772	704	795	937	1106	1307
France	2354	2849	2937	3196	4666	4748
Germany	2539	3134	3527	2986	4335	5549
Great Britain	4099	4593	4715	4651	5255	5979
Italy	1631	1746	2281	2531	3026	3444
Mexico	990	1157	1435	. . .	1489	1428
Russia / Soviet Union	925	1218	. . .	. . .	1386	2237
Spain	1847	2040	2096	2309	2947	2127
United States	3396	4096	4970	5559	6907	6568
Railway track (miles per square mile × 1,000)						
Argentina	6	10	15	21	22	24
Brazil	1	3	4	5	6	6
France	100	114	121	122	124	126
Germany	124	153	175	196	200	284
Great Britain	166	181	193	168	216	213
Italy	76	92	101	106	113	119
Mexico	7	12	20	11	21	15
Russia / Soviet Union	2	4	5	4	6	7
Spain	32	42	46	49	52	55
United States	46	53	66	70	69	65
Automobiles (per 1,000 population)						
Argentina	. . .	. . .	. . .	. . .	23.9	14.0
Brazil	. . .	. . .	. . .	. . .	3.0	2.4
France	. . .	0.1	1.4	3.4	22.6	47.5
Germany	. . .	. . .	. . .	0.9	6.7	20.6
Great Britain	. . .	. . .	1.2	4.0	21.5	42.6
Italy	. . .	. . .	. . .	. . .	4.5	6.6
Mexico	. . .	. . .	. . .	. . .	3.1	4.4
Russia / Soviet Union	. . .	. . .	. . .	. . .	0.1	0.6
Spain	. . .	. . .	. . .	. . .	5.2	2.7
United States	. . .	0.1	5.0	76.4	189.9	200.2

TABLE 7.2 (*Continued*)

	1890	1900	1910	1920	1929	1939
Steel production (tons per 1,000 population)						
Argentina	...	...	...	...	...	2
Brazil	...	...	...	...	1	3
France	18	41	86	69	236	199
Germany	45	118	212	138	251	342
Great Britain	95	117	140	192	208	272
Italy	4	4	21	21	52	52
Mexico	...	...	...	...	...	4
Russia/Soviet Union	3	17	21	1	32	103
Spain	5	3	13	18	43	23
United States	69	136	287	402	471	366
Cement production (tons per 1,000 population)						
Argentina	...	...	...	...	30	81
Brazil	...	...	...	...	3	17
France	...	...	...	37	151	99
Germany	...	...	...	133	109	210
Great Britain	...	...	...	50	104	175
Italy	...	...	...	29	86	139
Mexico	...	...	...	...	14	21
Russia/Soviet Union	...	...	...	...	15	30
Spain	...	...	...	28	78	47
United States	21	39	144	156	241	163
Urbanization (% population in cities greater than 100,000)						
Argentina	14.7	18.0	23.5	27.1	25.3	25.2
Brazil	4.7	8.3	9.5	9.5	11.7	13.3
France	11.8	13.0	14.4	15.1	15.7	19.5
Germany	12.1	16.2	21.1	24.9	28.4	32.1
Great Britain	32.9	32.5	33.0	34.5	38.6	43.7
Italy	7.8	8.7	10.3	9.8	15.9	18.4
Mexico	2.8	3.4	4.8	7.2	8.2	11.5
Russia/Soviet Union	4.4	5.7	6.6	10.6	11.8	15.8
Spain	7.4	9.4	10.2	11.9	13.2	18.6
United States	15.3	18.6	21.9	25.7	29.1	28.8

... missing data

Sources: Maddison 1995; Banks 2001.

did not make them shy away from designing and constructing modernist buildings. Thus, architectural modernism was not simply a function of economic development, miles of railway track, numbers of automobiles, tons of steel, or sacks of cement. Neither did modernism emerge more strongly in countries with a higher degree of urbanization. The United Kingdom and Argentina had greater proportions of their population living in cities than Germany, France, Italy or Russia (table 7.2).

Technological determinism cannot possibly explain why architects seized the opportunity to use cement and reinforced concrete once they became available in order to pursue very different aesthetic possibilities, ranging from classic revival all the way to machine-age modernism. Most architects used the new materials "to erect pseudo-monumental exteriors in the old modes. . . . [A]s long as scientific and technological advances were used in architecture without being absorbed by it, the engineer remained subordinate to and detached from the architect" (Giedion [1941] 1982, 183). Gaudí and Mendelsohn used the new materials and techniques to develop an expressionist aesthetic, while Garnier and Perret used them to revive certain aspects of classicism. In San Francisco, Victorian homes were erected using machine-made, catalogue-ordered parts. By contrast, the German, Russian, and Italian modernists used new industrial technologies to pursue a different aesthetic agenda that Le Corbusier later systematized and codified. Thus, cement and reinforced concrete did not cause modernist architecture, as Choisy would have it, though they certainly facilitated experimentation and renewal (Banham [1960] 1980, 202). New technologies did not dictate a specific style; designers and architects could, and did, exercise choice.

Perhaps the most defensible conclusion to draw is that industrial development had an ambiguous effect on architectural modernism as a movement. Economic advancements and technological breakthroughs certainly offered architects new possibilities for artistic expression. Oftentimes, however, it was relative backwardness rather than progress that encouraged architects to find a lost aesthetic in machinery, Taylorism, and Fordism, in an attempt to modernize their countries. For example, Behrens, Muthesius, and Gropius hoped their work would enhance the competitiveness of German firms (Buddensieg 1984; Muthesius [1914] 1971, 29; Gropius [1936] 1965, 30–32). The Soviet leadership believed that modernist design would improve product quality and the USSR's position on the "international exchange market" (Lodder 1983, 113; Kopp 1985, 27–28, 70–71). "Today we have to make an architecture which meets the needs and the means of production of our country," wrote the Mexican architect Guillermo Zárraga (quoted in Fraser 2000, 36). And the architects of Brasília, as well as its political supporters, hoped that modernist design would create a "new society," an economic boom, and a planned future (Holston 1989, 74–98).

The case of economically backward Spain, though, illustrates the fact that industrial retardation per se was no guarantee for the rise of a modernist aesthetic. Catalonia and, to a lesser extent, other parts of Spain fostered an arts and crafts movement similar to the English and German ones of the late nineteenth century. The movement's greatest achievements were the architectural works of Gaudí. As in England, however, Catalan and Spanish architects created a revivalist, nostalgic, and baroque movement during the 1910s that was the antithesis of the modernism developing elsewhere in Continental Europe: eclectic, given to creative ornamentation, conservative in outlook, and mildly opposed to mechanical production and to using the machine as a metaphor for artistic production (see chapter 5).

Sociopolitical Upheaval

A second contextual factor frequently linked to the rise of a modernist architecture is the occurrence of sociopolitical unrest. As outlined in chapter 3, social and political discontinuities may create conditions conducive to modernist architecture because such crises generate demand for low-cost buildings and also offer opportunities to overthrow the established artistic order.

The evidence presented in the preceding chapters is partly consistent with this argument. Consider the countries in which architectural modernism flourished early on. A crucial factor that set Germany, Italy, and the Soviet Union apart from other European countries during the late 1910s and early '20s was the occurrence of sociopolitical upheaval on a large scale. Germany, Italy, and Russia emerged weakened from World War I, while Britain and France were clear victors, and Spain remained neutral. Germany experienced military defeat, revolution, counterrevolution, and monetary and economic crises, a level of commotion and change that allowed artists to challenge traditional conceptions and practices (Herf 1984; Kaes, Jay, and Dimendberg 1994). As Gropius wrote in March 1919, one month before the founding of the Bauhaus, "political revolution must be used to liberate art from decades of regimentation" (quoted in Hochman 1989, 49). In spite of being part of the winning coalition in World War I, Italy was also reaching a critical juncture in the late 1910s. The Fascist March on Rome in 1922 provided the Italian avant-garde architects with a chance to influence industry, politics, and official artistic policies (Bowler 1991). In the Soviet Union, the October Revolution removed the entrenched traditional power structures in the arts that were preventing a variety of avant-garde movements from flourishing. Revolution and civil war offered architects and other artists an exposure to revolutionary ideology as well as experience in political agitation and in the management of artistic enterprises (Lodder 1983). In Germany, Russia, and Italy, sociopolitical turmoil created ample opportunities for the renewal of architectural practice, as predicted by theories of social movements emphasizing the importance of the structure of political opportunities and constraints for the emergence of collective action

(McAdam, McCarthy, and Zald 1996; Rao, Monin, and Durand 2003). Early experiments in modernism were stymied by political stability in some countries, namely, Britain and the United States. In Spain modernism only succeeded during the revolutionary phase of the Second Republic in the mid- and late 1930s, while in the case of France the modernist movement was relatively slow to develop.

While sociopolitical upheaval helps understand developments in Europe because it provided architects with the possibility of experimenting with new ideas, the Latin American cases serve as a reminder that political change, while conducive to architectural experimentation and renewal, did not necessarily produce modernism. Thus, in Mexico the initial thrust for architectural reform during the early postrevolutionary years came from the adoption of neocolonial and vernacular influences, rather than from international modernism. Likewise, Peronism in Argentina, while revolutionary in many respects, proved to be old-fashioned in terms of architectural taste and policy. Modernism flourished in Brazil to a greater extent than in either Argentina or Mexico, and yet political changes during the 1920s and 1930s were more gradual. The limitations of functionalist and conflict-centered views of the rise of architectural modernism invite a more nuanced approach focusing on more proximate conditions favoring the rise of an aesthetic based on the machine.

Class Dynamics and Artistic Production

As outlined in chapter 3, a number of social scientists have articulated the view that artistic production is linked to class dynamics. Bourdieu (1996) and Adorno (1997) proposed that new artistic movements emerge in situations in which the artist becomes autonomous from the market. Recently, Gartman (2000) applied this logic to the rise, during the 1920s, of modernist architecture in Germany, where the mass consumption market was underdeveloped and the state stepped in to become the most important patron of modernist architecture. By contrast, in the United States the alliance between the industrial bourgeoisie and the technocracy of engineers and managers developed a mass consumption market that thwarted modernism in favor of kitsch. In this view, architects could only become autonomous from the mass market and hence innovative with the help of the state.

The evidence presented in the preceding chapters suggests that an explanation based on class dynamics has serious shortcomings. For example, Gartman's (2000) comparison of the United States and Germany is somewhat overdrawn, for the German modernist movement in architecture and design did not originally emerge in the shadow of the state during the 1920s but twenty years earlier as the result of the close collaboration between artistic and industrial elites, as the examples of Behrens at the AEG and the Werkbund illustrate. Even during the 1920s, the most important experiment in modernism, the Bauhaus, benefited immensely from industry's support (see chapter 4).

The explanation based on the architect's autonomy within the class structure, while theoretically appealing, is also hard to square with the evidence from other national cases. For instance, Italian modernism did not benefit significantly from the state; it emerged mostly in the industrial North. France or Spain also lacked a mass consumption market, and yet modernism did not spring forth as vigorously there as it did in Germany. The two cases that could be explained by reference to class struggles and alliances, and to the impact of mass consumer preferences are Britain and Russia, where modernism was met by very different degrees of success, largely consistent with Gartman's variables in that Britain was more like the United States while Russia more similar to Germany. The Latin American cases, by contrast, do not seem to fit: the class alliances were similar to Germany's or Spain's, a mass consumption market was nowhere to be seen, and yet modernism succeeded in two countries (Brazil and Mexico), but not in the third examined here (Argentina).

In sum, a class-centered analysis seems to provide a satisfactory explanation for the rise of machine-age modernism in Russia and for its initial failure in Britain, Argentina, and the United States. It hardly helps, however, in the cases of Germany, Italy, France, Spain, Brazil, and Mexico. This explanation is nevertheless useful in that it focuses attention on the structure of constraints and opportunities faced by those architects and designers eager to introduce renewal and change into their stagnant field. A more refined analysis of the architect-as-professional will help pursue this line of argument to successfully account for cross-national differences in the emergence of modernist architecture.

A NEOINSTITUTIONAL ACCOUNT BASED ON SPONSORSHIP
AND PROFESSIONALIZATION

Contrary to the tenets of many architectural historians and social scientists, industrialization, sociopolitical upheaval, or class dynamics cannot fully explain the emergence of a modernist architecture cross-nationally. As indicated in chapter 3, one important problem associated with these "historical-contextual" arguments is that their explanatory power is supposed to come from relatively macro forces, without really delving into the issues of the social construction of problems, agency, and power dynamics in the spread of new practices. Neoinstitutional theory proposes to take a systematic look at the field of architecture, emphasizing the role that key actors play in it, especially those who produce it and those who pay for it.

The rise of modernism in architecture was intimately linked to the professionalization of architecture, which resulted from struggles between and within professional groups, that is, engineers versus architects, and academic versus modernist architects. Each group attempted to establish its claims to aesthetic authority and expert knowledge about architecture and building, with varying outcomes from country to country. Academic and modernist architects fought over the mission of architecture; the materials, methodology, and techniques to be used; the clients to be served; and the definition of the "architect," following the pattern observed by students of diversity and conflict within professional groups (Bucher and Strauss 1961).

Architecture became a separate profession late in the nineteenth century or early in the twentieth century, depending on the country, and always *after* engineering had consolidated itself as a profession linked to industry and public works. Until then, most builders were artisans or craftsmen with no formal training in their trade, while master architects tended to be educated in the Beaux-Arts tradition and have little, if any, contact with industry or knowledge about building methods and the construction business. The professionalization of architecture took place between 1890 and 1940 in the midst of a great debate about whether it was a decorative art or an application of technology, and whether the architect should remain an individualist, bohemian, and detached artist, or become involved in all aspects of the construction industry. Furthermore, the old conception of architecture as a decorative art assumed that only the state, the upper class, and perhaps the Church were legitimate patrons, while industry was derogated as an unworthy source of architectural commissions.

New Roles in Sponsorship

While changes in sponsorship were crucial to the development of modernism, no single type of sponsor predominated in all countries in which modernist architecture succeeded after reinterpreting scientific management, as pointed out above. Proposing the state as the key actor in the emergence of modernist architecture yields mixed results. In Germany, the Soviet Union, Brazil, Mexico, and, to a somewhat lesser extent, Italy, modernism developed during a period of rising state involvement in industry and art. In France, by contrast, state support for modernist projects and artistic experimentation was far less sustained (Lyon notwithstanding), but modernism nonetheless developed, albeit more slowly. This argument, however, helps to explain the failed modernist cases of Argentina and Britain, where the state played no role as a sponsor of architecture until after 1945.

Spain also fits this explanation in that modernism received no systematic support from the state until the mid-1930s, and then only briefly, until the Republic collapsed in the wake of the Civil War of 1936–39. In Madrid, Antonio Flórez worked for the Republic's Ministry of Education, in a policy context similar to postrevolutionary Mexico's, though smaller in scale. The central government launched several important projects, including the University City, the lengthening of La Castellana Avenue, and the New Ministries building complex. The purest modernist designs, however, popped up in and around Barcelona, where the Catalan autonomous government unambiguously supported a machine-age modernism (Bohigas 1998, 100–101). However, in the 1930s rare was the municipality in Catalonia or in Spain that tried to improve housing conditions in a systematic way. An exception was Bilbao, in the Basque country, which organized a competition aimed at "creating a rational dwelling following modernist designs, with the intention of satisfying a social need in its twin technical and sanitary aspects" (Pizza 1997, 58).

The German case lends stronger support to the thesis that state patronage was important to the development of modernism. The Bauhaus itself—perhaps the single most important seedbed of modernist ideas—was a state school, though it collaborated with myriad firms. The state-funded agency to promote industrial rationalization and scientific management (RKW) became the biggest and most active of that in any country (Merkle 1980; Guillén 1994). As documented in chapter 4, during the 1920s many German modernist architects collaborated with scientific management organizations affiliated to the RKW, and they benefited disproportionately from public funds for housing projects because they were willing to experiment with new concepts as well as money-saving ideas and techniques. Gropius was one of the vice-presidents of the National Society for Research into Efficiency in Construction and Housing (part of the RKW). Most of its funds were given to the Weissenhof Siedlung, the housing project in Dessau at which both Gropius and Mies worked,[1] as well as to May's Praunheim project (NGBK 1977, 41–108).

The influence of state economic planning and patronage on modernism in the early Soviet Union is even more apparent. State interventionism grew steadily from the "transitional state capitalism" stage immediately following the October Revolution to the output and price controls of 1921 and the First Five-Year Plan of 1928–32 (Parkins 1953). The Union of Contemporary Architects, a group that included Ginzburg and the Vesnin brothers, collaborated with the state economic planning agencies (Starr 1976). In particular, Ginzburg prepared housing projects for the Central Planning Agency, the Gosplan. Several architects and designers collaborated with the Council of the Scientific Organization of Labor (SovNOT), another state agency, or worked for the new state enterprises like the New Lessner Factory in Petrograd and the First State Textile Print Factory in Moscow (Lodder 1983; Senkevitch 1990). Following the German example, the state created a new school of architecture and design—the Higher State Artistic-Technical Workshops (VKhUTEMAS)—where many of the Russian modernist architects taught or

---

[1] Bauhaus-Archiv Berlin, Schrank 34, Inv.-Nr. 9153/1-12; RFGWBW 1929, 92–130; Wingler 1969, 126–27.

received their training (Lodder 1983, 109–44). It is important to note, however, that modernism was suppressed during the 1930s by the Nazi and Stalinist totalitarian regimes precisely at a time when economic and artistic planning intensified in scale and scope (Milward 1976).

The impact of state sponsorship should not be exaggerated because, except in the Soviet Union, industrialists were also important patrons of modernism in architecture and design. Germany is perhaps the clearest example of industry-art collaboration. The achievements of Behrens are unthinkable without the patronage of AEG, a firm that also employed Gropius and Mies. The German Federation of Artistic Workshops collaborated with such industrial powerhouses as AEG, Daimler, Krupp, Mannesmann, and Robert Bosch (Junghanns 1982, 24, 37). Gropius and his assistants did work for a variety of industrial firms: Fagus, Waggonfabrik of the Prussian State Railways, Hannoversche Papierfabriken, I-G Farben, Adler-Automobilwerke, Junkers, Mannesmann, AEG, and Siemens, among others. In 1925 Gropius created a limited liability company to attract consulting and design contracts, the Bauhaus GmbH, although revenues were lower than expected.[2] In France, Le Corbusier established myriad contacts with, and worked for, many industrial firms. The two most important links were with Aeroplanes Voisin, the world's largest aircraft manufacturer at the turn of the century, and with industrialist Ernest Mercier, the managing director of large utility and oil companies (McLeod 1983, 141–42; CGP 1987). In Italy, Luigi Figini and Gino Pollini designed several factory and office buildings for the electrical-machinery firm Olivetti (Savi 1990), while architect and engineer Giacomo Mattè-Trucco worked primarily for the FIAT automobile company. In Britain, by contrast, the leaders of industry were largely indifferent to modernist design (see chapters 4, 5, and 6).

Industry played a more modest role in Latin America, where state agencies (education, public works) were the key actors, especially in Brazil and Mexico (see chapter 6). Nonetheless, some architects collaborated with industrialists, like Warchavchik, who referred to them as the Medicis or the Louises of modern architecture (Warchavchik [1925] 1965, 39-D). As discussed in chapter 6, the Argentine case is fairly complex. By 1952 the state was spending nearly 6 percent of GDP on housing, with many of the projects sponsored by the Fundación Eva Perón. The increasing involvement of the state in the economy did not translate into a coherent architectural policy. As a result, various styles were promoted, sometimes simultaneously, while the continued use of traditional building techniques guaranteed the employment of unskilled labor (Eliash and San Martín 1998, 56–57; De Larranaga and Petrina 1987).

[2] See Bauhaus-Archiv Berlin, Schrank 58, GS 9/6-7; Bayer, Gropius, and Gropius 1975, 134–39; Wingler 1983, 46–49; Neumann 1993, 105.

What the new sponsorship roles of the state and industry clearly achieved was to place architects in close touch with the world of planning and of machines. The reconstruction of the architectural field along modernist lines was primarily undertaken by artists and architects trained in, or at least exposed to, engineering. Modernism first flourished after scientific management was reinterpreted in countries in which, early on, the emerging architecture profession developed linkages to engineering that were strong enough to allow for the creation of a differentiated body of technical and aesthetic knowledge about building but stopped short of subsuming architecture as an engineering specialty. Modernist architects developed a new professional conception based on the "subordination of technology to design" (Larson 1993, 4). Clearly, it was not enough that architects absorbed the new technological advances. They had to establish a legitimate claim over some area of expert knowledge (Freidson 1986), and in such a way that they would become different than other groups such as mere constructors or engineers (Abbott 1988).

The rivalry between a triumphant and powerful engineering profession and a troubled and less dynamic architectural profession-in-the-making resulted in the older generation of architects entrenching itself in tradition and history. By contrast, the younger generation saw in engineering not a threat but an opportunity to revitalize and eventually revolutionize architectural theory and practice. In so doing, they welcomed engineering and scientific management, making it very clear that design had to rule technology and building methods. That younger generations proved more receptive to modernism than older ones is reflected in the average year of birth of the leading architects of the 1890–1940 period listed in the appendix. Architects in Britain (whose mean year of birth is 1853), France (1865), and Spain (1868) were the oldest on average, while those in Germany (1881), Russia (1888), and Italy (1895) were the youngest. The United States (1874) lies in between both groups. In Latin America, a similar pattern obtains, with modernism being weaker in Argentina (mean year of birth 1892) than in Mexico (1899) and Brazil (1907).

Engineers were much more numerous relative to the size of the workforce during the 1910s and 1920s in the countries where modernism first emerged: Germany, Italy, the Soviet Union, and France, when compared to Britain and Spain. Figure 7.1 shows the most comparable and complete cross-national data on engineers available for the period. It should be noted, however, that the United States had the highest ratios of engineers in the world, and yet modernism in architecture lagged considerably behind.

Beyond the sheer numbers, a common experience among many French, German, Italian, and Russian/Soviet modernist architects was their early exposure to technology and engineering. Many of the architects listed in the appendix attended engineering school as part of their architectural training, or were

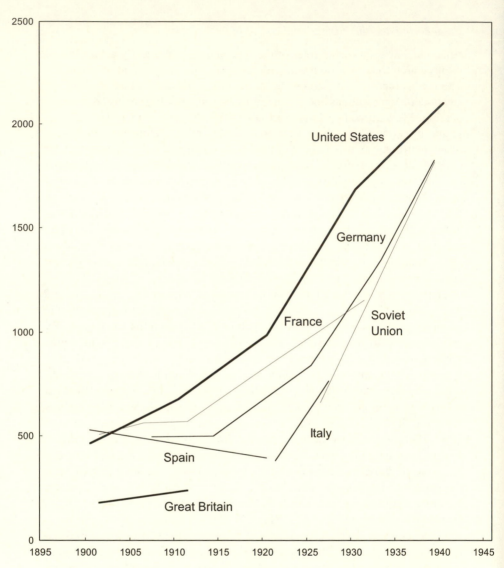

FIGURE 7.1 Certified Engineers (per 100,000 employed in mining, manufacturing, and construction). *Sources:* Ahlstrom 1982; Boltanski 1982, 121 n. 92; Buchanan 1989, 202–3; Jarausch 1990, 237; Markert 1965, 53–68; Mitchell 1980; *Censimento della Popolazione* 1921, 187; *Annuario Statistico Italiano*, several issues; *Censo de la población de España* 1900, 214, 1920, 424; *Historical Statistics of the United States* 1989, 139–40.

otherwise exposed to engineering. The "engineer-architects" were central to the rise of modernism. They were not only " 'modern' in their thought and actions," taking "novel building tasks" or "working and experimenting with iron, glass and concrete." They were "modern because [they] considered [their] discipline to be part of a whole, as a means to create structures of culture and social utility" (Pfammatter 2000, 12). They embraced method, standardization, and planning with a view to designing efficient buildings.

The impact of engineering on architecture, then, is to be found in the way in which architects were trained. Modernism in architecture represented a reaction against the traditional training received at the fine arts academies throughout Europe and the Americas, which were largely modeled after the École des Beaux-Arts in Paris. The impetus for change emerged not from the heritage of academic architecture but from cubist and abstract painting, and, most decisively, engineering (Gabetti and Marconi 1968). French builders and engineers pioneered the use of cement and reinforced concrete, later translated into a new theory of architecture in Germany, Italy, the Soviet Union, and subsequently in France, by Le Corbusier. In some European countries, engineering schools started to offer courses in building and architecture, and some of them even created specialized sections to train architects. As Phené Spiers, a Beaux-Arts graduate, put it in his 1884 speech at the Meeting of the General Conference of Architects in London, "in Germany, architects and engineers generally study together in the same school; in France, architects, painters and sculptors" (Spiers 1883–84, 124). And as Knill Freeman stated in his reply to Spier's lecture, "it would seem that the outcome of the French system is to develop the more artistic part of professional education, while the German system produces a 'cast-iron' development of it" (Spiers 1883–84, 129). No wonder machine-age modernism in architecture emerged in Germany and not in France, even though the technocratic elites in both countries offered Taylorism and Fordism a warm reception during the 1910s, and their principles were applied to industry during and after World War I (Merkle 1980, 136–58; Guillén 1994, 96–103).

French architectural education, while perceived as the best in the world, was consumed by rivalries between schools. The purest form of classical architectural education was offered by the École des Beaux-Arts in Paris, which privileged form over structure, and taught "geometrical regularity in order to achieve compositional unity" (Moore 1977, 145). It derived its theories of design from "literary and artistic sources of the Italian Renaissance, which in turn were largely based on classical Antiquity" (Egbert 1980, 99; Middleton 1982). At the Beaux-Arts "little formal education" in building construction was given (Collins [1965] 1998, 193). In a paper published in 1842, it was argued that "little concern is shown for the utilization of the different parts of a large building, and the students scarcely deign to bear in mind the purpose of the edifice" (quoted in Collins [1965] 1998, 221). The Beaux-Arts approach to architecture regarded the building as a monument to please the eye rather than as a construction to be used or to fulfill a purpose.

While the origins of the École go back to the reign of Louis XIV, it was officially founded as such by Napoleon Bonaparte in 1806 (see plate 7.1). Its nemesis was the École Polytechnique, founded in 1794 and devoted to the combination of theoretical and practical science with a view to facilitating industrial growth. Like the Polytechnique, the École Centrale des Arts et Manufactures (1829) also trained engineer-constructors, like Gustave Eiffel (Pfammatter 2000, 186). A "schism between architecture and construction" thus developed during the first half of the nineteenth century. It would set the training of architects on a distinct trajectory increasingly divergent from the world of industry and machines (Giedion [1941] 1982, 212–13; Lipstadt and Mendelsohn 1980; Lipstadt 1988). Another rift was the one between Beaux-Arts and the École des Arts Décoratifs, the school that pioneered art deco, which offered an architecture degree between 1922 and 1941. While the Déco architects did not share the academic and classicizing attitude of the Beaux-Arts, they were trained to "favor luxury production, which was incompatible with the values of mechanization that had been introduced by the modernists" (Martin 2001, 97). Moreover, the Déco school, because it trained interior decorators as well as architects, was in favor of ornamentation.

Some French architects—notably Viollet-le-Duc and his disciple Anatole de Baudot—attempted to reform architectural education at the École des Beaux-Arts during the 1860s. Although they had Napoleon III on their side, their efforts were met by stiff resistance. Their mistake was perhaps to introduce a "mimetic medieval historicism to counter the classical historicism of the École." Beaux-Arts classicism became the canon for artistic education "from grade school through university and professional levels" (Moore 1977, 151, 160; Lipstadt and Mendelsohn 1980). Moreover, the newly gained hegemony of the École des Beaux-Arts infiltrated the Polytechnique and the Arts Décoratifs schools at the turn of the century. As a result, the French "architect [became] not the *ingénieur* but rather the *constructeur*, a builder in stone whose knowledge of descriptive geometry (*stéréotomie*) allows him to turn structure into geometrical patterns" (Moore 1977, 168). Thus, until the end of World War II, French architects did not receive a strong engineering influence while at school. Of the ten most influential French architects in the appendix, only Choisy was trained at an engineering school, the Polytechnique.

In contrast to France, during the second half of the nineteenth century perhaps as many as 90 percent of all German architects were trained at technical schools together with engineers, and they were members of the same professional association until 1903 (Gaber 1966; Pfammatter 2000, 226–28; Zucker 1942). Not surprisingly, German architects were exposed to "a peculiar mixture of a dry pseudo-classical academism combined with an even drier technical rationalism" (Zucker 1942, 9). Rationalism and functionalism had been part of the German architect's training since at least 1830. "Prepared by Romanticism and Nationalism, helped by the revolt against Academism, the rediscovery of the Middle Ages and the adaptation of its forms were considered the redeeming stimuli for an authentic new architecture" (9). The link between engineering and architecture was so momentous because German engineering was a well-organized profession with a high degree of social and political prestige, and it fell in love with American scientific management at the turn of the century (Guillén 1994, 96–103; Gispen 1989, 1990; McClelland 1991, 91–94, 148–52, 186–88). The strong influences of engineering and scientific management would unambiguously channel the evolution of German architectural training and practice in the direction of modernism. Of the ten influential German architects in the appendix, seven were trained at engineering or construction schools (Gropius, Hilberseimer, May, Meyer, Muthesius, Taut, and Wagner).

Similar to the German pattern and influenced by it, in Italy there was a "mixture of types of training [that persisted] for a long time, and that would lead to the virtual inability to distinguish the training of architects from the training of engineers" until well into the 1920s (Gabetti and Marconi 1968; Bugarini 1987; Etlin 1991, 8–9; Krause 1996, 197). It was the polytechnic institutes in Milan and Turin, founded in the 1870s and 1880s (Cafagna 1971, 18; Minesso 1995), that trained six of the ten most influential Italian architects in the appendix (Figini, Griffini, Mattè-Trucco, Pagano, Pollini, and Terragni), with the others coming out of Academies of Fine Arts or Schools of Architecture in the Beaux-Arts tradition. Moreover, architects trained in the polytechnic tradition or those working for industrial firms were exposed to Taylorism, scientific management, and Fordism (Buselli, Finzi, and Predrocco 1976; Pedrocco 1976; Sapelli 1976, 1978; Steri 1979). Engineers also benefited from the Fascist regime's bias in favor of technical professions and occupations, even in the area of urban planning, at the expense of architects trained at the fine arts academies (Tacchi 1994).

In the Soviet Union technical education and scientific management were top priorities for the new regime given the chaotic state of industry and the country's isolation. Moreover, the need to train agricultural workers to perform jobs at factories called for a simplification of tasks along scientific-management or Fordist lines. The state created research institutes to explore the implementation of science in the workplace (Merkle 1980, 105–35). Moreover, several of the most influential Russian architects (including Ginzburg, Lissitzky, V. A. Vesnin, and A. A. Vesnin) had been trained at technical or engineering schools: St. Petersburg / Leningrad's Institution of Civil Engineers, Moscow's Higher Technical College, and Riga's Polytechnical University, among others (Cooke 1995, 160–77; Lodder 1983, 107, 122).

The training, certification, and professional organization of architects and engineers in Germany, Italy, and the Soviet Union overlapped so much that it should be no surprise that modernism first took shape in these countries after the turn of the century. Moreover, the modernist architects invested their energies in developing a new model of architectural education, as exemplified by the Bauhaus in Germany and the Higher State Artistic-Technical Workshops in the Soviet Union.

Unlike in Germany, Italy, and Russia/Soviet Union, in Spain not only were engineers less common and engineering schools relatively small, but industrial architecture was not taught at engineering schools until the end of the first decade of the twentieth century. Spanish engineers did not pay much attention to scientific management until after the Civil War of 1936–39 (Guillén 1994, 156–83). Engineers and architects were taught at separate schools throughout most of the nineteenth century, and the two groups engaged in a series of protracted debates and legislative battles over professional turf (Bonet Correa, Lorenzo Fornies, and Miranda Regojo 1985). Architectural instruction remained anchored in the Beaux-Arts tradition, with only a limited exposure to mathematics and engineering. The director of the Academy of Fine Arts stated in 1877 that "the architect is born, while the engineer is made" (quoted in Bonet Correa, Lorenzo Fornies, and Miranda Regojo 1985, 49). The faculty at the School of Architecture, founded in 1845 in Madrid, considered iron to be a "provisional material" (Bonet Correa, Lorenzo Fornies, and Miranda Regojo 1985, 57–58). An integration of technology and architecture faced enormous resistance even after the curriculum was reformed in 1914 (Cardellach i Avilés 1910; Fernández Alba 1975, 46–65; Freixa 1986, 75). During the 1910s and 1920s faculty and students at the School of Architecture were "curious" about European modernism, but hardly persuaded about its postulates. According to García Mercadal, the curriculum was "irrational and retrograde." Others argued that the faculty was devoted to "making pretty vignettes," that there was no reference in their teaching to the "technical aspects of construction," and that each subject was taught in isolation from the others, with little effort at curricular integration. One of the professors denounced the "eminently theoretical approach," proposing instead to have students "do practical assignments in the classroom and in the workshops, and learn about building practices, even by requiring them to work as assistants at an actual building site" (quoted in Diéguez Patao 1997, 19, 48–49). The educational reform of 1934 did introduce more modernist and technological subjects into the curriculum, but the victory of the right-wing nationalists in the Civil War of 1936–39 resulted in a return to traditionalism (López Otero 1951). The ten most influential Spanish architects in the appendix were trained at the traditional schools of architecture in Barcelona or Madrid. Only Cardellach i Avilés obtained an engineering degree in addition to one in architecture, but he actually opposed the precepts of modernism (Cardellach i Avilés 1916, 108).

In Britain, "the architectural profession was overwhelmed by a sense of inferiority" (Collins [1965] 1998, 190), the teaching of architecture was "chaotic and underfunded" during most of the period, engineering education was based on the apprenticeship system rather than formal training in technology and science at the universities, and educational and certification standards were mediocre or simply nonexistent (Ahlström 1982, 79–93; Glover and Kelly 1987, 99–115, 184–89; Powers 1993, 34; Buchanan 1989). Educational standards and professional credentials were the main issue. It was only as late as 1887 that the Royal Institute of British Architects established compulsory examinations for entry. In 1891 the Society of Architects, formed seven years earlier to improve professional standards, introduced formal registration procedures. In 1870 the Royal Academy established a School of Architecture in the Beaux-Arts tradition. At the turn of the century there was only one full-time university course in architecture being taught in the entire country, at Liverpool University (Powers 1993). Of the British architects and designers in the appendix only Mackintosh graduated from a formal program, at the Glasgow School of Art. The others received a rather general education, and then were apprenticed, or pursued a private education altogether (Howard). And they certainly were kept separate from the engineers. In 1865 Ruskin expressed a preference "to see the profession of an architect united, not with that of the engineer, but [with that] of the sculptor" (quoted by Wilton-Ely 2000, 200).

These attempts at professional education and certification in Britain were met by criticism. A protracted debate as to whether architecture was a profession or an art lingered on until World War I. William Morris and Walter Crane, among others, weighed in arguing that a student's "artistic qualifications (which really make the Architect)" could not be "brought to the test of examination, and that a diploma of architecture obtained by such means would be a fallacious distinction" (quoted in Wilton-Ely 2000, 203). Other Arts and Crafts architects, by contrast, took a slightly different position by proposing to require knowledge of construction and engineering in order to obtain certification as an architect. By 1915 their efforts were all but abandoned in the face of stiff resistance. Lethaby complained that British architectural training and registration had returned to the "catalogued styles" (quoted in Powers 1983, 69). After World War I, the traditional educational model of the Beaux-Arts was brought in from France to serve as the template (Kaye 1960, 156–69; Moore 1977, 162, 168, 174). Most British architects continued to be highly suspicious of the engineers and of formal education, and insisted that the architect was "born, not made" (Kaye 1960, 162). The ideal of the artist-architect was embraced, and that of the engineer-architect despised. Not that a closer link to engineering would have helped much anyway: British engineers reacted negatively to scientific management, labeling it "scientistic," "too rigorous," and "inhuman" (Guillén 1994, 213–27). As a result, the new engineering approach to architecture did not have much of an impact in Britain until after World War II.

As in Britain, few American architects appreciated the aesthetic potential offered by the methods of scientific management or by the revolutionary buildings that engineers were erecting throughout the industrial heartland. Frank Lloyd Wright, the most important exponent of early American modernism, remained isolated and failed to realize the critical importance of promoting a professional reconstruction of architecture along engineering lines (Wright 1932, 315). Several of the most noted American architects of the turn of the century remained eclectic in their designs, for example, Charles Greene (the pioneer of the California bungalow) and Bernard Maybeck. Even architect Albert Kahn—famous for his designs of Henry Ford's ultra-efficient factories—could not break with traditionalism, for he considered architecture "the art of building, adding to the mere structural elements distinction and beauty" (Smith 1993, 81; Bucci 1993). His factories were certainly functional but not wholeheartedly modernist, even though he was a German immigrant who returned frequently to his home country, and was in touch with one of the founders of modernist architecture, his compatriot Peter Behrens (Biggs 1996, 98–100; plate 1.5).

A majority of the most prominent American architects continued to receive their training in the Beaux-Arts tradition either in France or in the United States, as the Parisian model was being transplanted during the 1910s and '20s to Berkeley, Harvard, the University of Pennsylvania, even the Massachusetts Institute of Technology (Brain 1989; Moore 1977, 162, 168, 174; Pfammatter 2000, 281, 287–91; Hamlin 1908). When Le Corbusier lectured at Columbia, Yale, Harvard, MIT, Princeton, and Penn in 1935, his ideas were met by the hostility of many faculty members but the enthusiasm of the students (Bacon 2001, 91–101). Even Progressivism—a powerful advocate of scientific management in other walks of American life—sponsored a revival of the forms of colonial architecture. The so-called "modern colonial" style in housing continued to rely on naturalistic and organic themes rather than industrial, widening the rift between a historicist approach to form and an efficient approach to function (May 1991; Brain 1994). Government buildings were designed following the so-called "Federal classic" style (Fraser 2000, 145). Meanwhile, the Progressive movement in city planning and urban space management—heavily influenced by Taylorism—not only failed to bear fruit until the early 1930s but seemed to be concerned with purely technical issues to the exclusion of aesthetic ones (Fairfield 1994).

Intriguingly, American architectural modernism was a laggard relative not only to Europe but also to Mexico and Brazil (see chapter 6; Fraser 2000, 145; Goodwin 1943). American architecture proved receptive to modernism only after 1930 through the European rendition of the principles of building and organization that had been originally pioneered by American engineers but that only the European architects succeeded in blending with aesthetic theory and practice. Until then, skyscrapers continued to be designed according to premodernist tastes, forms, and motifs. The first genuinely modernist sky-scraper in the "international style," designed by George Howe and William Lescaze (Swiss born), was completed as late as 1932, the Philadelphia Saving Fund Society (PSFS) Building, "the most important American skyscraper be-tween Sullivan's work of the nineties . . . and the Seagram Building at the end of the fifties" (Jordy 1986, 163). It was a masterful integrated and "ultra-practical" design, with its projecting columns soaring into the sky from a base touched by a reticent expressionism (Gutheim 1949; Schulze 1992, 16:104–6; see plates 7.2 and 7.3). Other American architects pioneered "modernist" con-struction, as in the cases of Irving Gill in the use of reinforced concrete, and Raymond Hood in skyscrapers.

Modernism in the United States was encouraged by such new organizations as the Architecture Department at the Museum of Modern Art in New York (Philip Johnson was its first Director, 1930–36), the efforts of younger archi-tects exposed to European modernism (Hitchcock and Johnson 1995), the alignment of American architectural education with the Bauhaus model after the arrival of such exiled European architects as Albers (who taught at Yale), Mies van der Rohe (Illinois Institute of Technology), and Gropius, Wagner, and Sert (Harvard), the public housing projects of the New Deal (Bacon 2001, 160–69; Brain 1994; see plate 7.4), and the enthusiastic sponsorship of a handful of industrial companies (Giedion [1941] 1982; Mumford 1963; Wingler 1972; Allen 1983; Jordy 1986; Larson 1993; Harris 1996).

The education of architects in Latin America started in the European aca-demic tradition, but it then evolved differently in each country, with Mexico and, especially, Brazil gradually gravitating towards modernism, while Ar-gentina followed a more haphazard path. In Mexico the training of architects started in 1781 following the academic French and Spanish model. In 1857 a new curriculum of Italian influence was introduced, which integrated the study of engineering and architecture. In fact, graduates were called "engi-neer-architects," and an Association of Engineers and Architects was estab-lished in 1868. While other reforms took place during the Juárez presidencies (1861–63 and 1867–72), architects continued to be trained at the School of Engineering until 1910, when the teaching of architecture was transferred to the School of Fine Arts, modeled after the Parisian example and influenced by Ruskin's antimechanical themes.[3]

The Mexican Revolution of 1910–17 and the coming of age of the genera-tion of architects nurtured by the new regime created the conditions for a grad-ual rapprochement with modernism and technical subjects. The Association of Engineers and Architects proved to be better organized, better connected, and more influential than the Society of Mexican Architects, whose members were

[3] See the journal of the Society of Mexican Architects, *El Arquitecto: Revista de Arquitectura y Artes Mexicanas* 1 (3) (1923): 1–4.

fine arts graduates. The engineers argued that architectural education and design practices should incorporate a more technical approach, and invited architects to work together with them. They insisted on the importance of applying scientific methods (including those of Taylorism), of giving engineers a key planning and social role, and of involving the state in housing and urban projects. Some engineers even endorsed "modern architecture" because of its "elegance and sobriety," and made references to important buildings such as the Italian rationalists' Casa Elettrica (see chapter 5). Engineers had established professional accreditation examinations earlier than architects.[4] Meanwhile, architects trained in the Beaux-Arts tradition were busy cataloguing and analyzing Mexican pre-Columbian and colonial architecture, emphasizing that "feeling" should guide design, and yearning for a national Mexican style.[5]

Beginning in 1923, the architect José Villagrán García spearheaded the effort to align Mexican architectural education with the new modern functionalism, at a time when several of the most influential architects listed in the appendix were being trained, including Mora y Palomar, O'Gorman, Serrano, and Yáñez de la Fuente. In his class on the theory of architecture at the School of Fine Arts, Villagrán García would lecture on "utilitarianism, mechanical stability, and architectural beauty," and highlight the architect's "social role" (Alva Martínez 1983, 61). New educational institutions, like, for example, the School of Construction Technicians of the National Polytechnic Institute, headed by Juan O'Gorman, were created to train architects following the precepts of modernism (Fraser 2000, 50–51). These events took place in the midst of educational and economic reforms that placed a great value on engineering and technology, in a country ruled by a new revolutionary elite focused on economic development and social modernization (Lorey 1990).

The influence of engineering and scientific management on Mexican architecture, however, was not as strong as in Brazil. Curiously, in Brazil the Beaux-Arts tradition had a long history by Latin American standards. Rio de Janeiro's School of Fine Arts was originally founded in 1826 by a government-sponsored team of French artists. Few architects graduated from it until the early twentieth century, however. Meanwhile, industrial and urban growth prepared the ground for the creation of as many as ten engineering schools that granted the degree of "engineer-architect." These schools produced several times more graduates than the School of Fine Arts produced "architects." By

---

[4] See the journal of the Association of Engineers and Architects of Mexico, *Revista Mexicana de Ingeniería y Arquitectura* 1 (1923): 46–50, 374–84, 4 (1926): 101–4, 6 (1928): 396–405, 9 (1931): 234–57, 13 (1935): 168–86, 14 (1936): 450–53. See also the journal of the National School of Engineering, *Ingeniería* 2 (1928): 439, 6 (1932): 375, 8 (1934): 93.

[5] *El Arquitecto: Revista de Arquitectura y Artes Mexicanas* 1 (1) (1923): 1, 1 (3) (1923): 1–4, 1 (4) (1923): 9–10, 2 (1) (1924): 1–2. Only one article published during the 1920s, written by Alfonso Pallares, recommended including more scientific and technical subjects into the architectural curriculum: 2 (4) (1925): 4–10.

the mid-1920s Brazilian engineers were actively discussing Taylorism (Skidmore and Smith 1989, 153; Saenz Leme 1978; Guzzo Decca 1987; ROC 1932; Weinstein 1990). The critical moment came in the late 1920s, when a movement of neocolonialist architecture emerged at the National School of Fine Arts in Rio as a nationalistic response to the proliferation of eclectic styles. Le Corbusier's visit in 1929 gave impetus to the reform movement, and pointed it in the direction of modernism. Simultaneously, the new Vargas regime of 1930 placed a strong emphasis on technocracy and corporatism, and provided modernists with an institutional opportunity with the creation of the Ministry of Education and Health in 1931, headed by a politician well attuned to the avantgarde. Also in 1931 Lúcio Costa was appointed director of the National School of Fine Arts, to the delight of the students. He reformed the curriculum, and appointed Warchavchik as a professor (Deckker 2001, 15). The faculty's opposition, however, was intense, and Costa managed to remain in his post for a mere nine months (Durand 1991; Ferraz 1965, 35–37). He succeeded, though, at planting the seeds for a departure from academicism, which would benefit several of the younger influential Brazilian architects trained at the Rio school during the early 1930s (Moreira, Niemeyer, Reidy, and the Roberto brothers). Of the other architects included in the appendix, Bratke attended engineering school, and Levi and Warchavchik were educated in Italy before they moved to Brazil.

While in Mexico and Brazil the main precepts of modernism had become part of the curriculum by 1930, the situation in Argentina was rather different. The most influential Argentine architects of the turn of the century were trained in Europe in the Beaux-Arts tradition. The first degree in architecture was offered at the University of Buenos Aires back in 1878, and most of the curriculum was the same as for civil engineering. An Argentine-trained architect was "simply a civil engineer cut short" (De Paula 1984). In 1901 architectural education was separated from engineering with the creation of a School of Architecture in Buenos Aires firmly rooted in the Beaux-Arts tradition, where the next two generations of Argentine architects received their training. New subjects added to the curriculum included decorative composition, hygiene, and architectural history (Liernur 2000, 112–14). No innovative school of architecture emerged as an alternative institution to the traditional Beaux-Arts course of study. Engineering, itself an underdeveloped profession in Argentina, exerted a minuscule impact on architectural education. Tellingly, the number of practicing, certified architects grew faster between 1895 and 1914 than that of engineers (38–42). If any of the ten most influential Argentine architects listed in the appendix were influenced by engineering in any meaningful way, it was not during their time at school. (Prebisch, the most modernist of them all, earned a degree in mathematics as well as architecture.)

It seems safe to conclude that modernist architecture emerged first and most vigorously in countries in which the training of architects took place at engineering schools. This was especially true of Germany, Italy, and Russia/Soviet Union. In Mexico and Brazil the precepts of modernism were introduced into the architecture curriculum in the late 1920s, just in time to influence the new generation of architects that started to design and build before World War II. By contrast, modernism was slow to emerge in Britain, Spain, Argentina, and the United States precisely because of the lack of an engineering influence on architectural education. In France, the guardian of the Beaux-Arts tradition, reform did eventually succeed, but only after architects in Germany, Italy, and the early Soviet Union had shown the way. The argument can also be articulated at the individual level of analysis, for it was architects with a background in engineering or trained at educational institutions devoted to both engineering and architecture, who proved most receptive to the ideas of method, standardization, and planning. Among architects active and influential during the 1890–1940 period, those belonging to a younger generation, mostly trained during the first two decades of the twentieth century, were more receptive to modernist ideas. Because of prevailing patterns of architectural education and professionalization, it was architects in Germany, Italy, and Russia/Soviet Union who were more likely to adhere to the modernist principles derived from engineering and scientific management.

It is important, however, to avoid the simplistic and reductionist argument that modernism was the result of one single root cause. Machine-age modernism in architecture was neither a random process nor an idea whose time had necessarily come. It emerged out of very specific economic, political, and social conditions that provided the background for new experiments inspired by engineering, Taylorism, and Fordism. To be sure, the Industrial Revolution "created new patrons, generated new problems, supplied new methods of construction . . . and suggested new forms" (Curtis [1982] 1996, 22). It also seems clear that in Germany and the Soviet Union, even in Spain during the 1930s, sociopolitical upheaval helped architects mount an assault on the entrenched power structures within architectural education and practice. But the availability of funds and methods of construction, as well as the existence of social problems or political opportunities, did not guarantee the rise of a modernist architecture based on the machine aesthetic. The key agents of change were, for the most part, relatively small groups of architects and designers versed in engineering and with an exposure to the world of industry.

Undoubtedly, historical-contextual factors and problems provided the background, or the foundations, for the rise of modernist architecture. But as summarized in table 7.1, modernist architecture emerged in certain countries even in the absence of industrialization, sociopolitical upheaval, or favorable class dynamics. Machine-age modernism in architecture only took hold when new sponsors, such as industrial firms and the state and architects influenced by engineering and scientific management, promoted a new architecture based on new techniques and materials that offered a somewhat unified response to the demands of an era characterized by different combinations, depending on the country, of industrial achievements, social problems, political disruptions, and class dynamics. In some cases, of course, the architects themselves defined and reshaped those "demands" to fit their emerging professional template, especially if they could count on the collaboration of powerful patrons such as industrial firms or the state. As activists, the modernist architects engaged in a deliberate collective process of social construction (McAdam, McCarthy, and Zald 1996), framing problems and solutions in ways consistent with an engineering approach to design.

The Network of Modernist Architecture

The preceding chapters have documented that the emergence and subsequent diffusion of modernist architecture owed much to social contacts linking architects to one another. The early pioneers were connected to each other and played a key role in spreading modernist architecture beyond their home countries by virtue of ties that cut across national boundaries. Figure 7.2 shows the network of relationships between pairs of the one hundred most influential architects listed in the appendix. Three types of relationships are displayed: apprenticeship, collaboration, and attendance at the same educational institution (though not necessarily at the same time). Only the seventy-four architects with a tie to at least one other architect among the one hundred most influential are depicted in the figure. My approach here is similar to that of Collins (1998), who mapped the networks of philosophers over several hundred years as a way to ascertain how key ideas emerged and diffused. Unlike in his analysis, however, the conflict between different conceptions or schools of thought in architecture rarely manifested itself as dyadic disputes between the pairs of contemporaneous architects listed in the appendix. Rather, the most influential architects of the 1890–1940 period focused their criticisms on the architects, styles, ideas, and practices of times past. Hence, figure 7.2 cannot possibly reflect such criticisms and conflicts. As noted in chapters 4, 5, and 6, only a few polemics involved two or more of the most influential contemporaneous architects in the appendix: for instance, between the rationalists and the constructivists in Russia, internationalist and nationalist architects in Mexico, or Christophersen and Prebisch in Argentina.

The most significant feature of the network is that a majority of the ties are domestic, that is, do not cut across national boundaries. The few that do, however, turned out to be highly consequential. Peter Behrens was critical to the early spread of modernist ideas because Gropius, Mies, and Le Corbusier were apprenticed to his workshop. After moving to the United States, Gropius and Mies further disseminated modernism. Le Corbusier is clearly the most central architect in the network, and helped spread modernism not only throughout Europe but also to Latin America and Asia (not shown on the chart).

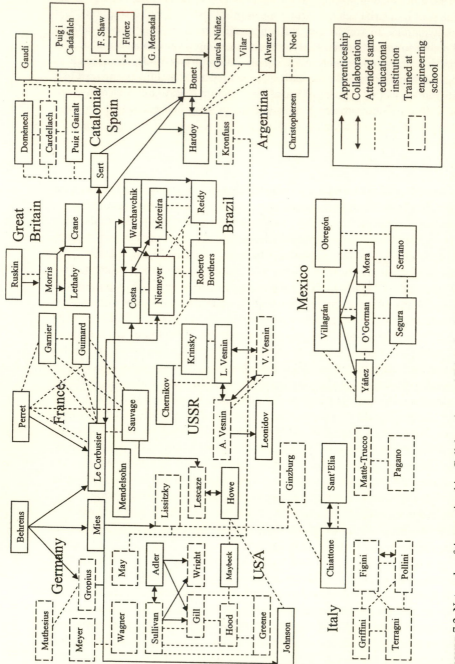

FIGURE 7.2 Networks of Apprenticeship, Collaboration, and Education in the Modernist Architecture Field, Ten Countries, 1890–1940. *Note:* Cross-national educational links between École des Beaux-Arts graduates not depicted: Argentina (Christophersen, Noel), France (Garnier, Le Corbusier, Perret, Sauvage), Mexico (Pani), and the United States (Hood, Howe, Maybeck, Sullivan). *Sources:* See the appendix.

A second noteworthy feature of the network is that there are relatively few apprenticeship and collaboration links between pairs of the most influential architects. By contrast, ties based on the attendance at the same educational institution, albeit not necessarily at the same time, are more numerous. The relative importance of educational institutions in the network highlights the effect of educational traditions and changes on the rise of modernist architecture. The key educational institutions in the spread of architectural modernism in various countries around the world included the Milan and Turin Politecnicos in Italy, some of the Technische Hochschulen in Germany, the VKhUTEMAS and several engineering schools in Russia / Soviet Union, the Escola Nacional de Belas Artes in Brazil, the Faculty of Architecture at the Universidad Nacional Autónoma de México, and Harvard and the Massachusetts Institute of Technology in the United States. Architects who attended engineering school figure prominently in the German, Italian, American, and Russian networks.

The network depicted in figure 7.2 should be complemented with an analysis of the ties that linked prominent scientific managers to modernist architects. While much of the comparative analysis in this chapter has revolved around macro-level correlations between developments in engineering and scientific management, on the one hand, and in architecture, on the other, the connections are also to be found at the dyadic, micro level. Thus, the most active German firm in scientific management, AEG, hired Peter Behrens as its chief designer. In turn, Le Corbusier, Gropius, and Mies van der Rohe (among the most influential architects of the twentieth century) worked with Behrens. Ernest Mercier of Compagnie Français des Petroles was a leading Taylorite in France, and he collaborated with Le Corbusier. In Italy, FIAT and Olivetti were the two most Taylorite firms. Mattè-Trucco designed factories for the former, and Figini and Pollini for the latter. In Brazil, Roberto Simonsen of Companhia Construtora de Santos was a key leader of the Brazilian scientific management movement, and he made arrangements for Warchavchik's arrival. And in Spain it was Sert—an architect linked to the technocratic and Taylorite socialist movement in Catalonia—who promoted, if fleetingly, machine-age modernism.

What is important to note about these social connections is that they played a dual role, although at slightly different moments in time. During the initial stages of the modernist movement in architecture, personal contacts between architects, and between industrialists or scientific managers and architects, helped create the template of modernist architecture. Later on, the preexisting linkages, and others that developed subsequently, helped diffuse that template throughout Europe and around the world. Thus, both the origins and the spread of modernist architecture owed much to the structure of the networks, but one should not discount the importance of industrialization, state activities, sociopolitical upheaval, and educational traditions as background conditions that facilitated the creation and sustainability of the networks of personal relationships.

The Modernist Reconstruction of Architecture

The complex coincidence of industrialization, sociopolitical upheaval, changing class dynamics, new sponsors, and shifting educational and professionalization patterns generated much change in the field of architecture. The rise of the modernist aesthetic came hand in hand with a reconfiguration of architecture, a development that was to facilitate the diffusion of the new practices and enhance their impact on society. As DiMaggio (1991) has observed, the rearrangement of organizational fields affects both practices and actors. The modernist reconstruction of architecture entailed the adoption not only of a new set of practices having to do with aesthetic design and construction methods, but also of a new category of authorized actors. The legitimate architect was no longer a decorator of buildings but an organizer of life, an expert versed in both technology and art (Larson 1993; Blau 1984; Brain 1994).

The modernist architect became the center of gravity of a revamped and more complex organizational field that included a number of interacting and highly specialized actors and institutions: professional schools of architecture teaching a unified curriculum in design and technology; separate professional associations for architects; industrial companies and the state as sponsors; a number of support occupations like surveyors, draftsmen, and structural engineers, among others; a great variety of manufacturing firms supplying such materials as steel, glass, and cement or providing specialized subsystems like elevators or lighting; construction subcontractors doing work under the coordination of the lead contractor; and the public, both as spectator and user of the resulting buildings. As the Mexican architect Mario Pani once observed, "the architect doesn't, cannot, work alone. . . . He must constantly extend and renew his lines of communication. He has his field commanders, his designers, draftsmen, mathematicians, contractors, suppliers, endless armies of workers, skilled craftsmen" (quoted in Smith 1967, 178). The new ideology, methods, and aesthetic of architectural modernism spread triumphantly after World War II thanks to the institutional blueprint for the reconstruction of the organizational field that had been produced in Continental Europe under the influence of American engineering and scientific management.

The Enduring Promise of Modernist Architecture

> Art is long and life is short, and . . .
> society must resign itself to having
> architects and engineers.
> —A. Melani (1890, 88).

> Less is a bore!
> —Robert Venturi

THE POINT OF THIS BOOK is not that a specific modernist architectural "style" coalesced and then spread throughout the world during the first third of the twentieth century. There is no agreement as to what exactly the "modern style" in architecture is all about, as discussed in chapter 1. The number of historical and national variations is so great that to identify a single, coherent style would be an elusive goal. In fact, so many different trends and events influenced modernism that it would be rather odd to tell the story as a linear path from eclectic classicism to modernism.

To avoid these difficulties, I have argued that machine-age modernism's unique contribution was to change the way we think about and experience architecture. What is distinctively and unambiguously "modern" about modernist architecture is the notion that the architect should concern him or herself with the user of the building (not the client), with planning and efficiency, and with improving living and working conditions. Architecture thus became a moral as well as a public art. The template of an architecture based on method, standardization, and planning geared towards the design of efficient buildings can be readily identified, and its diffusion around the world traced to a common origin in continental Europe during the early twentieth century.

Depending on the country, different forces coincided to produce modernism in architecture, including industrialization, sociopolitical upheaval, class dynamics, sponsors, and educational models. The common denominator to all countries in which modernism succeeded as a movement was the influence exerted by engineering and scientific management in the process of education and professionalization of architects. In turn, the impact of scientific management around the world was magnified by the spread of modernist architecture itself. Thus, architecture became a social as well as a public and moral art, with distinctive consequences for people's lives. The modernist reinterpretation of scientific management in aesthetic terms begs a revisiting of this cardinal organizational theory. Let us deal with each of these issues and consequences in turn.

As the Mexican Nobel Prize-winning poet Octavio Paz ([1987] 1993, 145) once put it, "the ambition to create a public art requires at least two conditions for its fulfillment: first, a community of beliefs, feelings, and images; second, a vision of humanity and of its place and mission in the world." Modernist architecture did become such a community, and it certainly entertained a vision, which made it a truly moral art espousing a specific vision, one driven by principles mostly borrowed from the world of engineering and scientific management, including method, standardization, and planning.

It is easy to get caught up in the colorful rhetoric employed by the most visionary of the modernist architects (see chapter 2) and forget that there was a moral vision embedded in it. By moral I do not mean, of course, that it was "right" or "good"; it was simply a vision, one among many others that competed for attention during the ideologically convulsive historical period covered in this book. It must be recognized that the modernists faced an uphill battle: an entrenched Beaux-Arts elite controlling the most prestigious architectural institutions in each country and a rampant eclecticism in practical design that they equated with bad taste. Gaudy and incisive rhetoric was a weapon they used to shake the foundations of the established institutions and ways of doing design.

But what was exactly their moral vision? A key point to keep in mind is that the modernist architects were technocrats, and they learned to apply science and method from the scientific managers, as documented in chapter 2. Modernism cannot be properly understood without the principles of method, standardization, and planning. The modernist architects were true believers in the potential of science and engineering to tackle social, industrial, and architectural problems. They were focused on improving living conditions in the city and the workplace: that was their moral vision. As true technocrats, they believed they were legitimate social reformers because of their (superior) claim to expert knowledge and good taste. They borrowed from Frederick Taylor the idea that the best way to solve social and economic problems was to give power to a class of impartial experts who would rise above the familiar bickering between employers and workers and actually make everyone better off. Or so they thought.

But then, how does one reconcile the modernist architects' technocratic ethos with the fact that they aspired to democratize architecture and to make good design available to everyone? The modernists were also populists, as it turns out. They learned from Henry Ford a second lesson, namely, that wide distribution and consumption of modernist architecture and artifacts was compatible with sobriety and sophistication in design. While it may be inaccurate to refer to the modernist architects as pure technocrats, it seems equally erroneous to classify them as mere populists. The label "populist technocrats" strikes a happy medium that captures their contained belief in science and planning, and their tempered desire to cater to the masses as opposed to the elite, even though several of them had elite social backgrounds (e.g., Gropius, Sert, or Niemeyer). They wished to improve the lot of the populace, but showed contempt for the populace's sense of aesthetics, mounting a blistering attack on kitsch art. As the modernist Austrian architect Adolf Loos once pointed out, "the lower the standard of a people, the more lavish are its ornaments" (quoted in Pevsner [1936] 1960, 30).

A long discussion could be kept going as to whether the modernists were moved to democratize good design out of professional self-interest or because of an altruistic inclination. Their desire to shake the foundations of the art world and to take over the field of architecture in their respective home countries points in the direction of self-interest. Modernist architecture was, after all, a revolutionary movement that attempted to overthrow the traditional structures of power within the profession, and the modernists themselves stood much to gain from such a change. And given their close ties to firms and the state, it is possible that they may have eventually abdicated their aesthetic and social convictions in favor of their patrons' (Blau 1984; see also Alexander 1996a, 1996b for art in general).

It is only fair to point out, however, that many of the modernist architects were deeply concerned with social justice, and committed to rather utopian and radical political projects, including versions of Socialism, Communism, Anarchism, or Fascism; most of them were willing to pay allegiance to those beliefs with their own careers and social position, going into exile if necessary; and a few of them were willing to put their lives on the line. Thus, the modernist architects were simultaneously technocratic and populist, elitist and plebeian, and egoistic and altruistic, with the caveat that it was the architect— and not the user or consumer—who should make the decision as to what qualified as good taste. As true technocrats, they presented themselves as "despotic but disinterested" (Gartman 2000, 87). And the impact of the modernist view of the architect has been long-lasting in this respect, for contemporary architects, at least in the United States, "have neither succumbed to art for art's sake nor is their economic dependence on clients matched by an ideological identification with them" (Blau 1984, 15). I now turn to the thorny issue of how the users of modernist architecture experienced it.

THE CONSUMPTION OF MODERNIST ARCHITECTURE AND DESIGN

The analysis of modernist architecture contained in this book has emphasized the production of cultural artifacts (buildings), and relegated the consumption of the artifacts to the background. The explanations for the rise of modernism discussed in chapters 3 and 7 had to do with factors driving the production of modernist artifacts, not with the ways in which they may have been experienced by the user. It is germane to ask what happened to the user or the consumer of the finished artifacts. This is, of course, the question critics of modernism enjoy asking the most. They have tended, for the most part, to answer it in terms of the failures of modernism in architecture and urban planning: dehumanization, alienation, dislocation, impoverishment. While there surely is some truth to these accusations, it is only fair to point out that the modernists never gave too much importance to how their designs would be received by the end user. They thought they had a better claim to design and to define good taste than anyone else, including the users or consumers of their artifacts. This approach represents yet another influence of scientific management and Fordism: the technocrat knows better than the employers, the workers, and the consumers, what they really want. Perhaps modernist architects would not object to this book's focus on the production of the artifact rather than on its consumption because the modernists themselves cared about the production of art and did not systematically seek to incorporate feedback from the user. They did, however, employ techniques and methods to make buildings more user-friendly, and they designed from the point of view of the user, though without actually asking users about their preferences.

If the modernist architects strived to democratize good design, to make it available to the masses, however, it is legitimate to ask how the working-class users of their artifacts were expected to react and how they actually did react. There are two conflicting views of working-class tastes in the sociology of culture (Gartman 2000). First, the Frankfurt School of sociology has suggested that the working class, alienated by scientific management and Fordism, seeks to escape from the rationalized world of the factory by consuming cultural artifacts with the opposite characteristics (Adorno 1994, 1997; Fromm 1984). This "compensating hypothesis" essentially means that workers would prefer to consume a kitsch sort of art and architecture, one that makes them more socially connected by enhancing their sense of belonging to a community, while simultaneously helping them develop a more individualized existence.

In contrast to this view, the French sociologist Pierre Bourdieu (1984) has argued that a taste for immediate gratification is part of the durable dispositions (*habitus*) of the working class, one that is most likely fulfilled with unadorned, functionalist artifacts (see also Veblen [1899] 1934). Bourdieu builds his argument on the Kantian distinction between "that which pleases" and "that which gratifies." The "popular aesthetic," according to Bourdieu, provides a "continuity between art and life, which implies the subordination of form to function." "Working-class people . . . expect every image to fulfill a function," because they have a sense of aesthetics that "bases appreciation on informative, tangible or moral interest." In other words, "necessity imposes a taste for necessity" (Bourdieu 1984, 32, 41, 42, 372). Naturally, the modernists would rather agree with Bourdieu than with Adorno, and any indication of a compensating effect would have compelled them to try even harder to make "good" design more widely available.

There is some research on the actual reaction to modernism of occupants that may help shed some light on the Adorno-Bourdieu debate. Residents of Le Corbusier's working-class apartment settlement at Pessac, near Bordeaux—designed and built during the mid-1920s with his five modernist principles in mind (see chapter 4)—made alterations to the apartments that suppressed some of the most conspicuous modernist features, including an expansion of the kitchen into the parlor to create a communal area, the dissimulation of industrial motifs with ornaments, and the division of the continuous ribbonlike windows into smaller ones so as to create a more private and cozy interior (Boudon 1972). Gartman (2000, 92) interprets these alterations as proof that the workers sought to escape from the rationalized world of the factory by individualizing and humanizing their standardized modernist dwellings, a view that is consistent with Adorno's (1994) approach rather than Bourdieu's (1984).

The residents of Pessac, however, were ambivalent about their homes, liking some of their features very much and others not so well. For instance, one resident noticed: "From the outside I didn't like it very much, and then, once I had looked over the house, really, I was completely won over by the design, by the layout of the rooms, which were large, very bright, very airy and well aligned . . ." (Boudon 1972, 89; see also 113). Not all occupants were so positive in their remarks, but the majority did not seem to reject the basic elements of Corbusian design. Quite on the contrary, after interviewing the residents, the neighbors, and several architects, Boudon (1972, 114–23, 161–63) concludes that, although Le Corbusier would not have approved of all of the alterations, they should be interpreted as a sign that the occupants were able to take advantage of his free-plan interiors so as to better satisfy their needs by rearranging walls, concealing certain elements, or reallocating space. Specifically, Le Corbusier's standardized design left degrees of freedom for permutation of the various elements so that individualized requirements could be met. Thus, it seems that the complex set of reactions of the residents of Pessac to Le Corbusier's design included both the compensating actions anticipated by Adorno and the functionalist behaviors predicted by Bourdieu.

It is important to keep in mind another important influence of modernism on consumption. Several of the modernist designers in Europe made enduring contributions to the artistic techniques underlying mass marketing. The Bauhaus had workshops for typography and photography, and did advertising design for several firms. The Russian modernists refined the art of revolutionary propaganda, especially in the form of posters. Modernist principles inspired the generation of typographers, photographers, and advertisers that came of age after World War II in the United States, and later in Europe. Thus, another important chapter in the consumption of modernist cultural artifacts remains to be written.

ARCHITECTURE AS SOCIAL ART

Whether consumers of modernism found it beautiful or not is largely beside the point. What really matters is that modernist architecture aspired to shape the lives of millions, and it actually succeeded at that, for better or worse. The founders of modernist architecture contributed decisively to the legitimate application of scientific management techniques to the construction industry. Moreover, the industrialization, mechanization, and Taylorization of architecture spearheaded by European modernism came together with the formulation of a modernist aesthetic whose impact transcended the organization of the building activity itself. The scientific-management content underlying modernist architecture has exerted a widespread, profound, and lasting effect on the people living, studying, or working in the myriad of Taylorized, machine-like buildings that were erected during the booming 1945–65 period on both sides of the Atlantic and that still dominate the configuration of the modern city, the industrial complex, and the university campus.

The new technical, social, and organizational roles of the architect proposed by the modernists have endured as part of the architectural profession's ethos. In her excellent study, *Architects and Firms*, Judith Blau (1984, 66–67, 80–81) reports that the New York City architects she surveyed in the 1970s either "strongly agreed" or "agreed" with several key modernist themes related to the architect's social role, including that architecture should be designed for users not clients, and that serviceability of buildings should be given top priority. Moreover, while more than 80 percent agreed with Sullivan's aphorism "form follows function," and about 60 percent with Mies van der Rohe's "less is more," only 23 percent did with Venturi's "less is a bore!" Of the eight twentieth-century architects they reported admiring the most, four were among the founders of machine-age modernism: Le Corbusier, Aalto, Mies van der Rohe, and Gropius.

The modernist architect pursued the ideas of regularity, continuity, and speed by applying the scientific principles of method, standardization, and planning. Thus, scientific management unobtrusively invaded our homes and workplaces and, most importantly, the culture. Although the most visionary and utopian proposals of the European modernist architects were not realized, they succeeded at turning many of our buildings into efficient—and arguably beautiful—machines to live or work in. If architecture is a ubiquitous fact of life, then scientific management became truly rampant after the spread of modernist architectural design. Therefore, the impact of scientific management in contemporary society and industry cannot be thoroughly assessed without taking the modernist architectural revolution into consideration. It is in this sense that architecture, in addition to being a public and moral art, also became a social art, one with immediate consequences for the ways in which social life unfolds in space and time. From a Durkheimian sociological perspective, modernist architecture affected the density and pattern of social relationships in ways that must have made a difference, if only we could sociologically conceptualize and measure them. The relationship between scientific management and modernist architecture illustrates that organizations and organization theory have the potential of shaping social life and thus have become an important element of contemporary society (Perrow 1991).

THE AESTHETIC IMPLICATIONS OF ORGANIZATIONAL THEORIES

Recent years have witnessed a flourishing interest in the social, political, and cultural roots and implications of organizational theories (Yates 1989; Barley and Kunda 1992; Guillén 1994; Shenhav 1995; Abrahamson 1997; Martin 2003). Little attention, though, has been paid to their aesthetic message and impact, that is, to notions of the beautiful that may be associated with specific ways of organizing.[1] The formulation by modernist architects of an aesthetic based on the beauty of the machine and on the new scientific management methods of the turn of the century provides an excellent laboratory for exploring the aesthetic content of organizational theories.

Traditionally, scientific management has been seen as a highly constraining, overtly exploitative, and ideologically conservative model of organization. It has been portrayed as a paradigm of reckless deskilling, impersonal production, and mediocre quality (Braverman 1974; Edwards 1979; Piore and Sabel 1984; Perrow 1986; MacDuffie 1991; Scott 1995b). At first sight this conception of scientific management appears to be at odds with artistic creation and re-creation. Besides, aesthetics have to do with emotions and sensations, however rationalized, while this organizational theory seems to underscore practical and utilitarian aspects alone.

Organizational scholars have come to accept that their main theories—including scientific management—contain ideological as well as technical considerations (Bendix 2001; Barley and Kunda 1992; Kilduff 1993; Guillén 1994; Shenhav 1995, 1999), but the aesthetic message of scientific management or other organizational theories has received scant attention from organizational

[1] For exceptions see: Brady (1986), who writes about the aesthetic dimension of management ethics without delving into the actual link between the two; and Dean, Ottensmeyer, and Ramirez (1997) and Strati (1992, 1999), who explore how people's aesthetic perceptions of an organization may affect their behavior (including their decision to participate, job satisfaction, resistance to change, and leadership style).

researchers, largely because its theoretical elaboration did not take place in the United States but in Europe, and because modernist architecture has not been studied by organizational scholars.

The evidence and analysis presented in this book challenges familiar images of scientific management in two respects. First, it suggests that the impact of scientific management has been much more pervasive and enduring than previously assumed. The European architects' sweeping reinterpretation of scientific management took place in the midst of the reconstruction of architecture as an organizational field along a new set of professional ideals and techniques. This new institutional blueprint facilitated the diffusion of modernist architectural practice throughout the world after World War II. The result of this most consequential and lasting change was a drastic reconfiguration of the modern metropolis, a development that continues to affect the lives of hundreds of millions of people around the world who live or work in modernist buildings.

In identifying scientific management's "lost" aesthetic, this book exposes a forgotten cultural implication of this organizational theory: European modernist architects found an aesthetic message in scientific management, producing an unlikely synthesis between art and the rationalized world of machines. Thus, the view held by many social scientists and organizational researchers that scientific management intrinsically leads to seamy, unpleasant, or stultifying outcomes needs to be reconsidered or at least qualified. This organizational model has not ceased to arouse extreme passions ever since its inception a century ago. Its most zealous supporters and detractors may find it startling—or bizarre—that scientific management contributed crucially to a new aesthetic order in architecture and design. It is important to realize that scientific management is much richer and more complex an organizational theory than either the cold proponents of its technical postulates or its unwavering critics are willing to admit. To be sure, scientific management has served as a draconian instrument of domination and condemned many people to dreadful working conditions. I do not wish to extol scientific management but to show how its impact on society has been more widespread than previously assumed by organizational researchers, and to suggest that an aesthetic message may be derived even from the most alienating of organizational theories. If the prevailing images of scientific management's qualities and impact need to be revised, what are the wider implications for organizational research down the road?

A most tantalizing question for future research is whether one can expect other of our organizational theories to harbor the same potential for aesthetic reinterpretation as scientific management does. Recent work has underlined that organizational theories seem to oscillate between rational and normative approaches (Barley and Kunda 1992). In this view, scientific management belongs to a class of theories heralding rational, futuristic, and mechanical themes. Accordingly, the rise of human relations as an organizational theory during the 1930s and 1940s could be further explored by reference to the naturalistic, nostalgic, and organic motifs expounded by architects and artists as well as management intellectuals in England, Spain, and some segments of the artistic community in the United States (Guillén 1994). Some of the issues raised by the industrial welfare movement in the United States or in Great Britain could be reinterpreted in aesthetic terms, as could the famous Hawthorne investigations of the 1920s, which often addressed aspects having to do with the arrangement of physical space at the workplace (Biggs 1996, 59–61). In the late 1960s and early '70s a movement of "office landscaping" developed both in America and Europe in an attempt to make life at work more productive and satisfactory (Martin 2003, 91–95). The corporate-culture trend of the 1980s may lend itself to a similar analysis. While the postmodern architecture of the 1960s through the '80s entertained naturalistic and organic motifs, the linkage to such organizational approaches as human relations or corporate culture seems to have been rather weak. Whether other organizational theories correlate with different aesthetic conceptions in architecture deserves further empirical investigation.

One promising area for future research lies in the influence of electrical engineering and computer science on art and on organizational theory, beginning with the work of Herbert Simon. The "informational aesthetic" developed at the Ulm School of Design in Germany during the 1950s and '60s and at Carnegie Mellon University's Design Research Center during the '70s has been traced back to operations research, systems analysis, and Simon's theory of programmed design (March 1981; Simon 1981, 150–59; Lindinger 1991; Demes et al. 1993; Kilduff 1993; Selle 1994, 290–300; Martin 2003, 174–77). More recently, electronic and cybernetic metaphors have become legal tender both in the field of organization—the networked organization, the learning organization, the virtual organization, and so on—and in the visual arts with the new expressive possibilities offered by the electronic media, as evidenced by artistic production and consumption on the World Wide Web. Nowadays, both organizational theory and art seem to be emphasizing virtuality and networks, ideas that share in common their origin in electrical engineering and computer science. For example, Barry and Rerup (2002) have noted that there is an affinity between network theories of organization, on the one hand, and the paintings of Joan Miró and the mobile sculptures of Alexander Calder, on the other. The commonality lies in the emphasis on relationships, modular design, and movement. These emerging affinities between organization and art in the context of a revolutionary electronic age are intriguing enough to merit future empirical research, especially because the linkage between scientific management and avant-garde modernism was forged in the midst of an equally sweeping mechanical transformation. In either case, engineering seems to be the common denominator.

In general, the evidence and analysis presented in this book opens a new area of discussion and research in the field of organizational theory. We have long neglected the aesthetic context of organizational behavior. Are job performance and satisfaction influenced by aesthetic factors, as Gropius suggested back in 1911, or by the allocation of space in the workplace?[2] Are different authority structures consistent with specific aesthetic orders? Is decision making in organizations affected by aesthetic considerations in addition to ideological and instrumental ones? Do organizational cultures and occupational communities contain aesthetic elements? Research on organizational design, decision making, occupations, conflict, and leadership can benefit from an explicit consideration of the aesthetic dimension as a cultural variable, a possibility occasionally noted by some management theorists and organizational researchers (Ackoff 1981, 39–45, 117–19; Strati 1992, 1999; Darr 2000) but rarely brought to fruition. Future organizational studies on these topics could explore the impact of aesthetics not only with comparative-historical methods similar to the ones used throughout this book but also with other approaches, such as survey research or ethnography.

Perhaps this book will help to make one proposition about the field of organizational studies more widely accepted. It is the notion that organizational theories may have aesthetic as well as technical and ideological underpinnings and implications. I hope that this book has rescued the modernist aesthetic message of scientific management from oblivion. An aesthetic is not necessarily a rational element, but it is a rationalized one, and it is as intuitive and emotional as it is pervasive in human character. People seem to yearn for beauty as intensely as they pursue instrumental methods and morally acceptable conditions. Our understanding of the inner logic of organizational theories, as well as of their effectiveness and impact, is likely to be enhanced by taking the aesthetic dimension into account.

■■■

What needs to be grasped about modernist architecture is not the specific style or outlook of the buildings but rather its commitment to planning for a better world and its ability to realize that promise, even if many would not perceive it as necessarily or objectively "better." The most important, albeit unintended, consequence of the industrialization and Taylorization of architecture during the first third of the twentieth century was that it became a social art with enormous implications for all of us. Architecture was changed forever, even though the aesthetic dogmas of "form follows function" and "less is more" may have been partially abandoned in favor of the less restrictive, though

[2] On this debate, see Pfeffer (1997, 198–202), and Cohen (2002).

potentially eclectic, "less is a bore!" The future will surely bring new trends, transitions, even styles, which may spread throughout the world following distinctively local patterns. And yet architecture will continue to play the moral role that the modernists envisioned and perhaps also some social role that nobody anticipated.

Leading Architects in the Six Largest European Countries and the Four Largest Countries in the Americas

THIS APPENDIX lists the ten most influential architects in Argentina, Brazil, France, Germany, Great Britain, Italy, Mexico, Russia/Soviet Union, Spain/Catalonia, and the United States during the 1890–1940 period, for a total of one hundred architects. To generate the lists I used five well-established histories of modernist or contemporary architecture (Banham [1960] 1980; Benevolo [1960] 1977; Curtis [1982] 1996; Hitchcock [1958] 1971; Weston 1996), and five encyclopedias (Lampugnani [1964] 1986; Midant 1996; Muriel [1980] 1994; Placzek 1982; Sharp [1967] 1981). I also used more specialized sources for some countries to complete the list of the ten most influential architects, as follows: France (McLeod 1983); Germany (Lane 1985); Great Britain (Pevsner 1937); Italy (Etlin 1991); Russia / Soviet Union (Kopp 1985; Bowlt 1988; Cooke 1995); and Spain/Catalonia (Freixa 1986; Flores 1989; Pizza 1997). For Latin America, I relied on the encyclopedic dictionary contained in *Arquitectura Latinoamericana en el Siglo XX* (Gutiérrez 1998b), and on a wide variety of country-specific sources.

When available, I include the educational background of each architect. I also assigned each architect a code depending on whether he welcomed or opposed mechanization and standardization in art and architecture and whether he explicitly accepted or rejected scientific management, under the assumption that endorsing the latter implied acceptance of the former. The resulting four-point scale is as follows:

— Reacted against scientific management
– Reacted against mechanization and standardization
+ Reacted favorably to mechanization and standardization
++ Reacted favorably to scientific management

Citations:

[a] Cited in Banham [1960] 1980, *Theory and Design in the First Machine Age.*
[b] Cited in Benevolo [1960] 1977, *History of Modern Architecture.*
[c] Cited in Curtis [1982] 1996, *Modern Architecture since 1900.*
[d] Cited in Hitchcock [1958] 1971, *Architecture: Nineteenth and Twentieth Centuries.*
[e] Cited in Weston 1996, *Modernism.*
[f] Entry in Lampugnani [1964] 1986, *Encyclopedia of 20th-Century Architecture.*
[g] Entry in Midant ed. 1996, *Dictionnaire de l'architecture du XXe siècle.*
[h] Entry in Muriel ed. [1980] 1994, *Contemporary Architects.*
[i] Entry in Placzek ed. 1982, *The MacMillan Encyclopedia of Architects.*
[j] Entry in Sharp ed. [1967] 1981, *Sources of Modern Architecture: A Critical Bibliography.*

Argentina

	Architect	Lifespan	Educational Background	Citations
+	Mario Roberto Álvarez	1913–?	Architect, University of Buenos Aires, UBA	f g h i
+	Antonio Bonet, Spanish born	1913–1989	Architect, University of Barcelona	c g i
–	Alejandro Christophersen, Spanish born	1866–1946	Architect, École des Beaux-Arts	g i
–	Julián Jaime García Núñez	1875–1944	Apprenticed architect	g i
–	Ángel Guido	1896–1960	Architect, University of Córdoba	g i
+	Jorge Ferrari Hardoy	1914–1976	Architect, UBA	g i
–	Juan Kronfuss, Hungarian born	1872–1944	Engineer and architect, Technische Hochschule, Munich	g i
–	Martín Noel	1888–1963	Architect, École des Beaux-Arts	g i
+	Alberto Prebisch	1899–1970	Architect and mathematician, UBA	g
+	Antonio Ubaldo Vilar	1888–1966	Architect, UBA	g i

Brazil

	Architect	Lifespan	Educational Background	Citations
+	Oswaldo Bratke	1907–1997	Engineer and architect, University of Mackenzie	g i
+	Lúcio Costa	1902–1998	Architect, Escola Nacional de Belas Artes, ENBA, Rio	b c f h g i
+	Rino Levi	1901–1965	Architect, Milan and Rome	g h i
+	Jorge Moreira	1904–1992	Architect, ENBA Rio	g h i
+	Oscar Niemeyer	1907–	Architect, ENBA Rio	b c d e f g h i j
+	Affonso Eduardo Reidy	1909–1964	Architect, ENBA Rio	b c d g h i
+	Marcelo Roberto	1908–1964	Architect, ENBA Rio	b d g h i
+	Milton Roberto	1914–1953	Architect, ENBA Rio	d g h i
+	Mauricio Roberto	1921–?	Architect, ENBA Rio	b d g h i
++	Gregori Warchavchik, Russian born	1896–1972	Architect, Academia de Belle Arti, Rome	f g h i

France

	Architect	Lifespan	Educational Background	Citations
+	Anatole de Baudot	1834–1915	Apprenticed architect	a b c e f g i
++	Georges Benoit-Lévy	1880–1971	Urban planner	i
+	Auguste Choisy	1841–1910	Architect (Polytechnique), engineer (Ponts et Chaussées)	a c e i
+	Tony Garnier	1869–1948	architect (École des Beaux-Arts)	a b c e f g i j
–	Héctor Guimard	1867–1942	architect (École des Beaux-Arts)	b c d e f g i j
+	François Hennebique	1842–1921	Apprenticed architect, entrepreneur, inventor	a b c d e g i
++	Le Corbusier (Charles Édouard Jeanneret), Swiss-born	1887–1965	Painter, architect (École des Beaux-Arts)	a b c d e f g h i j
+	Rob. Mallet-Stevens	1886–1945	Architect and designer (École Spéciale d' Architecture)	a b c d e f g i
+	Auguste Perret, Belgian-born	1874–1954	architect (École des Beaux-Arts)	a b c d e f g h i j
+	Henri Sauvage	1873–1932	architect (École des Beaux-Arts)	a d e f g h i

Germany

	Architect	Lifespan	Educational Background	Citations
++	Peter Behrens	1869–1940	Architect (Kunstschule Karlsruhe), painter, designer	a b c d e f g h i j
++	Walter Gropius	1883–1969	Architect, engineer, designer (Königliche Technische Hochschule Berlin-Charlottenburg)	a b c d e f g h i j
++	Ludwig Hilberseimer	1885–1967	Architect (Technische Hochschule Karlsruhe)	a b c e f g h i j
++	Ernst May	1886–1970	Architect, doctor in engineering (Technische Hochschule Darmstadt and Munich)	a b d e g h i j

Germany (*Continued*)

	Architect	Lifespan	Educational Background	Citations
+	Erich Mendelsohn	1887–1953	Architect (University of Munich)	a b c d e f g h i j
+	Hannes Meyer, Swiss born	1889–1954	Architect (Gewerbeschule Berlin; Landswirtschaftsakademie; Technische Hochschule Berlin)	a b c d e f g h i j
+	Ludwig Mies van der Rohe	1886–1969	Apprenticed architect	a b c d e f g h i j
+	Hermann Muthesius	1861–1927	Architect, doctor in engineering (Technische Hochschule Berlin-Charlottenburg)	a b c d e f g i j
++	Bruno Taut	1880–1938	Architect (Baugewerkschule Königsberg, Technische Hochschule Stuttgart)	a b c e f g h i j
++	Martin Wagner	1885–1957	Architect, doctor in engineering, professor (Technische Hochschule Berlin)	c f g i

Great Britain

	Architect	Lifespan	Educational Background	Citations
+	Charles Robert Ashbee	1863–1942	Aprenticed architect, decorator	a b c d e g i
−	Walter Crane	1845–1915	Aprenticed architect, designer, painter	b e i
−	Sir Ebenezer Howard	1850–1928	Stenographer, city planner	b c e f g i
− −	William Richard Lethaby	1857–1931	Aprenticed architect	a b e g j
−	Charles Rennie Mackintosh	1888–1928	Architect (Glasgow School of Art), designer	b d e f g h i j
−	William Morris	1834–1896	Architect, painter, poet, writer (Oxford)	a b c d e f i
−	John Ruskin	1819–1900	Professor of art, architectural theorist (Oxford)	a b c d e i

Great Britain (*Continued*)

	Architect	Lifespan	Educational Background	Citations
−	Geoffrey Scott	1885–1929	Architect, art and architecture critic	a c
−	Richard Norman Shaw	1831–1912	Aprenticed architect, designer (Royal Academy, London)	a b d e f i j
+	Charles F. Annesley Voysey	1857–1941	Aprenticed architect	a b c d e f g i j

Italy

	Architect	Lifespan	Educational Background	Citations
+	Mario Chiattone, Swiss born	1891–1957	Architect and painter (Accademia de Belle Arti, Brera and Bologna)	a c f g i
+	Luigi Figini	1903–1984	Architect (Milan Politecnico)	b c d e g h i j
+	Enrico Griffini	1887–1952	Architect (Milan Politecnico)	i
+	Adalberto Libera	1903–1963	Architect, mathematician (Scuola Superiore, University of Rome)	b c f g i
+	Virgilio Marchi	1895–1960	Architect (Siena), scenographer	a g i
+	Giacomo Mattè-Trucco	1869–1934	Architect, engineer (Turin Politecnico)	c g i
+	Giuseppe Pagano	1896–1945	Architect (Turin Politecnico)	b g j
+	Gino Pollini	1903–1991	Architect, studied engineering (Milan Politecnico)	b c e f g h I j
+	Antonio Sant'Elia	1888–1916	Architect (Technical School in Como, Accademia di Brera, Scuola di Belle Arti in Bologna)	a b c e f g i j
+	Giuseppe Terragni	1904–1943	Architect, diploma in physics and mathematics (Milan Politecnico)	a b c d e f g h i j

Mexico

	Architect	Lifespan	Educational Background	Citations
–	Luis Barragán	1902–1988	Civil engineer, Escuela Libre de Ingenieros, Guadalajara	c f g h i
–	Adamo Boari, Italian born	1865–1928	Architect	i
+	Enrique de la Mora y Palomar	1907–1978	Architect, Universidad Nacional Autónoma de México, UNAM	g
–	Carlos Obregón Santacilia	1896–1961	Architect, UNAM	
++	Juan O'Gorman	1905–1982	Architect, UNAM	c d f g h i j
+	Mario Pani	1911–1993	Architect, École des Beaux-Arts	g h i
+	Juan Segura Gutiérrez	1898–1989	Architect, UNAM	g
+	Francisco Serrano	1900–1982	Engineer and architect, UNAM	g
–	José Villagrán García	1901–1992	Architect, UNAM	f g h i
+	Enrique Yáñez de la Fuente	1908–1992	Architect, UNAM	g

Russia / Soviet Union

	Architect	Lifespan	Educational Background	Citations
+	Yakov Chernikhov	1889–1951	Architect, painter (Odessa Art School, and St. Petersburg Academy of Arts)	e
+	Aleksei Gan	1889–1942	Architect, painter (Odessa Art School, and St. Petersburg Academy of Arts)	e g
++	Moisei Yakovlevich Ginzburg	1892–1946	Architect, engineer (Academia de Belle Arti, Milan, and Riga Polytechnical University)	b c e i j
++	Vladimir Fedorovich Krinsky	1890–1971	Architect (St. Petersburg Academy of Arts)	g

Russia / Soviet Union (*Continued*)

	Architect	Lifespan	Educational Background	Citations
+	Nikolai Aleksandrovich Ladovsky	1881–1941	Architect (Moscow Institute of Painting, Sculpture, and Architecture)	c e g i
+	Ivan Leonidov	1902–1959	Architect (Tver' Art School, and VKhUTEMAS)	e f g i j
+	El Lissitzky	1890–1941	Architect, painter (Technische Hochschule Darmstadt, and Riga Polytechnical University)	a c e f g i j
+	Leonid A. Vesnin	1880–1933	Architect (Academy of Fine Arts, St. Petersburg)	b e g i
+	Viktor A. Vesnin	1882–1950	Architect, engineer (Institution of Civil Engineering, St. Petersburg)	b c e g i
++	Alexandr A. Vesnin	1883–1959	Architect, engineer (Institution of Civil Engineering, St. Petersburg)	b c e g i

Spain/Catalonia

	Architect	Lifespan	Educational Background	Citations
−	Félix Cardellach i Avilés	1875–1919	Architect, engineer (Universidad de Barcelona)	
−	Josep Domènech i Estapà	1858–1917	Architect, PhD in mathematics (Universidad de Barcelona)	
+	Casto Fernández Shaw	1896–1978	Architect (Universidad de Madrid)	i
+	Antonio Flórez	1877–1941	Architect (Universidad de Madrid)	
+	Fernando García Mercadal	1896–1985	Architect (Universidad de Madrid)	g i
−	Antoni Gaudí	1852–1926	Architect (Universidad de Barcelona)	b c d e f g h i j

Spain/Catalonia (*Continued*)

	Architect	Lifespan	Educational Background	Citations
+	Lluís Muncunill i Parellada	1868–1931	Architect (Universidad de Barcelona)	c
−	Josep Puig i Cadafalch	1867–1956	Architect, PhD in physics and mathematics, politician (Universidad de Barcelona and Universidad de Madrid)	g h i
−	Antoni Puig i Gairalt	1888–1935	Architect (Universidad de Barcelona)	
+	Josep Lluís Sert	1902–1983	Architect (Universidad de Barcelona)	e f g h i j

United States

	Architect	Lifespan	Educational Background	Citations
+	Dankmar Adler, German-born	1844–1900	Architect (Detroit and Chicago)	b c d e f g i
+	Irving John Gill	1870–1936	Architect (MIT)	c d f g i j
−	Charles Sumner Greene	1868–1957	Architect (MIT)	c d f g h i j
−/+	Raymond Hood	1881–1934	Architect (MIT, École des Beaux-Arts)	b c d f h i
+	George Howe	1886–1955	Architect (Harvard, École des Beaux-Arts)	b c d e f g h i j
+	Philip Johnson	1906–2005	Architect (Harvard, BA in philology, degree in architecture)	c d e f g h i j
+	William Lescaze	1896–1964	Engineer (Eidgenössische Technische Hochschule Zürich)	b c d e f g h i j
−	Bernard Maybeck	1862–1957	Architect (École des Beaux-Arts)	c d f g i
+	Louis H. Sullivan	1856–1924	Architect (MIT, but did not graduate; École des Beaux-Arts)	b c d e f g h i j
−/+	Frank Lloyd Wright	1867–1959	Apprenticed architect, engineer (University of Wisconsin, as a special student)	a b c d e f g h i j

Illustration Credits for Plates

References

Abbott, Andrew. 1988. *The System of Professions: An Essay on the Division of Expert Labor.* Chicago: University of Chicago Press.

Abrahamson, Eric. 1997. "The Emergence and Prevalence of Employee Management Rhetorics." *Academy of Management Journal* 40:491–533.

Ackoff, Russell L. 1981. *Creating the Corporate Future.* New York: Wiley.

Ackroyd, Peter. 1996. "Blooming Genius: William Morris Emerges from the Flowers and Vines as a Visionary." *New Yorker*, September 23, 90–94.

Adorno, Theodor. 1994. *Philosophy of Modern Music.* New York: Continuum.

———. 1997. *Aesthetic Theory.* Minneapolis: University of Minnesota Press.

Ahlström, Göran. 1982. *Engineers and Industrial Growth.* London: Croom Helm.

Alexander, Victoria D. 1996a. *Museums and Money: The Impact of Funding on Exhibitions, Scholarship, and Management.* Bloomington: Indiana University Press.

———. 1996b. "Pictures at an Exhibition: Conflicting Pressures in Museums and the Display of Art." *American Journal of Sociology* 101 (4) (January): 797–839.

Allen, James Sloan. 1983. *The Romance of Commerce and Culture.* Chicago: University of Chicago Press.

Alva Martínez, Ernesto. 1983. "La enseñanza de la arquitectura en México en el siglo XX." *Cuadernos de Arquitectura y Conservación del Patrimonio Artístico* 26–27: 47–112.

Andel, Jaroslav. 1990. "The Constructivist Entanglement: Art into Politics, Politics into Art." In *Art into Life: Russian Constructivism, 1914–1932*, edited by Richard Andrews and Milena Kalinovska, 223–39. New York: Rizzoli.

Anderson, Stanford. 2000. *Peter Behrens and a New Architecture for the Twentieth Century.* Cambridge, MA: MIT Press.

Bacon, Margdes. 2001. *Le Corbusier in America: Travels in the Land of the Timid.* Cambridge, MA: MIT Press.

Bailes, Kendall E. 1977. "Alexei Gastev and the Soviet Controversy over Taylorism, 1918–24." *Soviet Studies* 29:373–94.

Baliero, Horacio, and Ernesto Katzenstein. 1984. "Le Corbusier en la ciudad sin esperanza." In *Documentos para una historia de la arquitectura argentina*, edited by Marina Waisman, 183–86. Buenos Aires: Ediciones Summa.

Banham, Reyner. [1960] 1980. *Theory and Design in the First Machine Age.* Cambridge, MA: MIT Press.

———. 1986. *A Concrete Atlantis: U.S. Industrial Building and European Modern Architecture.* Cambridge, MA: MIT Press.

Banks, Arthur S. 2001. *Cross-National Time-Series Data Archive.* www.databanks .sitehosting.net/.

Barley, Stephen R., and Gideon Kunda. 1992. "Design and Devotion: Surges of Rational and Normative Ideologies of Control in Managerial Discourse." *Administrative Science Quarterly* 37:363–99.

Barr, Alfred H., Jr. 1995. Preface to *The International Style*, by Henry-Russell Hitchcock and Philip Johnson, 27–32. New York: W.W. Norton.

Barragán Foundation. 2002. *Guía Barragán.* Mexico City: Arquine + RM.

Barron, Stephanie, ed. 1991. *Degenerate Art: The Fate of the Avant-Garde in Nazi Germany.* New York: Harry N. Abrams.

Barry, David, and Claus Rerup. 2002. "Calder and the Network: Towards Movement and Individual Sensibility within Organizational Network Theory." Working paper, Wharton School.

Bassegoda Nonell, Juan. 1992. *Aproximación a Gaudí.* Madrid: Doce Calles.

Baumgarten, Franciska. 1924. *Arbeitswissenschaft und Psychotechnik in Russland.* Munich: R. Oldenbourg.

Bayer, Herbert, Walter Gropius, and Ise Gropius, eds. 1975. *Bauhaus, 1919–1928.* New York: Museum of Modern Art.

Behrens, Peter, and H. de Fries. 1918. *Vom sparsamen Bauen.* Berlin: Verlag der Bauwelt.

Bell, Daniel. [1976] 1978. *The Cultural Contradictions of Capitalism.* New York: Basic.

Bendix, Reinhard. 2001. *Work and Authority in Industry: Managerial Ideologies in the Course of Industrialization.* New Brunswick, NJ: Transaction.

Benevolo, Leonardo. [1960] 1977. *History of Modern Architecture.* Cambridge, MA: MIT Press.

Benton, Tim. 1984. "Villa Savoye and the Architects' Practice." In *The Le Corbusier Archive*, edited by H. Allen Brooks, 7:ix–xxxi. New York: Garland Architectural Archives.

Bigazzi, Duccio. 1987. "Management Strategies in the Italian Car Industry 1906–1945: Fiat and Alfa Romeo." In *The Automobile Industry and Its Workers*, edited by Steven Tolliday and Jonathan Zeitlin, 76–96. New York: St. Martin's.

Biggs, Lindy. 1996. *The Rational Factory.* Baltimore: Johns Hopkins University Press.

Blake, Peter. [1960] 1996. *The Master Builders: Le Corbusier, Mies van der Rohe, Frank Lloyd Wright.* New York: W. W. Norton.

Blau, Judith R. 1984. *Architects and Firms.* Cambridge, MA: MIT Press.

Bohigas, Oriol. 1973. *Reseña y catálogo de la arquitectura modernista.* Barcelona: Lumen.

———. 1998. *Modernidad en la arquitectura de la España republicana.* Barcelona: Tusquets.

Boltanski, Luc. 1982. *Les Cadres.* Paris: Editions de Minuit.

Bonet, Juan Manuel. 1999. *Diccionario de las vanguardias en España, 1907–1936.* Madrid: Alianza Editorial.

Bonet Correa, Antonio, Soledad Lorenzo Fornies, and Fátima Miranda Regojo. 1985. *La polémica ingenieros-arquitectos en España: Siglo XIX.* Madrid: Colegio de Ingenieros de Caminos, Canales y Puertos, Ediciones Turner.

Boudon, Philippe. 1972. *Lived-In Architecture: Le Corbusier's Pessac Revisited.* Cambridge, MA: MIT Press.

Bourdieu, Pierre. [1972] 1977. *Outline of a Theory of Practice*. Cambridge: Cambridge University Press.

———. 1984. *Distinction: A Social Critique of the Judgment of Taste*. Cambridge, MA: Harvard University Press.

———. 1996. *The Rules of Art: Genesis and Structure of the Literary Field*. Stanford, CA: Stanford University Press.

Bowler, Anne. 1991. "Politics as Art: Italian Futurism and Fascism." *Theory and Society* 20:763–94.

Bowlt, John E., ed. 1988. *Russian Art of the Avant Garde*. New York: Thames and Hudson.

Bozdoğan, Sibel. 2001. *Modernism and Nation Building: Turkish Architectural Culture in the Early Republic*. Seattle: University of Washington Press.

Brady, F. Neil. 1986. "Aesthetic Components of Management Ethics." *Academy of Management Review* 11 (2): 337–44.

Brain, David. 1989. "Discipline and Style: The École des Beaux-Arts and the Social Production of an American Architecture." *Theory and Society* 18:807–68.

———. 1994. "Cultural Production as 'Society in the Making': Architecture as an Exemplar of the Social Construction of Cultural Artifacts." In *The Sociology of Culture*, edited by Diana Crane, 191–220. Cambridge, MA: Blackwell.

Braverman, Harry. 1974. *Labor and Monopoly Capital*. New York: Monthly Review Press.

Brecht, Bertolt. [1925–28] 1979. "The Impact of the Cities." In *Poems, 1913–1956*, 105–64. New York: Routledge.

Brooks, H. Allen, ed. 1987. *Le Corbusier*. Princeton, NJ: Princeton University Press.

Bucci, Federico. 1993. *Albert Kahn: Architect of Ford*. New York: Princeton Architectural Press.

Buchanan, R. A. 1989. *The Engineers: A History of the Engineering Profession in Britain, 1750–1914*. London: Jessica Kingsley.

Bucher, Rue, and Anselm Strauss. 1961. "Professions in Process." *American Journal of Sociology* 66 (4) (January): 325–34.

Buddensieg, Tilmann. 1984. *Industriekultur: Peter Behrens and the AEG, 1907–1914*. Cambridge, MA: MIT Press.

Bugarini, Fabio. 1987. "Ingegneri, architetti, geometri: La lunga marcia delle professioni tecniche." In *Le libere professioni in Italia*, edited by Willem Tousijn, 305–35. Bologna: Mulino.

Bullrich, Francisco. 1963. *Arquitectura argentina contemporánea*. Buenos Aires: Nueva Visión.

———. 1969. *New Directions in Latin American Architecture*. New York: George Braziller.

Burian, Edward R. 1997. "The Architecture of Juan O'Gorman: Dichotomy and Drift." In *Modernity and the Architecture of Mexico*, edited by Edward R. Burian, 127–49. Austin: University of Texas Press.

Buselli, G., R. Finzi, and G. Predrocco. 1976. *Materiali per lo studio dell'organizzazione del lavoro durante il regime fascista*. Bologna: Cooperativa Libraria Universitaria Editrice.

Cafagna, Luciano. 1971. "The Industrial Revolution in Italy, 1830–1914." In *The Fontana Economic History of Europe*, vol. 4. London: Collins.

Callahan, Raymond E. 1962. *Education and the Cult of Efficiency*. Chicago: University of Chicago Press.

Campbell, Joan. 1978. *The German Werkbund*. Princeton, NJ: Princeton University Press.

Campbell, John L. 2004. *Institutional Change and Globalization*. Princeton, NJ: Princeton University Press.

Cardellach i Avilés, Félix. 1910. "La enseñanza de la construcción en las escuelas de ingenieros." *Anuario de la Universidad de Barcelona 1909 à 1910*: 229–346.

———. 1916. *Las formas artísticas en la arquitectura técnica*. Barcelona: Agustín Bosch.

Castronovo, Valerio. 1977. *Giovanni Agnelli: La Fiat dal 1899 al 1945*. Turin: Einaudi.

CEDODAL (Centro de Documentación de Arquitectura Latinoamericana). 1999. *Alberto Prebisch: Una Vanguardia con Tradición*. Buenos Aires: CEDODAL.

Cetto, Max L. 1961. *Modernist Architecture in Mexico. Arquitectura moderna en México*. New York: Praeger.

CGP (Centre Georges Pompidou). 1987. *Le Corbusier: Une Encyclopédie*. Paris: CGP.

Christophersen, Alejandro. [1927] 1999. "Un rato de charla con un futurista." *Revista de Arquitectura* 77 (May). Reprinted in *Alberto Prebisch: Una Vanguardia con Tradición*, 175–77. Buenos Aires: CEDODAL. Also available from http://www.almargen.com.ar/sitio/seccion/arquitectura/prebisch/disputa1.html.

CIAM (Congrès Internationaux d'Architecture Moderne). [1928a] 1979. *Vorbereitender internationaler Kongress für Neues Bauen. Die Wohnung für das Existenzminimum*. Nedeln, Liechtenstein: Kraus Reprint.

———. [1928b] 1971. "La Sarraz Declaration." In *Programs and Manifestoes on 20th-Century Architecture*, edited by Ulrich Conrads, 109–13. Cambridge, MA: MIT Press.

Ciucci, Giorgio. 1989. *Gli architetti e il fascismo*. Turin: Piccola Biblioteca Einaudi.

Cohen, Linda. 2002. "Bridging Two Streams of Corporate Office Design Research: A Comparison of Articles Appearing in Design/Behavior and Management Journals, 1980–2001." Working paper, Wharton School.

Collins, George R., and Carlos Flores. 1968. *Arturo Soria y la Ciudad Lineal*. Madrid: Revista de Occidente.

Collins, Peter. [1965] 1998. *Changing Ideals in Architecture*. Montreal: McGill-Queen's University Press.

Collins, Randall. 1998. *The Sociology of Philosophies: A Global Theory of Intellectual Change*. Cambridge, MA: Harvard University Press, Belknap Press.

Conrans, Ulrich, ed. 1970. *Programs and Manifestoes on 20th-Century Architecture*. Cambridge, MA: MIT Press.

Cooke, Catherine. 1995. *Russian Avant-Garde*. London: Academy.

Cooper, Jackie, ed. 1977. *Mackintosh Architecture: The Complete Buildings and Selected Projects*. London: Academy; New York: St. Martin's.

Costa, Lúcio. 1991. *Relatório do plano piloto de Brasília*. Brasília: Governo do Distrito Federal.

Crane, Diana. 1989. "Reward Systems in Avant-Garde Art: Social Networks and Stylistic Change." In *Art and Society: Readings in the Sociology of the Arts*, edited by Arnold W. Foster and Judith R. Blau, 261–72. Albany: State University of New York Press.

Crispiani, Alejandro. 1999. "Alejandro Christophersen y el desarrollo del eclecticismo en la Argentina." *Arquitectura en línea.* http://www.arquitectura.com/historia/protag/christoph/christoph.asp.

Curtis, William J. R. [1982] 1996. *Modern Architecture since 1900.* London: Phaidon Press.

Darr, Asaf. 2000. "Technical Labor in an Engineering Boutique: Interpretive Frameworks of Sales and R&D Engineers." *Work, Employment, and Society* 14 (2): 205–222.

Davis, Diane. 2004. "Wither the Public Sphere: Local, National and International Influences on the Planning of Downtown Mexico City, 1910–1950." *Space & Culture* 7 (2) (May): 193–222.

De Larrañaga, María Isabel, and Alberto Petrina. 1987. "Arquitectura de masas en la Argentina (1945–1955): Hacia la búsqueda de una expresión propia." *Anales del Instituto de Arte Americano e Investigaciones Estéticas* 25:107–15.

De Matteis, Federico. 2001. "Giuseppe Pagano, 1896–1945." http://www.phys.uniroma1.it/DOCS/LIB/Giuseppe_Pagano.html.

De Paula, Alberto S. J. 1984. "Kronfuss en la universidad y 'lo nacional' en el diseño arquitectónico." In *Documentos para una historia de la arquitectura argentina,* edited by Marina Waisman, 153–54. Buenos Aires: Ediciones Summa.

De Paula, Alberto S. J., and Raúl Arnaldo Gómez. 1984. "El Art Déco: Orígenes y proyecciones en nuestro país." In *Documentos para una historia de la arquitectura argentina,* edited by Marina Waisman, 163–66. Buenos Aires: Ediciones Summa.

Dean, James W., Jr., Edward Ottensmeyer, and Rafael Ramirez. 1997. "An Aesthetic Perspective on Organizations." In *Creating Tomorrow's Organizations,* edited by C. L. Cooper and S. E. Jackson, 419–37. New York: John Wiley and Sons.

Deckker, Zilah Quezado. 2001. *Brazil Built: The Architecture of the Modern Movement in Brazil.* London: Spon Press.

Demes, Georgette H. et al. 1993. "The Engineering Design Center of Carnegie Mellon University." *Proceedings of the IEEE* 81:10–24.

Devinat, Paul. 1927. *Scientific Management in Europe.* International Labour Office Studies and Reports, Series B, no. 17. Geneva: International Labour Office.

Diéguez Patao, Sofía. 1997. *La Generación del 25: Primera arquitectura moderna en Madrid.* Madrid: Cátedra.

DiMaggio, Paul J. 1979. "Review Essay: On Pierre Bourdieu." *American Journal of Sociology* 84 (6) (May): 1460–74.

———. 1987. "Classification in Art." *American Sociological Review* 52:440–55.

———. 1988. "Interest and Agency in Institutional Theory." In *Institutional Patterns and Organizations,* ed. L. G. Zucker, 3–22. Cambridge, MA: Ballinger.

———. 1991. "Constructing an Organizational Field as a Professional Project: U.S. Art Museums, 1920–1940." In *The New Institutionalism in Organizational Analysis,* edited by Walter W. Powell and Paul J. DiMaggio, 267–92. Chicago: University of Chicago Press.

Dobb, Maurice. 1966. *Soviet Economic Development since 1917.* London: Routledge and Kegan Paul.

Dorfman, Adolfo. 1995. "Taylorismo y Fordismo en la industria argentina de los '30 y '40." *Realidad Económica* 132 (May): 87–96.

Dos Passos, John. [1933] 1979. *The Big Money.* New York: New American Library.

Droste, Magdalena. 1990. *Bauhaus 1919–1933*. Cologne: Benedikt Taschen.

Durand, Jose Carlos. 1991. "Political Negotiation and the Renovation of Architecture: Le Corbusier in Brazil." *Actes de la Recherche en Sciences Sociales* 88 (June): 61–77.

Ebbinghaus, Angelika. 1975. "Taylor in Russland." *Autonomie* 1:3–15.

Eckstein, Hans, ed. 1958. *50 Jahre Deutscher Werkbund*. Frankfurt: Alfred Metzner.

Edwards, Richard. 1979. *Contested Terrain: The Transformation of the Workplace in the Twentieth Century*. New York: Basic Books.

Egbert, Donald Drew. 1980. *The Beaux-Arts Tradition in French Architecture*. Princeton, NJ: Princeton University Press.

Eggener, Keith L. 1999. "Towards an Organic Architecture in Mexico." In *Frank Lloyd Wright: Europe and Beyond*, edited by Anthony Alofsin, 166–83. Berkeley: University of California Press.

———. 2000. "Contrasting Images of Indentity in the Post-War Mexican Architecture of Luis Barragán and Juan O'Gorman." *Journal of Latin American Cultural Studies* 9 (1): 27–45.

Eliash, Humberto, and Eduardo San Martín. 1998. "La vivienda social y la construcción de la periferia urbana en América Latina." In *Arquitectura latinoamericana en el siglo XX*, edited by Ramón Gutiérrez, 53–64. Barcelona: Lunwerg Editores.

Erfurth, Helmut. 1985. *Hugo Junkers: Leben und Werk, 1859–1935*. Dessau: Stadtgeschichte Dessau.

Estivill i Pascual, Jordi, and Josep R. Tomàs i Llacuna. 1978. "Orientación profesional en Cataluña." *Cuadernos de Pedagogía* 4 (47) (November): 44–47.

Etlin, Richard A. 1991. *Modernism in Italian Architecture, 1890–1940*. Cambridge, MA: MIT Press.

Fairfield, John D. 1994. "The Scientific Management of Urban Space: Professional City Planning and the Legacy of Progressive Reform." *Journal of Urban History* 20:179–204.

Fernández Alba, Antonio, ed. 1975. *Ideología y enseñanza de la arquitectura en la España contemporánea*. Madrid: Túcar.

Fernández Ordoñez, José Antonio, and José Ramón Navarro Vera. 1999. *Eduarto Torroja: Ingeniero, Engineer*. Madrid: Ediciones Pronaos.

Ferraz, Geraldo. 1965. *Warchavchik e a introdução da nova arquitetura no Brasil: 1925 a 1940*. São Paulo: Museu de Arte de São Paulo.

Ficher, Sylvia, and Marlene Milan Acayaba. 1982. *Arquitetura moderna brasileira*. São Paulo: Projeto.

Fischer, Wend, ed. 1975. *Zwischen Kunst und Industrie: Der Deutsche Werkbund*. Munich: Staatliches Museum fur angewandte Kunst.

Flores, Carlos. 1989. *Arquitectura española contemporánea, I: 1880–1950*. Madrid: Aguilar.

Ford, Henry. 1926. "Henry Ford Expounds Mass Production." *New York Times*, September 19, sec. 10.

Forty, Adrian. 1986. "Taylorism and Modern Architecture." *Transactions/Royal Institute of British Architects* 5 (1): 73–81.

Frampton, Kenneth. [1980] 1992. *Modern Architecture: A Critical History*. London: Thames and Hudson.

———. 2001. *Le Corbusier*. New York: Thames & Hudson.

Fraser, Valerie. 2000. *Building the New World: Studies in the Modern Architecture of Latin America, 1930–1960*. London: Verso.

Freidson, Eliot. 1986. *Professional Powers: A Study of the Institutionalization of Formal Knowledge*. Chicago: University of Chicago Press.

Freixa, Jaume. 1997. *Josep Ll. Sert: Obras y proyectos / Works and Projects*. Barcelona: Gustavo Gili.

Freixa, Mireia. 1986. *El Modernismo en España*. Madrid: Cátedra.

———. 1996. *Lluís Muncunill (1868–1931), Arquitecte*. Barcelona: Lunwerg.

Frickel, Scott, and Neil Gross. 2005. "A General Theory of Scientific/Intellectual Movements." *American Sociological Review* 70 (April): 204–32.

Fromm, Erich. 1984. *The Working Class in Weimar Germany*. Cambridge, MA: Harvard University Press.

Gaber, Bernhard. 1966. *Die Entwicklung des Berufsstandes der freischaffenden Architekten*. Essen: Verlag Richard Bacht.

Gabetti, Roberto, and Paolo Marconi. 1968. *L'insegnamento dell' architettura nel sistema didattico franco-italiano 1789–1922*. Turin: Quaderni di Studio.

Galison, Peter. 1990. "Aufbau/Bauhaus: Logical Positivism and Architectural Modernism." *Critical Inquiry* 16 (Summer): 709–52.

Gantt, Henry L. 1911. *Work, Wages, and Profits: Their Influence on the Cost of Living*. New York: Engineering Magazine.

———. 1919. *Organizing for Work*. New York: Harcourt, Brace.

García Hernández, Miguel Ángel. 1997. "Mister Le Corbusier." In *Le Corbusier y España*, edited by Juan José Lahuerta, 39–82. Barcelona: Centre de Cultura Contemporània de Barcelona.

García Hernández, Ramón, and Jesús Calvo Barrios. 1981. *Arturo Soria: Un urbanismo olvidado*. Madrid: Junta Municipal del Distrito de Ciudad Lineal.

Gartman, David. 2000. "Why Modern Architecture Emerged in Europe, Not in America: The New Class and the Aesthetics of Technology." *Theory, Culture & Society* 17 (5): 75–96.

GATEPAC. 2001. "GATEPAC." http://members.es.tripod.de/basarte/gatepac.htm.

Gaudí, Antoni. [1878] 2002. "Ornamentación." In *Antoni Gaudí: Escritos y documentos*, edited by Laura Mercader, 41–72. Barcelona: El Acantilado.

———. [1878–83] 2002. "La construcción del Templo." In *Antoni Gaudí: Escritos y documentos*, edited by Laura Mercader, 127–31. Barcelona: El Acantilado.

———. [N.d.] 2002. "Conversaciones con Bergòs." In *Manuscritos, artículos, conversaciones y dibujos*, edited by Marcià Codinachs, 85–128. Murcia: Colegio Oficial de Aparejadores y Arquitectos Técnicos de la Región de Murcia.

Gazaneo, Jorge O., and Mabel M. Scarone. 1984. "Arquitectura de la revolución industrial en la Argentina." In *Documentos para una historia de la arquitectura argentina*, edited by Marina Waisman, 113–16. Buenos Aires: Ediciones Summa.

Gerschenkron, Alexander. 1962. *Economic Backwardness in Historical Perspective*. Cambridge, MA: Harvard University Press.

Giedion, Siegfried. [1941] 1982. *Space, Time, and Architecture: The Growth of a New Tradition*. Cambridge, MA: Harvard University Press.

———. [1948] 1969. *Mechanization Takes Command*. New York: W. W. Norton.

Gilbreth, Frank B. 1909. *Bricklaying System*. New York: Myron C. Clark.

————. 1911. *Motion Study: A Method for Increasing the Efficiency of the Workman.* With an introduction by Robert Thurston Kent. New York: D. Van Nostrand.

————. 1912. *Primer of Scientific Management.* With an introduction by Louis D. Brandeis. New York: D. Van Nostrand.

Gilbreth, Frank B., and Lillian M. Gilbreth. 1917. *Applied Motion Study: A Collection of Papers on the Efficient Method to Industrial Preparedness.* New York: Sturgis & Walton.

Giner de los Ríos, Bernardo. [1952] 1980. *50 años de arquitectura española II.* Madrid: Adir Editores.

Ginzburg, Moisei. 1982. *Style and Epoch.* Cambridge, MA: MIT Press.

Gispen, Kees. 1989. *New Profession, Old Order: Engineers and German Society, 1815–1914.* Cambridge: Cambridge University Press.

————. 1990. "Engineers in Wilhelmian Germany: Professionalization, Deprofessionalization, and the Development of Nonacademic Technical Education." In *German Professions, 1800–1950,* edited by Geoffrey Cocks and Konrad H. Jarausch, 104–22. New York: Oxford University Press.

Glover, Ian A., and Michael P. Kelly. 1987. *Engineers in Britain: A Sociological Study of the Engineering Dimension.* London: Allen & Unwin.

Golomstock, Igor. 1990. *Totalitarian Art in the Soviet Union, the Third Reich, Fascist Italy and the People's Republic of China.* New York: IconEditions / HarperCollins.

Gomá Lanzón, Javier. 2003. *Imitación y experiencia.* Valencia, Spain: Pre-Textos.

Goodwin, Philip L. 1943. *Brazil Builds: Architecture New and Old, 1652–1942.* New York: Museum of Modern Art.

Gorelik, Adrián. 1987. "La arquitectura de YPF, 1934–1943: Notas para una interpretación de las relaciones entre Estado, modernidad e identidad en la arquitectura argentina de los años 30." *Anales del Instituto de Arte Americano e Investigaciones Estéticas* 25:97–106.

Gray, Camilla. 1986. *The Russian Experiment in Art, 1863–1922.* London: Thames and Hudson.

Gropius, Walter. [1926] 1971. "Principles of Bauhaus Production [Dessau]." In *Programs and Manifestoes on 20th-Century Architecture,* edited by Ulrich Conrads, 95–97. Cambridge, MA: MIT Press.

————. 1927. "Erfolge der Baubetriebsorganisation in Amerika." Bauhaus-Archiv Berlin, Schrank 34, Inv. Nr. 9153/1–12.

————. [1936] 1965. *The New Architecture and the Bauhaus.* London: Faber and Faber.

Güell, Carmen. 2001. *Gaudí y el Conde de Güell: El artista y el mecenas.* Barcelona: Editorial Martínez Roca.

Guggenheim Museum. 1992. *The Greate Utopia: The Russian and Soviet Avant-Garde, 1915–1932.* New York: Guggenheim Museum.

Guillén, Mauro F. 1994. *Models of Management: Work, Authority, and Organization in a Comparative Perspective.* Chicago: University of Chicago Press.

————. 1996. "Arte, Cultura y Organización: La Influencia de Ortega y Gasset en la Élite Empresarial Española." *Revista Española de Investigaciones Sociológicas* 74 (April–June): 115–26.

————. 1997. "Scientific Management's Lost Aesthetic: Architecture, Organization, and the Taylorized Beauty of the Mechanical." *Administrative Science Quarterly* 42 (4) (December): 682–715.

————. 2004. "Modernism without Modernity: The Rise of Modernist Architecture in Mexico, Brazil and Argentina, 1890–1940." *Latin American Research Review* 39 (2) (June): 6–34.

Gutheim, Frederick. 1949. "The Philadelphia Saving Fund Society Building: A Re-Appraisal." *Architectural Record* (October).

Gutiérrez, Ramón. 1984a. "Una nueva propuesta: El renacimiento colonial." In *Documentos para una historia de la arquitectura argentina*, edited by Marina Waisman, 151–54. Buenos Aires: Ediciones Summa.

————. 1984b. "La arquitectura imperial." In *Documentos para una historia de la arquitectura argentina*, edited by Marina Waisman, 205–6. Buenos Aires: Ediciones Summa.

————. 1998a. "Arquitectura latinoamericana: Haciendo camino al andar." In *Arquitectura latinoamericana en el siglo XX*, edited by Ramón Gutiérrez, 17–39. Barcelona: Lunwerg Editores.

————. 1998b. "Diccionario enciclopédico." In *Arquitectura latinoamericana en el siglo XX*, edited by Ramón Gutiérrez, 187–440. Barcelona: Lunwerg Editores.

Gutiérrez, Ramón, and Graciela M. Viñuales. 1998. "Grances Voces." In *Arquitectura latinoamericana en el siglo XX*, edited by Ramón Gutiérrez, 95–185. Barcelona: Lunwerg Editores.

Guzzo Decca, Maria Auxiliadora. 1987. *A vida fora fábricas: Cotidiano operário em São Paulo, 1920–1934*. Rio de Janeiro: Paz e Terra.

Haber, Samuel. 1964. *Efficiency and Uplift: Scientific Management in the Progressive Era, 1890–1920*. Chicago: University of Chicago Press.

Hamlin, A.D.F. 1908. "The Influence of the Ecole des Beaux-Arts on Our Architectural Education." *Architectural Record* 23 (4) (April): 241–47.

Harris, Neil. 1996. "Architecture and the Business Corporation." In *The American Corporation Today*, edited by Carl Kays, 436–86. New York: Oxford University Press.

Hays, K. Michael. 1992. *Modernism and the Posthumanist Subject: The Architecture of Hannes Meyer and Ludwig Hilberseimer*. Cambridge, MA: MIT Press.

Herbert, Gilbert. 1984. *The Dream of the Factory-Made House: Walter Gropius and Konrad Wachsmann*. Cambridge, MA: MIT Press.

Herf, Jeffrey. 1984. *Reactionary Modernism: Technology, Culture, and Politics in Weimar and the Third Reich*. Cambridge: Cambridge University Press.

Hilberseimer, Ludwig. 1927. *Groszstadt Architektur*. Stuttgart: Verlag Julius Hoffmann.

Hinrichs, Peter, and Lothar Peter. 1976. *Industrieller Friede? Arbeitswissenschaft, Rationalisierung und Arbeiterbewegung in der Weimarer Republik*. Cologne: Pahl-Rugenstein.

Hitchcock, Henry-Russell. [1958] 1971. *Architecture: Nineteenth and Twentieth Centuries*. Harmondsworth, UK: Penguin.

Hitchcock, Henry-Russell, and Philip Johnson. [1932] 1995. *The International Style*. New York: W. W. Norton.

Hochman, Elaine S. 1989. *Architects of Fortune: Mies van der Rohe and the Third Reich*. New York: Weidenfeld & Nicolson.

Hoff, Andreas. 1978. "Gewerkschaften und Rationalisierung: Ein Vergleich gewerkschaftlicher Argumentationsmuster Heute und vor fünfzig Jahren." *Mehrwert* 15–16:167–208.

Holston, James. 1989. *The Modernist City: An Anthropological Critique of Brasília.* Chicago: University of Chicago Press.

Hounshell, David A. 1984. *From the American System to Mass Production 1800–1932: The Development of Manufacturing Technology in the United States.* Baltimore: Johns Hopkins University Press.

Huxley, Aldous. [1932] 1989. *Brave New World.* New York: Harper & Row.

Isaacs, Reginald. 1991. *Gropius: An Illustrated Biography of the Creator of the Bauhaus.* Boston: Little, Brown.

Isac, Ángel. 1997. " 'Eso no es arquitectura': Le Corbusier y la crítica adversa en España, 1923–1935." In *Le Corbusier y España*, edited by Juan José Lahuerta, 189–214. Barcelona: Centre de Cultura Contemporània de Barcelona.

Jablonowski, Ulla. 1983. " 'Wo berühren sich die Schaffensgebiete des Technikers und Künstlers?' (Walter Gropius). Beziehungen zwischen dem Dessauer Bauhaus und den Werken des Junkerskonzerns." *Dessauer Kalender*, 13–30.

James, Daniel. 1981. "Rationalisation and Working Class Response: The Context and Limits of Factory Floor Activity in Argentina." *Journal of Latin American Studies* 13 (2) (November): 375–402.

Jarausch, Konrad. 1990. *The Unfree Professions.* New York: Cambridge University Press.

Jardí, Enric. 1975. *Puig i Cadafalch: Arquitecte, polític i historiador de l'art.* Mataró: Caixa d'Estalvis Laietana.

Jencks, Charles. 1973. *Modern Movements in Architecture.* Garden City, NY: Anchor Books.

Jordy, William H. 1986. *The Impact of European Modernism in the Mid-Twentieth Century.* New York: Oxford University Press.

Jullian, René. 1989. *Tony Garnier: Constructeur et Utopiste.* Paris: Philippe Sers.

Junghanns, Kurt. 1982. *Der Deutsche Werkbund: Sein erstes Jahrzehnt.* Berlin: Henschelverlag.

Kabat, Marina. 1999. "El ojo del amo: Primeras inquietudes en torno al taylorismo en la Argentina, 1920–1930." *Estudios del Trabajo* 17:113–24.

Kadushin, Charles. 1976. "Networks and Circles in the Production of Culture." *American Behavioral Scientist* 19:769–84.

Kaes, Anton, Martin Jay, and Edward Dimendberg, eds. 1994. *The Weimar Republic Sourcebook.* Berkeley: University of California Press.

Kahn, Selirn O. 1982. *Pioneers of Soviet Architecture.* New York: Rizzoli.

Kaye, Barrington. 1960. *The Development of the Architectural Profession in Britain.* London: Allen & Unwin.

Kern, Stephen. 1983. *The Culture of Time and Space 1880–1918.* Cambridge, MA: Harvard University Press.

Kilduff, Martin. 1993. "Deconstructing Organizations." *Academy of Management Review* 18:13–31.

Kirsch, Karin. [1927] 1989. *The Weissenhofsiedlung: Experimental Housing Built for the Deutscher Werkbund.* Stuttgart. Repr., New York: Rizzoli.

Kocka, Jürgen. 1969. "Industrielles management: Konzeptionen und modelle in Deutschland vor 1914." *Vierteljahrschrift für Sozial- und Wirtschaftsgeschichte* 56 (3) (October): 332–72.

Kopp, Anatole. 1985. *Constructivist Architecture in the USSR.* New York: St. Martin's.

Krause, Elliott A. 1996. *Death of the Guilds: Professions, States, and the Advance of Capitalism, 1930 to the Present*. New Haven, CT: Yale University Press.

Lahuerta, Juan José. 1997. "Federico García Lorca, Salvador Dalí y *L'Esprit Nouveau*." In *Le Corbusier y España*, edited by Juan José Lahuerta, 23–37. Barcelona: Centre de Cultura Contemporània de Barcelona.

Lampugnani, Vittorio Magnago. [1964] 1986. *Encyclopedia of 20th-Century Architecture*. New York: Harry N. Abrams.

Lane, Barbara Miller. 1985. *Architecture and Politics in Germany, 1918–1945*. Cambridge, MA: Harvard University Press.

Larson, Magali Sarfatti. 1972–73. "Notes on Technocracy: Some Problems of Theory, Ideology and Power." *Berkeley Journal of Sociology* 17:1–34.

———. 1977. *The Rise of Professionalism*. Berkeley: University of California Press.

———. 1993. *Behind the Postmodern Facade: Architectural Change in Late Twentieth-Century America*. Berkeley: University of California Press.

Le Corbusier (Charles Édouard Jeanneret). [1923] 1986. *Towards a New Architecture*. New York: Dover

———. [1924] 1987. *The City of To-Morrow and Its Planning*. New York: Dover.

Le Corbusier, and Jeanneret, Pierre. [1926] 1971. "Five Points towards a New Architecture." In *Programs and Manifestoes on 20th-Century Architecture*, edited by Ulrich Conrads, 99–101. Cambridge, MA: MIT Press.

———. [1935] 1967. *The Radiant City*. New York: Orion Press.

Lethaby, W. R. 1922. *Form in Civilization: Collected Papers in Art & Labour*. London: Oxford University Press.

Levine, A. L. 1967. *Industrial Retardation in Britain 1880–1914*. New York: Basic.

Lewchuk, Wayne A. 1984. "The Role of the British Government in the Spread of Scientific Management and Fordism in the Interwar Years." *Journal of Economic History* 44 (2) (June): 355–61.

Lieberstein, Samuel. 1975 "Technology, Work, and Sociology in the USSR: The NOT Movement." *Technology and Culture* 16 (1) (January): 48–66.

Liernur, Jorge Francisco. 2000. *Arquitectura en la Argentina del siglo XX: La construcción de la modernidad*. Buenos Aires: Fondo Nacional de las Artes.

Lindinger, Herbert, ed. 1991. *Ulm Design*. Cambridge, MA: MIT Press.

Lipstadt, Hélène. 1988. "The Building and the Book in César Daly's *Revue Générale de l'Architecture*." In *ArchitectureProduction*, edited by Beatriz Colomina, 25–55. Princeton, NJ: Princeton Architectural Press.

Lipstadt, Hélène, and Harvey Mendelsohn. 1980. *Architectes et Ingenieur dans la Presse: Polemique, Debat, Conflit*. Paris: CORDA-IERAU.

Lissitzky-Küppers, Sophie, ed. 1967. *El Lissitzky*. London: Thames & Hudson.

Littler, Craig R. 1982. *The Development of the Labour Process in Capitalist Societies: A Comparative Study of the Transformation of Work Organization in Britain, Japan, and the USA*. London: Heinemann.

Lodder, Christina. 1983. *Russian Constructivism*. New Haven, CT: Yale University Press.

———. 1984. "Constructivism and Productivism in the 1920s." In *Art into Life: Russian Constructivism 1914–1932*, edited by Richard Andrews and Milena Kalinovska, 99–167. New York: Rizzoli.

López Otero, M. 1951. "Cincuenta años de enseñanza." *Revista Nacional de Arquitectura* 11:9–16.

López Rangel, Rafael. 1986. *Diego Rivera y la arquitectura mexicana*. Mexico City: Dirección General de Publicaciones y Medios.

Lorey, David E. 1990. "The Development of Engineering Expertise for Social and Economic Modernization in Mexico since 1929." In *Society & Economy in Mexico*, edited by James W. Wilkie, 71–102. Los Angeles: UCLA Latin American Center Publications.

Ludwig, Armin K. 1980. *Brasilia's First Decade: A Study of its Urban Morphology and Urban Support Systems*. Amherst: International Area Studies Programs, University of Massachusetts at Amherst.

Luna Arroyo, Antonio. 1973. *Juan O'Gorman: Autobiografía, antología, juicios críticos y documentación exhaustiva sobre su obra*. Mexico City: Cuadernos Populares de Pintura Mexicana Moderna.

Lyttelton, Adrian. 1976. "Italian Fascism." In *Fascism: A Reader's Guide*, edited by Walter Laqueur, 125–50. Berkeley: University of California Press.

MacDuffie, John Paul. 1991. "Beyond Mass Production." Ph.D. diss. MIT Sloan School of Management.

Mackay, David. 1989. *Modern Arquitecture in Barcelona (1854–1939)*. New York: Rizzoli.

Maddison, Angus. 1995. *Monitoring the World Economy 1820–1992*. Paris: OECD.

Maier, Charles S. 1970. "Between Taylorism and Technocracy: European Ideologies and the Vision of Industrial Productivity in the 1920s." *Journal of Contemporary History* 5 (2): 27–61.

March, Lionel. 1981. "The Aesthetic State." *Design*, September, 37.

Marinetti, F. T. [1909] 1973. "The Founding and Manifesto of Futurism." In *Futurist Manifestos*, edited by Umbro Apollonio, 19–24. Boston: MFA Publications.

Markert, Werner, ed. 1965. *Sowjetunion: Das Wirtschaftssystem*. Cologne: Böhlau.

Martin, Reinhold. 2003. *The Organizational Complex: Architecture, Media, and Corporate Space*. Cambridge, MA: MIT Press.

Martin, Sylvie. 2001. "The École Nationale des Arts Décoratifs in Paris: Architecture and the Applied Arts between the World Wars." *Studies in Decorative Arts* (Spring–Summer): 77–104.

Marzá, Fernando. 1997. "Visita a la Casa Milà, 'La Pedrera': Gaudí y el movimiento moderno." In *Le Corbusier y España*, edited by Juan José Lahuerta, 215–20. Barcelona: Centre de Cultura Contemporània de Barcelona.

Maure Rubio, Miguel Angel. 1991. *La Ciudad Lineal de Arturo Soria*. Madrid: Colegio Oficial de Arquitectos de Madrid.

May, Bridget A. 1990. "Progressivism and the Colonial Revival." *Winterthur Portfolio* 26 (Summer–Autumn): 107–22.

McAdam, Doug, John D. McCarthy, and Mayer N. Zald. 1996. Introduction to *Comparative Perspectives on Social Movements*, edited by Doug McAdam, John D. McCarthy and Mayer N. Zald, 1–20. Cambridge: Cambridge University Press.

McClelland, Charles E. 1991. *The German Experience of Professionalization: Modern Learned Professions and Their Organizations from Early Nineteenth Century to the Hitler Era*. Cambridge: Cambridge University Press.

McLeod, Mary. 1983. "Architecture or Revolution: Taylorism, Technocracy, and Social Change." *Art Journal* 43 (2): 132–47.

————. 1985. "Urbanism and Utopia: Le Corbusier from Regional Syndicalism to Vichy." Ph.D. diss. Princeton University.

Melani, A. 1890. "Architectural Education in Italy." *The American Architect and Building News* 28 (750) (May 10): 86–88.

Méndez-Vigatá, Antonio E. 1997. "Politics and Architectural Language: Post-Revolutionary Regimes in Mexico and their Influence on Mexican Public Architecture, 1920–1952." In *Modernity and the Architecture of Mexico*, edited by Edward R. Burian, 61–89. Austin: University of Texas Press.

Merkle, Judith A. 1980. *Management and Ideology: The Legacy of the International Scientific Management Movement.* Berkeley: University of California Press.

Merton, Robert K. 1968. *Social Theory and Social Structure.* Glencoe, IL: Free Press.

Meyer, David S., and Suzanne Staggenborg. 1996. "Movements, Countermovements, and the Structure of Political Opportunity." *American Journal of Sociology* 101 (6) (May): 1628–60.

Meyer, Jean. 1991. "Revolution and Reconstruction in the 1920s." In *Mexico since Independence*, edited by Leslie Bethell, 125–200. Cambridge: Cambridge University Press.

Midant, Jean-Paul, ed. 1996. *Dictionnaire de l'architecture du XXe siècle.* Paris: Institut Français d'Architecture.

Middleton, Robin, ed. 1982. *The Beaux-Arts and Nineteenth-Century French Architecture.* Cambridge, MA: MIT Press.

Mies van der Rohe, Ludwig. [1923] 1971. "Working Theses." In *Programs and Manifestoes on 20th-Century Architecture*, edited by Ulrich Conrads, 74–75. Cambridge, MA: MIT Press.

————. [1924] 1971. "Industrialized Building." In *Programs and Manifestoes on 20th-Century Architecture*, edited by Ulrich Conrads, 81–82. Cambridge, MA: MIT Press.

Mijares Bracho, Carlos G. 1997. "The Architecture of Carlos Obregón Santacilia." In *Modernity and the Architecture of Mexicco*, edited by Edward R. Burian, 151–61. Austin: University of Texas Press.

Milward, Alan S. 1976. "Fascism and the Economy." In *Fascism: A Reader's Guide*, edited by Walter Laqueur, 379–412. Berkeley: University of California Press.

Minesso, Michela. 1995. "The Engineering Profession 1802–1923." In *Society and the Professions in Italy, 1860–1914*, edited by Maria Malatesta, 175–220. New York: Cambridge University Press.

Minnaert, Jean-Baptiste, ed. 1994. *The Architectural Drawings of Henri Sauvage.* New York: Garland Architectural Archives.

Mitchell, B. R. 1980. *European Historical Statistics 1750–1975.* New York: Facts On File.

Monteys, Xavier. 1997. "Le Corbusier en España: Los viajes por Levante y Mallorca." In *Le Corbusier y España*, edited by Juan José Lahuerta, 101–7. Barcelona: Centre de Cultura Contemporània de Barcelona.

Montolíu, Cipriano. [1915] 1916. *El sistema de Taylor y su crítica.* Barcelona: Casa Editorial Estudio.

Moore, Richard A. 1977. "Academic *Dessin* Theory in France after the Reorganization of 1863." *Society of Architectural Historians Journal* 36 (3) (October): 145–74.

Morgan, Gareth. 1986. *Images of Organization.* Newbury Park, CA: Sage.

Morris, William. [1888] 1902. "The Revival of Architecture." In *Architecture, Industry, and Wealth: Collected Papers*, 198–213. New York: Longmans, Green.

Mumford, Eric. 2000. *The CIAM Discourse on Urbanism, 1928–1960*. Cambridge, MA: MIT Press.

Mumford, Lewis. 1963. *Technics and Civilization*. New York: Harcourt Brace Jovanovich.

Münsterberg, Hugo. 1913. *Psychology and Industrial Efficiency*. Boston: Houghton Mifflin.

Muriel, Emanuel, ed. [1980] 1994. *Contemporary Architects*. New York: St. James' Press.

Muthesius, Hermann. [1914] 1971. "Werkbund Theses." In *Programs and Manifestoes on 20th-Century Architecture*, edited by Ulrich Conrads, 28–29. Cambridge, MA: MIT Press.

Myers, I. E. 1952. *Arquitectura Moderna Mexicana. Mexico's Modern Architecture*. New York: Architectural Book Publishing.

Nelson, Daniel. 1980. *Frederick W. Taylor and the Rise of Scientific Management*. Madison: University of Wisconsin Press.

Nerdinger, Winfried. 1985. "Walter Gropius—From Americanism to the New World." In *Walter Gropius*, edited by Winfried Nerdinger, 4–28. Berlin: Gebrüder Mann Verlag.

Neumann, Eckhard. 1993. *Bauhaus and Bauhaus People*. New York: Van Nostrand Reinhold.

NGBK, ed. 1977. *Wem gehört die Welt. Kunst und Gesellschaft in der Weimarer Republik*. Berlin: Neue Gesellschaft für Bildende Kunst.

Niemeyer, Oscar. 2000. *The Curves of Time: The Memoirs of Oscar Niemeyer*. London: Phaidon.

Noelle Merles, Louise. 1997. "The Arcthitecture and Urbanism of Mario Pani: Creativity and Compromise." In *Modernity and the Architecture of Mexico*, edited by Edward R. Burian, 177–89. Austin: University of Texas Press.

Nolan, Mary. 1994. *Visions of Modernity: American Business and the Modernization of Germany*. New York: Oxford University Press.

Olivetti, Adriano. [1928] 1976. "L'Organizzazione in una fabbrica italiana de macchine per scrivere." *L'Organizzazione Scientifica del Lavoro* 10:616–28. Reprinted in *Materiali per lo studio dell'organizzazione del lavoro durante il regime fascista*, edited by G. Buselli, R. Finzi, and G. Predrocco, 119–31. Bologna: Cooperativa Libraria Universitaria Editrice.

Oller i Foixench, Joan Manel, and M. Àngels Rodulfo i Giménez, eds. 2002. *El modernismo en Terrassa*. Barcelona: Lunwerg.

Ortega y Gasset, José. [1954] 1983. "Una vista sobre la situación del gerente o 'manager' en la sociedad actual." In *El "manager" en la sociedad actual*. With an introduction by Julián Marías. Madrid: Asociación para el Progreso de la Dirección.

Ortiz, Federico F. 1984. "Resumen de la arquitectura argentina desde 1925 hasta 1950." In *Documentos para una historia de la arquitectura argentina*, edited by Marina Waisman, 191–94. Buenos Aires: Ediciones Summa.

Ortiz, Federico F., and Ramón Gutiérrez. 1973. *La arquitectura en la Argentina, 1930–1970*. Special issue of *Hogar y Arquitectura*, no. 103.

References

Ortiz, Federico F., Juan C. Mantero, Ramón Gutiérrez, and Abelardo Levaggi. 1968. *La arquitectura del liberlismo en la Argentina*. Buenos Aires: Editorial Sudamericana.

Orwell, George. [1946] 1968. "James Burnham and the Managerial Revolution." In *The Collected Essays, Journalism and Letters of George Orwell*, vol. 4, *In Front of Your Nose, 1945–1950*, 160–81. London: Secker & Warburg.

———. 1949. *Nineteen Eighty-Four*. London: Secker & Warburg.

Padovan, Richard. 2002. *Towards Universality: Le Corbusier, Mies, and De Stijl*. New York: Routledge.

Parkins, Maurice Frank. 1953. *City Planning in Soviet Russia*. Chicago: University of Chicago Press.

Paz, Octavio. 1961. *The Labyrinth of Solitude*. New York: Grove Press.

———. [1987] 1993. *Essays on Mexican Art*. New York: Harcourt Brace.

Pedrocco, G. 1976. "Introduzione: L'Organizzazione Scientifica del Lavoro in Italia dal Decollo Industriale all Seconda Guerra Mondiale." In *Materiali per lo studio dell'organizzazione del lavoro durante il regime fascista*, edited by G. Buselli, R. Finzi, and G. Predrocco, 5–16. Bologna: Cooperativa Libraria Universitaria Editrice.

Perrow, Charles. 1986. *Complex Organizations*. New York: Random House.

———. 1991. "A Society of Organizations." *Theory and Society* 20 (6) (December): 725–62.

Pevsner, Nikolaus. [1936] 1960. *Pioneers of Modern Design: From William Morris to Walter Gropius*. Harmondsworth, UK: Penguin.

———. 1937. *An Enquiry into Industrial Art in England*. Cambridge: Cambridge University Press.

Pfammatter, Ulrich. 2000. *The Making of the Modern Architect and Engineer*. Berlin: Birkhäuser.

Pfeffer, Jeffrey. 1997. *New Directions in Organization Theory*. New York: Oxford University Press.

Pinchon, Jean-François. 1990. *Rob. Mallet-Stevens: Architecture, Furniture, Interior Design*. Cambridge, MA: MIT Press.

Piore, Michael J., and Charles F. Sabel. 1984. *The Second Industrial Divide*. New York: Basic Books.

Pizza, Antonio. 1997. *Guía de la arquitectura del siglo XX: España*. Milan: Electa.

Placzek, Adolf K., ed. 1982. *The Macmillan Encyclopedia of Architects*. New York: Free Press.

Poggioli, Renato. 1968. *The Theory of the Avant-Garde*. Cambridge, MA: Harvard University Press, Belknap Press.

Pommer, Richard, David Spaeth, and Kevin Harrington. 1988. *In the Shadow of Mies: Ludwig Hilberseimer, Architect, Educator, and Urban Planner*. New York: Art Institute of Chicago and Rizzoli.

Powers, Alan. 1983. "Architectural Education and the Arts and Crafts Movement in Britain." *Architectural Education* 3:42–70.

———. 1993. "Arts and Crafts to Monumental Classic: The Institutionalization of Architectural Education 1900 to 1914." In *The Education of the Architect*, edited by Neil Bingham, 34–38. London: Society of Architectural Historians of Great Britain.

Pozzetto, Marco. *La Fiat-Lingotto: Un'architettura torinese d'avanguardia*. Turin: Centro Studi Piemontesi.

Prebisch, Alberto. 1927. "Carta abierta a Alejandro Christophersen." *Martín Fierro* (May). Reprinted in *Alberto Prebisch: Una Vanguardia con Tradición*, 178–79. Buenos Aires: CEDODAL. Also available from http://www.almargen.com.ar/sitio/seccion/arquitectura/prebisch/disputa2.html.

Rabinbach, Anson. 1990. *The Human Motor: Energy, Fatigue, and the Origins of Modernity*. New York: Basic.

Rao, Hayagreeva, Phillipe Monin, and Rodolphe Durand. 2003. "Institutional Change in Toque Ville: Nouvelle Cuisine as an Identity Movement in French Gastronomy." *American Journal of Sociology* 108 (4): 795–843.

Read, Herbert. 1954. *Art and Industry*. New York: Horizon.

Reeves, Terrie C., W. Jack Duncan, and Peter M. Ginter. 2001. "Motion Study in Management and the Arts: A Historical Example." *Journal of Management Inquiry* 10 (2) (June): 137–49.

RFG (Reichsforschunggesellschaft). 1929. *Technische Tagung in Berlin. 15. Bis 17. April*. Berlin: RFG.

RFGWBW (Reichsforschunggesellschaft für Wirtschaftlichkeit im Bau- und Wohnungswesen). 1929. *Bericht über die Versuchssiedlung in Dessau*. Berlin: RFG-WBW.

ROC. 1932. "Instituto de Organisação Racional do Trabalho de São Paulo." *Revista de Organisação Científica* 1 (1) (January): 35–38.

Rochon, Thomas R. 1998. *Culture Moves: Ideas, Activism, and Changing Values*. Princeton, NJ: Princeton University Press.

Rodrigo Alharilla, Martín. 2000. "Eusebio Güell Bacigalupi, 1846–1918." In *Los 100 empresarios españoles del siglo XX*, edited by Eugenio Torres, 48–52. Madrid: LID Editorial Empresarial.

Rodríguez Leirado, Eduardo. 2001. "Alberto Prebisch y la modernidad argentina." Buenos Aires: Sitio al Margen. http://www.almargen.com.ar/sitio/seccion/arquitectura/prebisch/.

Ruskin, John. [1849] 1891. *The Seven Lamps of Architecture*. New York: John Wiley and Sons.

Rybczynski, Witold. 2004. "The Triumph of a Distinguished Failure." *New York Review of Books*, October 21, 30–32.

Saenz Leme, Marisa. 1978. *A ideologia dos industriais brasileiros, 1919–1945*. Petrópolis: Vozes.

Sant'Elia, Antonio. [1914] 1973. "Manifesto of Futurist Architecture." In *Futurist Manifestos*, edited by Umbro Apollonio, 160–72. Boston: MFA Publications.

Sapelli, Giulio. 1976. "Appunti per una storia dell'organizzazione scientifica del lavoro in Italia." *Quaderni di Sociologia* 25 (April–September): 154–71.

———. 1978. *Organizzazione lavoro e innovazione industriale nell'Italia tra le due guerre*. Turin: Rosenberg & Sellier.

Savi, Vittorio. 1990. *Figini e Pollini: Architetture 1927–1989*. Milan: Electa.

Scheidig, Walther. [1966] 1967. *Weimar Crafts of the Bauhaus, 1919–1924: An Early Experiment in Industrial Design*. New York: Reinhold.

Schein, Edgar H. 1988. *Organizational Psychology*. Englewood Cliffs, NJ: Prentice-Hall.

Schulze, Franz, ed. 1992. *The Mies van der Rohe Archive*. New York: Garland Architectural Archives.

Schumacher, Thomas. 1992. *Giuseppe Terragni 1904–1943*. Milan: Electa.

Scott, W. Richard. 1995a. *Institutions and Organizations*. Thousand Oaks, CA: Sage.

———. 1995b. *Organizations*. Englewood Cliffs, NJ: Prentice-Hall.

Scully, Vincent. [1961] 1974. *Modern Architecture: The Architecture of Democracy*. New York: George Braziller.

Selle, Gert. 1994. *Geschichte des Design in Deutschland*. Frankfurt: Campus Verlag.

Senkevitch, Anatole, Jr. 1983. "Aspects of Spatial Form and Perceptual Psychology in the Doctrine of the Rationalist Movement in Soviet Architecture during the 1920s." In *VIA 6: Architecture and Visual Perception*, edited by Alice Gray Read and Peter C. Doo, 78–115. Cambridge, MA: MIT Press.

———. 1990. "The Sources and Ideals of Constructivism in Soviet Architecture." In *Art into Life: Russian Constructivism, 1914–1932*, edited by Richard Andrews and Milena Kalinovska, 169–211. New York: Rizzoli.

Sharp, Dennis, ed. [1967] 1981. *Sources of Modern Architecture: A Critical Bibliography*. London: Granada.

Shenhav, Yehouda. 1995. "From Chaos to Systems: The Engineering Foundations of Organization Theory, 1880–1930." *Administrative Science Quarterly* 40:557–85.

———. 1999. *Manufacturing Rationality: The Engineering Foundations of the Managerial Revolution*. Oxford: Oxford University Press.

Simon, Herbert A. 1981. *The Sciences of the Artificial*. Cambridge, MA: MIT Press.

Skidmore, Thomas E., and Peter H. Smith. 1989. "Brazil: Development For Whom?" In *Modern Latin America*, edited by Thomas E. Skidmore and Peter H. Smith, 140–80. New York: Oxford University Press.

Smith, Clive Bamford. 1967. *Builders in the Sun: Five Mexican Architects*. New York: Architectural Book Publishing.

Smith, Terry. 1993. *Making the Modern: Industry, Art, and Design in America*. Chicago: University of Chicago Press.

Sobrino, Julián. 1996. *Arquitetura industrial en España, 1830–1990*. Madrid: Cátedra.

Solà-Morales, Ignasi de. 1990. " 'Orderly, monumental city' . . . The Architecture of Josep Puig i Cadafalch in the Age of the Mancomunitat." In *J. Puig i Cadafalch: L'arcuitectura entre la casa i la ciutat*, 36–63. Barcelona: Fundació Caixa de Pensions.

———. 1992. *Arquitectura modernista: Fin de siglo en Barcelona*. Barcelona: Gustavo Gili.

Sonderéguer, Pedro Conrado. 1986. *Arquitectura y modernidad en la Argentina*. Buenos Aires: Centro de Estudios de la Sociedad Central de Arquitectos.

Soria y Mata, Arturo. 1894. *Conferencia dada en el Ateneo Científico y Literario de Madrid*. Madrid: Sucesores de Rivadeneyra.

———. 1907. *Buen Negocio*. Madrid: Compañía Madrileña de Urbanización.

Spiers, R. Phené. 1883–84. "The French Diplôme d'architecte and the German System of Architectural Education." In *Transactions/Royal Institute of British Architects*, 121–32. London: The Institute.

Starr, S. Frederick. 1976. "OSA: The Union of Contemporary Architects." In *Russian Modernism: Culture and the Avant-Garde, 1900–1930*, edited by George Gibian and H. W. Tjalsma, 188–208. Ithaca, NY: Cornell University Press.

Steri, Francesco. 1979. *Taylorismo e fascismo*. Rome: Editrice Sindacale Italiana.

Stewart, Richard. 1987. *Design and British Industry*. London: John Murray.

Stites, Richard. 1989. *Revolutionary Dreams: Utopian Vision and Experimental Life in the Russian Revolution*. New York: Oxford University Press.

Stollberg, Gunnar. 1981. *Die Rationalisierungsdebatte, 1908–1933: Freie Gewerkschaften zwischen Mitwirkung und Gegenwehr*. Frankfurt: Campus Verlag.

Strati, Antonio. 1992. "Aesthetic Understanding of Organizational Life." *Academy of Management Review* 17:568–81.

———. 1999. *Organization and Aesthetics*. London: Sage Publications.

Sussman, Herbert L. 1968. *Victorians and the Machine: The Literary Response to Technology*. Cambridge, MA: Harvard University Press.

Sward, Keith. [1948] 1972. *The Legend of Henry Ford*. New York: Atheneum.

Sweeney, James Johnson, and Josep Lluís Sert. 1960. *Antoni Gaudí*. New York: Praeger.

Tacchi, Francesca. 1994. "L'ingegnere, il tecnico della 'nuova' società fascista." In *Libere Professioni e Fascismo*, edited by Gabriele Turi, 177–227. Milan: Franco Angeli.

Tafuri, Manfredo. 1976. *Architecture and Utopia*. Cambridge, MA: MIT Press.

Taylor, Frederick W. [1903] 1972. *Shop Management*. With an introduction by Henry R. Towne. In *Scientific Management*. Westport, CT: Greenwood.

———. [1911] 1967. *The Principles of Scientific Management*. New York: W. W. Norton.

———. [1912] 1972b. *Taylor's Testimony Before the Special House Committee*. In *Scientific Management*. Westport, CT: Greenwood.

Termes, Josep. 1990. "Josep Puig i Cadafalch (1867–1956): Between Architecture and Politics." In *J. Puig i Cadafalch: L'arcuitectura entre la casa i la ciutat*, 90–103. Barcelona: Fundació Caixa de Pensions.

Toca Fernández, Antonio. 1997. "Juan Segura: The Origins of Modern Architecture in Mexico." In *Modernity and the Architecture of Mexicco*, edited by Edward R. Burian, 163–76. Austin: University of Texas Press.

Tomàs, Josep R., and Jordi Estivill. 1979. "Apuntes para una historia de la organización del trabajo en España, 1900–1936." *Sociología del Trabajo* 1:17–43.

Traub, Rainer. 1978. "Lenin and Taylor: The fate of 'Scientific Management' in the (Early) Soviet Union." *Telos* 37 (Fall): 82–92.

Tselos, Dimitri. 1967. "The Chicago Fair and the Myth of the 'Lost Cause.'" *Journal of the Society of Architectural Historians* 26 (4): 259–68.

Ucelay-Da Cal, Enric. 1997. "Le Corbusier i les rivalitats tecnocràtiques a la 'Catalunya revolucionària.'" In *Le Corbusier y España*, edited by Juan José Lahuerta, 121–88. Barcelona: Centre de Cultura Contemporània de Barcelona.

Ucha Donate, Rodolfo. 1980. *50 años de arquitectura española I (1900–1950)*. Madrid: Adir Editores.

Urwick, L. 1956. *The Golden Book of Management: A Historical Record of the Life and Work of Seventy Pioneers*. London: Newman Neame Limited.

Van Casteele-Schweitzer, Sylvie. 1987. "Management and Labour in France, 1914–39." In *The Automobile Industry and its Workers*, edited by Steven Tolliday and Jonathan Zeitlin, 57–75. New York: St. Martin's.

Van de Velde, Henry. [1907] 1971. "Credo." In *Programs and Manifestoes on 20th-Century Architecture*, edited by Ulrich Conrads, 18. Cambridge, MA: MIT Press.

Van Hensbergen, Gijs. 2001. *Gaudí*. London: HarperCollins.

Vasconcelos, José. 1963. *A Mexican Ulysses*. Bloomington: Indiana University Press.

Veblen, Thorstein. [1899] 1934. *The Theory of the Leisure Class*. New York: Modern Library.

Villalón, Teclo, and Pedro Plasencia. 1992. "La estela de Gaudí." *Sobremesa* 9 (96) (October): 55–65.

Vogt, Adolf Max. 1998. *Le Corbusier, the Noble Savage: Toward an Archaeology of Modernism*. Cambridge, MA: MIT Press.

Warchavchik, Gregori. [1925] 1965. "Acerca da Architetura Moderna." In *Warchavchik e a introdução da nova arquitetura no Brasil: 1925 a 1940*, by Geraldo Ferraz, 39-D. São Paulo: Museu de Arte de São Paulo. [Translated as "Apropos of Modern Architecture," pp. 264–66.]

Weinstein, Barbara. 1990. "The Industrialists, the State, and the Issues of Worker Training and Social Services in Brazil, 1930–1950." *Hispanic American Historical Review* 70 (3) (August): 379–404.

Weston, Richard. 1996. *Modernism*. New York: Phaidon.

White, Harrison C., and Cynthia A. White. [1965] 1993. *Canvasses and Careers: Institutional Change in the French Painting World*. Chicago: University of Chicago Press.

Whitford, Frank. 1984. *Bauhaus*. London: Thames and Hudson.

Whitston, Kevin. 1997a. "The Reception of Scientific Management by British Engineers, 1890–1914." *Business History Review* 71 (Summer): 207–29.

———. 1997b. "Worker Resistance and Taylorim in Britain." *International Review of Social History* 42:1–24.

Wichmann, Hans. 1992. *Deutsche Werkstätten und WK-Verband, 1898–1990: Aufbruch zum neuen Wohnen*. Munich: Prestel.

Wilton-Ely, John. 2000. "The Rise of the Professional Architect in England." In *The Architect: Chapters in the History of the Profession*, edited by Spiro Kostof, 180–208. Berkeley: University of California Press.

Wingler, Hans M., ed. 1969. *The Bauhaus: Weimar, Dessau, Berlin, Chicago*. Cambridge, MA: MIT Press.

———. 1972. *Bauhaus in America*. Berlin: Bauhaus-Archiv.

———. 1983. *The Bauhaus-Archiv Berlin: Museum of Design*. Braunschweig: Westermann.

Wright, Frank Lloyd. [1928] 1992. "In the Cause of Architecture: Purely Personal." In *Frank Lloyd Wright Collected Writings*, vol. 1, *1894–1930*, edited by Bruce Brooks Pfeiffer, 255–58. New York: Rizzoli.

———. [1929] 1944. *When Democracy Builds*. Chicago: University of Chicago Press. (Originally published as *The Disappearing City*)

———. 1932. *An Autobiography*. London: Longmans.

Wurster, Catherine Bauer. 1934. *Modern Housing*. Boston: Houghton Mifflin.

———. 1965. "The Social Front of Modern Architecture in the 1930s." *Journal of the Society of Architectural Historians* 24 (1) (March): 48–52.

Xavier, Alberto, Alfredo Britto, and Ana Luiza Nobre. 1991. *Arquitetura moderna no Rio de Janeiro*. São Paulo: Editora Pini.

Yates, JoAnne. 1989. *Control through Communication: The Rise of System in American Management*. Baltimore: Johns Hopkins University Press.

Zald, Mayer N, and Bert Useem. 1987. "Movement and Countermovement Interaction." In *Social Movements in an Organizational Society*, edited by Mayer N. Zald and John D. McCarthy, 247–72. New Brunswick, NJ: Transaction.

Zevi, Bruno. [1973] 1994. *The Modern Language of Architecture*. New York: Da Capo Press.

———. 1980. *Giuseppe Terragni*. Bologna: Zanichelli Editori.

Zucker, Paul. 1942. "Architectural Education in Nineteenth Century Germany." *American Society of Architectural Historians Journal* 2 (July): 6–13.

Index

Philosophy, and modernist architecture, 12n.6, 13n.7

Piacentini, Marcelo, 88, 99

Picasso, Pablo, 57, 88

Pirelli SpA, 70

Planning. *See* scientific management

Politecnicos (Italy), 125, 135

Pollini, Gino, 72–73, 120, 125, 135

Polytechnical University (Riga), 125

Popova, Lyubov', 28, 79

Populism, and the modernist architects, 138–39

Postal Center (Libera), 73

Prebisch, Alberto, 104–5, 131, 133

President Alemán Urban Hosing Project (Pani), 97

Princeton University, 128

Principles of Scientific Management (Taylor), 5, 6, 19, 46

Professionalization: as a cause of modernist architecture, 41–44, 117–18, 121–23; and social movements, 42–44, 115–16

Progressivism, 7, 128

Proletkult, 75

Psychology and Industrial Efficiency (Münsterberg), 6

Puig i Cadafalch, Josep, 81, 83, 84, 90

Puig i Gairalt, Antoni, 82

Purism, 63–64, 84

Radical Party (Argentina), 92

Rathenau, Walther, 60–61

Rationalism: in Italian architecture, 72–74; in Russian architecture, 76–78

Rationality, defined, 14n.8

Redressment Français, 65

Reichskuratorium für Wirtschaftlichkeit (RKW), 60–61, 119

Reidy, Affonso Eduardo, 100, 101, 131

Renault, Louis, 65

Rentas Baratas, 97n.7

Repetto, Bartolomé, 106

Research Society for Economical Construction Business (Germany), 61

Residencia de Estudiantes, 85

Revista de Occidente, 84

Rivera, Diego, 93–96, 98

Rivera-Kahlo House (O'Gorman), 96

Robert Bosch GmbH, 120

Roberto, Marcelo, 100, 131

Roberto, Mauricio, 100, 131

Roberto, Milton, 100, 131

Royal Academy, 127

Royal Institute of British Architects, 127

Rue Franklin, apartment building in (Perret), 53

Ruppelwerk, 58

Ruskin, John, 16, 47–48, 51, 80, 83, 104, 127, 129

Sánchez, Lagos y de la Torre, Arquitectos, 105

Sant'Elia, Antonio, 11, 16, 30, 71–72

Santos Dumont Airport terminal (Roberto and Roberto), 100

Sauvage, Henri, 28, 65

Schawinsky, Xanti, 73

Schlemmer, Oskar, 28, 58

Schönberg, Arnold, 58

School of Applied Arts (Weimar), 58

School of Architecture, Buenos Aires, 103, 104, 131

School of Architecture, Madrid, 85, 126

School of Construction Technicians, National Polytechnic Institute (Mexico), 96

School of Engineering and Architecture, National Polytechnic Institute (Mexico), 96

School of Fine Arts (Mexico), 130

School of Fine Arts (Rio de Janeiro), 130–31, 135

Scientific management: 18–32; and aesthetics, 29–32, 142–46; defined, 5; in Argentina, 103; in Brazil, 99–101; in Britain, 46–47; in France, 54, 64–65; in Germany, 55, 60–62; in Italy, 70–71, 73; in Mexico, 95; in Russia, 75–76; in Spain, 80–81; in the United States, 18–32. *See also* Fordism and Taylorism

Scott, Geoffrey, 50

Scully, Vincent, 36

Seagram Building (Mies van der Rohe), 60, 129

Secretariado del Aprendizaje, 81

Segura, Juan, 96–97

Sellier, Henri, 65

Serrano, Francisco, 97, 130

Sert, Josep Lluís, 87–88, 90, 105, 129, 135, 139

Seven Lamps of Architecture (Ruskin), 47–48

Severini, Gino, 12n.5

Shaw, Richard Norman, 50

Shop Management (Taylor), 5

A Note about the Type

This book has been set in the Adobe Times Roman font family.

In 1931, *The Times* of London commissioned the Monotype Corporation, under the direction of Stanley Morison, to design a newspaper typeface. According to Morison: "*The Times*, as a newspaper in a class by itself, needed not a general trade type, however good, but a face whose strength of line, firmness of contour, and economy of space fulfilled the specific editorial needs of *The Times*." Times New Roman, drawn by Victor Lardent and initially released in 1932, was the result. Research into legibility and readability led to a design that was unique in newspaper typography; it was based on old style (or Garalde) types, had greater contrast, and was more condensed than previous newspaper types.

When the *The Times*, for whom Monotype designed Times New Roman, switched to machine-set type, they used Linotype equipment. Monotype licensed Times New Roman to Linotype, who optimized it for the new technology. Adobe's main Times Roman font family uses Linotype's 12-point design. There are a variety of differences between the Linotype and Monotype cuts of Times, though most are very subtle.